AF600232

GENDER, NARRATIVE, AND DISSONANCE IN THE MODERN ITALIAN NOVEL

Gender, Narrative, and Dissonance in the Modern Italian Novel

SILVIA VALISA

UNIVERSITY OF TORONTO PRESS
Toronto Buffalo London

Toronto Buffalo London
www.utppublishing.com

ISBN 978-1-4426-4922-4 (cloth)

Toronto Italian Studies

Publication cataloguing information is available from Library and Archives Canada

University of Toronto Press acknowledges the financial assistance to its publishing program of the Canada Council for the Arts and the Ontario Arts Council, an agency of the Government of Ontario.

Canada Council for the Arts Conseil des Arts du Canada

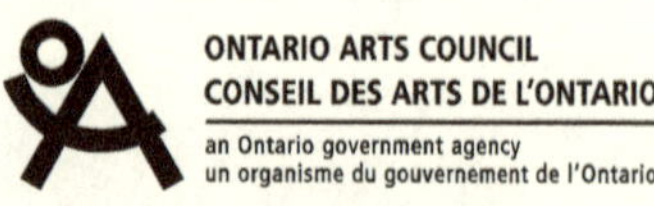

University of Toronto Press acknowledges the financial support of the Government of Canada through the Canada Book Fund for its publishing activities.

Contents

Acknowledgments

Writing is arguably a lonely enterprise. But all that surrounds it – researching, reading drafts, rewriting, procrastinating, editing, proofreading, whining, and celebrating – are very much group exercises. Many people kept me company throughout the various phases of making this book, and I am deeply grateful to them all.

I want to thank Barbara Spackman, Albert R. Ascoli, and Debarati Sanyal at Berkeley for their attentive reading, their support, and encouragement and my great colleagues Bill Cloonan, Mark Pietralunga, and Irene Zanini-Cordi at Florida State University for their amazing patience and their help at every step of the process. I also want to thank Suzanne Stewart-Steinberg, Massimo Riva, Evie Lincoln, and the participants of the Cogut Center for the Humanities seminar at Brown for the wonderful and productive time I spent there in 2009.

During my five years at FSU, many colleagues and staff members have cheered me on, offered their expertise, lent a hand, and often made everyday tasks much easier. Among many people, the staff of the Modern Languages and Linguistics Department, in particular Kathy Wimberly and Brian Ruscher, have always been ready to go the extra mile to help me. I deeply appreciate their care and patience. I thank Sarah Buck Kachaluba, the humanities librarian at Strozier Libraries, and the delivery staff of my beloved FEDS (the Faculty Book Delivery System at FSU), who promptly delivered to my office, often with less than an hour's notice, any and all books that I requested.

This book would not exist without the tireless care of the late Ron Schoeffel, editor at the University of Toronto Press (UTP). He worked to connect my writing with readers who might appreciate what was good in it and help me rework what was not needed. He will be greatly missed. I thank Merrie Bergman and Barbie Halaby, my amazing copy editors, because their professional advice made a huge difference during the revision process. I thank the UTP readers for their precious feedback at the different stages of writing and my new editor, Richard Ratzlaff, for so graciously taking on this project and helping me bring it to completion.

I am deeply grateful to Adriana Cavarero for being one of my early readers. Angela Matilde Capodivacca, Nora Stoppino, Rebecca Falkoff, Rhiannon N. Welch, and Araceli Hernandez-Laroche all read parts of this project; their suggestions and thoughts were sorely needed and much appreciated. I also want to thank Luisa Colicchio, Alessandra Raffieri, Kim Harley, Stacey Rutledge, Edward Gray, Helene Bilis, Ayelet Ben-Yishai, Lisa Wakamiya, and Rob Romanchuk for their friendship and support throughout the years. Finally, I thank the Zimmer and Valisa families – Karl, Catherine, Roni, my mother, and my father. And I thank Paul, Serafina, and Lucas for being here, even when they would rather have been somewhere else. This book is dedicated to them.

GENDER, NARRATIVE, AND DISSONANCE IN THE MODERN ITALIAN NOVEL

Introduction

> I have always fondly remembered a remark that I heard fall years ago from the lips of Ivan Turgenieff in regard to his own experience of the usual origin of the fictive picture. It began for him almost always with the vision of some person or persons, who hovered before him, soliciting him, as an active or passive figure, interesting him and appealing to him just as they were and by what they were. He saw them, in that fashion, as *disponibles*, saw them subject to the chances, the complications of existence, and saw them vividly.
>
> (James 613)

On 14 January 1824, Giulia Beccaria Manzoni, the mother of Alessandro Manzoni, wrote a letter to Monsignor Luigi Tosi. A close friend of her son, Tosi had been following Manzoni's new literary enterprise, along with other intellectuals such as Claude Fauriel, Ermes Visconti, and Victor Cousin. Tosi had, like the others, read the first draft of a historical novel that Manzoni was writing – the text that is now known under the title *Fermo e Lucia* – and had expressed a favourable opinion, albeit with some reservations. In her letter, Beccaria Manzoni informed Tosi that her son was about to begin revising the novel. She then briefly confided, "[S]ia detto fra noi M.r Fauriel, certamente uno dei più gran letterati, dice che è una cosa ammirabile e si è incontrato con lei dicendogli di togliere affatto *l'Episodio della Monaca*" (90; to be said between you and me: Mr. Fauriel, certainly one of the greatest writers, says that [the novel] is admirable, and agrees with you in suggesting to him that the *Story of the Nun* be completely removed).[1] With this comment, she made it clear that the two intellectuals agreed on one major revision that should be made to *Fermo e Lucia*: the character of Geltrude, the *monaca di Monza*, should be totally eliminated.

Geltrude's story, based on the historical vicissitudes of Virginia Maria de Leyva, the daughter of Monza's seventeenth-century feudal lord who revolted – to no avail – against her father's decision to cloister her, was indeed extravagantly rich in the first version of what would later become *I promessi sposi*. The story occupied about a fifth of the novel, a novel in which she was supposedly only a secondary character for the purpose of the main plot – serving to nudge the fate of the female protagonist, Lucia, towards her encounter with the Innominato and his subsequent conversion.

Manzoni did, in one sense, follow his friends' advice. He condensed the *monaca*'s story and changed the overall tone substantially. He pared down the Gothic elements and limited the role of several characters who interacted with her. However, he did not submit to Tosi's and Fauriel's drastic suggestions that Geltrude be eliminated altogether. He did quite the opposite, in fact. He entrusted the *monaca* with a more realistic psychology and an independent cognitive project. He turned her into a much more modern, complex character than she had been. In so doing, Manzoni dramatically enhanced the complexity of his novel and created the first real "problematic" character in the modern Italian novel. Gertrude (the *l* changed to *r* by 1827) not only became, as Anna Banti has argued, "la figura poetica più alta" (35; the highest poetic figure) of the novel; she also turned into the locus of a crucial tension between different narrative desires.

Gender, Narrative, and Dissonance is a book about characters. With one (concluding) exception, it is a book about female characters – problematic characters in Georg Lukács's formulation, wilful characters in Sarah Ahmed's definition – and the gender dissonance that they define and articulate by virtue of their narrative existence. I use the works of Alessandro Manzoni and Elsa Morante to frame the works of three less widely known authors: Neera, Marchesa Colombi (with a detour via Giovanni Verga), and Paola Masino, who conjugate and narrate gender dissonance in different ways through different structural arrangements in their texts. The questions each chapter poses in relation to characters may strike the reader as initially unrelated: why, for example, does Gertrude so clearly *not* die (or disappear) in *I promessi sposi*? Why does Masino's *Massaia* narrator keep insisting that her character has changed, when this is obviously false? And why does one identical narrative technique of knowledge (revelation) provide such strikingly different outcomes in Neera's three novels? This book argues that we can read these apparently disparate narrative accidents, incongruences, and dissonances along a common interpretive line, one that connects gender ideology to both character creation and narrative structure. Most crucially, it asks readers to dispose of an easy notion of characters as the "people" of books and to think of them instead as the critical intersection of different narrative desires, namely the ambition to solve ideological contradictions and the engagement to narratively survive such solutions.

Gender, Narrative, and Dissonance combines my fascination with novelistic characters, the subjects of literature, with a specific interest in literary theory, the ideological and epistemological structures of the novel. By focusing on the intersection between the thematic and structural levels of fictional texts, between gender, epistemology, and narrative, I aim to show how these novels work, that is, to illustrate how signifying operations – be they narrative paradigms, the characters' existential parables, or epistemological biases – are arranged by these authors into stories.

Post-Marxist literary scholar Fredric Jameson has famously defined literature as "a socially symbolic act" (20), that is, "an ideological act … with the function of inventing imaginary or formal 'solutions' to unresolvable social contradictions" (79). Each literary text stages dramatic conflicts within its pages while simultaneously trying to propose a plausible solution. Following Jameson's formulation, I analyse and decipher these conflicts across the multiple levels at which they occur because the most interesting ideological discoveries are often made by juxtaposing and comparing different narrative layers. Thus, for example, I will underscore significant connections between specific narrative directives and a character's dissonant behaviour, or between an epistemological project and the character who brings it forth "against" the rest of the novel. The solution that each novel offers is ultimately less conciliatory than we might hope – it is always characterized by ideological dissonance rather than reconciliation. Gender ideology emerges here as the most unsettling organizing principle of narrative, one that both conservatively frames and explicitly subverts the discourse of identity in narrative.

In ideological terms, *Gender, Narrative, and Dissonance* proposes a journey through the modernity of gender – from the problematic status of gendered subjects within narrative frames still proposed as viable, still passing as "neutral," to the conscious undermining of narrative instances and cognitive patterns that is evident in Masino's and Morante's texts. Manzoni's gesture towards Gertrude's character is in this respect a symbolic overture to the complexities of modernity and to the ideological dissonances it brings forth and an acknowledgment of the relevance of a more heterogeneous poetics of gender in the discourse of the novel. Morante's protagonist, Manuele, provides the strongest example of the structural impasse that occurs in projects that represent reality in traditionally gendered terms.

An ideological analysis of these stories requires, first and foremost, engaging in understanding gender ideology as a structurally and thematically fundamental concept. As Teresa de Lauretis and Barbara Spackman – two of the scholars most relevant to my research – have illustrated, gender is not a uniquely existential category that determines the appearance and behaviour of individuals or, in the case of fictional texts, novelistic characters. It is, rather, a cognitive structure that heavily conditions our attitude towards the world, shaping the way we approach – and represent – reality: "[T]he ways we know, and the ways we position ourselves as knowers are not neutral but bear the traces of those who constructed them" (Spackman, "Monstrous Knowledge" 298). In the case of patriarchal societies such as the one in question in this book – Italian society during the nineteenth and twentieth centuries – white male subjects have historically been the epistemological point of reference, their authority enforcing a "sexualization of knowledge," in philosopher Elizabeth Grosz's words (*Space, Time and Perversion* 26). This "projection of male sexualized bodies onto the structure of knowledge" is, in the end, difficult to detect because it is presented as "neuter, neutral, disembodied" (Spackman, "Monstrous Knowledge" 298). Indeed, one of the common traits of the characters analysed in the following chapters is their unease in inhabiting epistemological and narrative structures that leave them little "room for maneuver" (to use Ross Chambers's apt expression in his book of the same title), structures which exhibit an ideological bias that always already frames the subjects' "imaginary relation … to the real relations in which they live" (Althusser 125).

In his classic essay "Ideology and Ideological State Apparatuses (Notes Toward an Investigation)," Louis Althusser presented ideology as a phantasmatic notion regulating individuals' actual interactions with the rest of the world. He also characterized ideology as "itself endowed with a material existence" (126), born of actions and practices that subsequently condition the individual's ideological framework: "Pascal says, more or less: 'Kneel down, move your lips in prayer, and you will believe'" (127). The material nature of ideological performance is helpful to keep in mind when thinking of literature as a signifying practice that actively engages the individual in a negotiation of his phantasmatic relation with his real conditions of existence (and I use the masculine pronoun intentionally here, since it is of a male individual that Althusser was thinking).

Yet, as Teresa de Lauretis's analysis of his discussion of ideology points out, there is something paradoxical about Althusser's own blindness to such a specific and powerful ideological construct as that of gender: "the Althusserian subject of ideology ... is ungendered," that is, falsely proposed as neutral, as it does not contemplate the possibility " – let alone the process of constitution – of a female subject" (de Lauretis, *Technologies of Gender* 6). Althusser remains within a patriarchal tradition of thought that takes for granted the equivalence between man and (neutral) subject and thereby uncritically endorses that same system of thought.

Nonetheless, one of Althusser's central theses – that "there is no ideology except by subjects and for subjects" (128) or, in de Lauretis's words, that "ideology needs a subject, a concrete individual or person to work on" (*Technologies of Gender* 9) – remains extremely useful when applied to analysis of gender ideology. The thesis has aesthetic implications, as well, that directly bear on my project: it pinpoints why a novel's ideological framework needs characters: it needs embodied expressions of "the imaginary relation" of individuals to their actual conditions of existence. It would be impossible, otherwise, to be ideologically (and aesthetically) effective.[2]

On Characters

> Mark Twain (or was it Charles Dudley Warner?) said that everybody talks about the weather but nobody does anything about it. Something of the sort could be said about characterization in fiction.
>
> (Walcutt 5)

Theoretically speaking, the notion of character appeared for centuries to be defined by, and limited to, the characterization found in Aristotle's discussion of tragedy. The single work to which all of the literature on characters refers, either *en passant* or at length, is Aristotle's *Poetics*, most specifically by citing his famous formulation that subordinates characters to action: "[P]lot ... is the first principle, and, as it were, soul of tragedy, while character is secondary" (53).[3] Although a renewed interest in characters, and their importance in the creative act, was promoted by realist novelists from the mid-nineteenth century, as the modern novel took shape, it was only in the second half of the twentieth century that critics started focusing expressly on characters and questioning the critical and theoretical tradition within which they found themselves working: "[W]hy is the criticism of fiction forever dealing with structures, values, point of view, social and psychological implications – all of which relate to character – without coming firmly to grips with the question of what *is* character exactly and *how* exactly it is formulated, depicted, developed in a novel?" (Walcutt 5).[4]

I turned to this international, character-driven tradition as I searched for theoretical models that could account for the complexity of the relationship between *personaggi* ("characters" in Italian) and structure in the novels I was exploring, but fairly early on in my research, I realized that there existed no sustained reflection on the relationship among characters, gender, and novels as such. As for theorization about the character within the Italianist tradition, the elaboration and application of different hermeneutical approaches (structuralism, narratology, psychoanalysis, ideological critique), whether in Italy or abroad, seldom called for a specific and direct focus on characters – and certainly not for the sort of focus I was interested in: one that would not limit itself to the notion of character as a human type and to a specific interest in tying the character back to the referential world it supposedly replicates.

Looking at the study of Italian literature, we can see that scholars such as Giovanni Getto and Ezio Raimondi have in fact offered brilliant analyses and explorations of specific characters in, for example, Manzoni's canonical novel. (Perhaps not surprisingly, *I promessi sposi* is one of the books in the Italian canon that seems to "provoke" studies of its characters.) However, neither Getto nor Raimondi was subsequently tempted to elaborate a theory of characters. Generally speaking, most critics perceive the concept of character as so straightforward, transparent, and self-explanatory that even works explicitly devoted to the study of characters (e.g., Enzo Noé Girardi's *Struttura e personaggi dei Promessi Sposi*) do not offer a preliminary discussion or even a definition. Scholars are clearly referring to and inserting themselves within a critical tradition that has had no disagreements about this notion.

It is arguable that such disagreements have not arisen, at least among Italian scholars, because Italy has never had a "serious theoretical debate" (16) about the novel, as Remo Ceserani and Pierluigi Pellini have recently argued. Even the critical material that Franco Moretti assembled about novels around the world in his five-volume *Il romanzo* accounts for the notion of character only secondarily – most contributions about characters are located in the fourth volume, tellingly entitled "Luoghi, temi, eroi" (Places, themes, heroes). The one remarkable exception in terms of theoretical contribution is the work of Alex Woloch, to which I will return.

Why, throughout the history of literary critique and theory, and especially in Italy, has so little room been devoted to characters or a theory of characters, and why does the notion of character appear to be so slippery, so hard to define? Although several factors may be at play here, there seems to be widespread agreement among critics that the key lies in the perceived limitations, that is, the referentiality, of characters – in other words, it has to do with their being "people." Even more precisely, it has to do with their perceived (fictional) bodily nature. As Mieke Bal has argued, "That no satisfying, coherent theory of character is available is due to this anthropomorphic aspect. The character is not a human being, but it resembles one" (113). Bal means to remind us that "literature is written by, for, and about people" and that as such it needs people within; but she also warns that the humanity we often take for granted in characters is "fabricated ... made up" (113). Once we start thinking about the novel in critical terms, it is the duplicitous status of characters, as both referential and abstract notions, that lies at the heart of what is wrong with them.

What does it mean, exactly, to say that the problem with characters is their human aspect? Why can't the "people" who shape novels also become part of a theoretical discussion? Perhaps it is because their problematic status is tied to ideological limitations – more specifically, to a gendered framing of the problem: not the gender of characters and not the fact that characters *are* gendered, although at times that might come into play, but rather the gendering of epistemological structures and the gender bias that is inscribed in critical approaches. In what follows, I will first briefly outline how, in the theory of literature, the troubled status of humanity within texts is quite often tied to a gendered devaluation of characters as mere matter, and then I will outline my goal of performing a different, less referential type of gender criticism, one that looks at the gendering of characters and structures as a coextensive, inextricably interconnected ideological process.

Bodies and Literature

What are the ultimate relations between natural forms (bodies, plants, geological formations) and abstract representations, social constructions, and the built environment? At what price do we ignore the pathways between the concrete, corporeal realm and the realm of intellectual activity?

(Shemek 10–11)

In literary studies, it is the conventional understanding of character as the most referential element of narrative – to put it bluntly, the most corporeal element – that accounts for the relative absence of a focus on characters as such. They are often theoretically neglected in literary discussions because they directly evoke the physical and because, in the hierarchical organization of knowledge, bodies do not fare as well as "minds." Whenever a discursive dichotomy between discourse and matter is formulated, the status of characters within the narrative is devalued, reflecting a perspective that is connected to a gendered hierarchy of knowledge.[5]

As Elizabeth Grosz reminds us, there is

> [a] correlation and association of the mind/body opposition with the association of male and female, where man and mind, woman and body, become representationally aligned. Such a correlation is not contingent or accidental but is central to the ways in which philosophy has historically developed and still sees itself even today. Philosophy has always considered itself a discipline concerned primarily or exclusively with ideas, concepts, reason, judgment – that is, by terms clearly framed by the concept of mind, terms which marginalize or exclude considerations of the body. (*Volatile Bodies* 4)

Literary criticism concerning characters often resorts to the same hermeneutic categories: although characters certainly do not have actual bodies, it is nevertheless their materiality, and their "accidentality" – again, in the Aristotelian sense – to which theory objects.

Reviewing the theoretical trends concerning characters, Seymour Chatman describes the striking proximity between Aristotle's categorizations and those proposed by many modern scholars. For the Russian Formalists and Vladimir Propp, for example, "[i]t is as if the differences in appearance, age, sex, life concerns, status, and so on were *mere* differences, and the similarity of function were the only important thing" (11). Describing the structuralist take on character, Jonathan Culler writes that "[t]he most intense and satisfying reading experiences may depend upon what we call involvement with characters, but successful critical investigation of the structure and effects of a novel, as a literary construct, may require thinking of characters as sets of predicates grouped under proper names" (5). It is only as non-humans, that is, as functional paradigms stripped of any specific connotations, that characters can enter the rarefied realm of discourses on literature.

Reviewing the literature on character that preceded his important contribution to the field, Alex Woloch summarizes this widespread theoretical attitude: "[T]he decoupling of literary characters from their implied humanness becomes the price of entry into a theoretical perspective in characterization" (15). Along with Woloch, Chatman and James Phelan are among the few theorists who have openly reevaluated characters within their systems of the literary, with Chatman arguing for an "open theory of character" – one that can "preserve openness and treat characters as autonomous beings, not as mere plot functions" (119) – and Phelan contending, concerning his distinction between three "components" of novelistic characters (synthetic, mimetic, and thematic; 2–3), "that the multiple possible relationships among the three components do not fall neatly into a hierarchy of aesthetic value" (Scholes, Phelan, and Kellogg 314). Woloch's own book proposes a theory of character that accounts for both structural and referential notions and interpretations of characters. It is within this new, more flexible orientation that I situate my study, although with a specific concern about gender.

In the Italian tradition, as well, in literary histories and theoretical essays about Italian literature, the understanding of characters is most often split between two perspectives, two hermeneutical trends that are uneasily balanced between the humanity of characters and their functionality within complex structures that "transcend" the human. The guiding passion for characters as people that one encounters in the first trend leads to an interesting proliferation of traditional dictionaries of characters – encyclopedic works that list the names and occurrences of all the significant characters in literary history and that handle them as human types – along with lively critical investigations of characters as literal figures, human topoi that replicate (and at times improve upon) actual human beings.[6] A work of this second kind is Salvatore Battaglia's *Mitografia del personaggio*, in which he accounts for the evolution of human subjectivity in chapters on "La 'persona' medievale" (the medieval person), "l'attore amletico" (the Hamletic actor), and "il protagonista dilettante" (the amateur protagonist). Battaglia's analysis is anything but simple, yet his terminology still alludes to an instrumental notion of characters' bodies: he identifies characters as "dimore esistenziali" (existential abodes), containers, as it were, of thought and artistic invention.

Dictionaries and monographs are usually not concerned with epistemological projects that allow readers to understand how novels actually work; rather, they involve the analysis of individual and individualized human types. Needless to say, these are easy targets for those who believe that the humanity in literature should be the last element under consideration and for criticisms that aim "low" to show the shortcomings of texts. Knights's *How Many Children Had Lady Macbeth?* famously opposed such anthropomorphizations, while George Bernard Shaw offered a memorable definition of opera as "the story of a tenor and a soprano who want to go to bed with each other, and a baritone who wants to prevent them" (Hadlock 68). The humour here lies in his unexpected conflation of the person with the character; although the theatrical dimension of melodrama provided even more leeway for such fusion, Shaw's wit lies precisely in unmasking (and exaggerating) a connection between character and person that we know is always, somehow, there though it never, somehow, should be there.

While the second hermeneutical approach to characters is committed to understanding them as elements of a narrative structure that go beyond referentiality, the key semantic field used to analyse the relationship between characters and other structural elements is often one of abstraction, with an analytical path moving from characters towards more complex matters, or one that posits a dichotomy between two irreconcilable hermeneutic levels. Girardi's *Struttura e personaggi dei Promessi Sposi*, for example, already refers to a discursive separation between "bodies" and discourses, as do the title and content of Giuseppe Savoca's similarly organized volume, *Strutture e personaggi: Da Verga a Bonaviri*. Savoca's book offers cogent character-based analyses of several Italian novels, yet in the final note he feels compelled to explain that he does not aim to solve narratological problems but prefers instead to follow a "direzione *concreta* di indagini" (a *concrete* direction for investigations, emphasis mine): "il nodo teorico che qualcuno dovrà illuminare ... riguarda i rapporti tra ciò che passa attraverso le strutture dei personaggi e ciò che, invece, sfuggendo ad esse, costituisce tuttavia

... qualcosa di importante ed ineliminabile, e cioé ancora struttura" (191; the theoretical knot that someone will have to shed light on ... concerns the relationships between that which passes through the characters' structures and that which, instead, eluding them, nonetheless constitutes ... something important and ineliminable, that is still structure). Clearly, here "characterology" is not a satisfactory approach to literature; it cannot account for the totality of the literary experience.

A different example comes from Luigi Pirandello, a hybrid figure in literary reflection – a novelist, playwright, and essayist – and an author who had a whole lot to say, in fact, about characters. Here is a striking pronouncement by one of Pirandello's narrators, Dr Fileno (who is, in fact, a "meta-character," a precursor of the self-referential protagonists of *Sei personaggi in cerca di autore*) from "La tragedia di un personaggio": "Si nasce alla vita in tanti modi, caro signore; e lei sa bene che la natura si serve dello strumento della fantasia umana per proseguire la sua opera di creazione. E chi nasce mercé questa attività creatrice che ha sede nello spirito dell'uomo, è ordinato da natura a una vita di gran lunga superiore a quella di chi nasce dal grembo mortale d'una donna" (717; "There are so many ways of coming to life, sir; and you know very well that nature makes use of the human imagination as a tool for pursuing its work of creation. And anyone who is born thanks to this creative activity which has its seat in the human spirit is ordained by nature for a life that is higher than the life of those born from the mortal womb of a woman"; trans. Appelbaum 153).[7] In Pirandello's perspective, the lives of characters are bound to be superior to those of actual people because the gendered mediation of the maternal body in real life is dispensed with once the literary parthenogenesis is completed: the people of literature are less bodily than people in real life. Indeed, the description of such a gendered hierarchy placing spirit above body brings with it the suspicion that there is an even higher, more resolutely abstract level of nature's work to which creation can aspire, one that can completely do away with the mere accidents of matter and individualities.

In establishing and rehearsing an approach to the text that begins with flesh only to move on towards more meaningful forms, many modern literary scholars – and authors – replicate a dichotomous, gendered approach to literature. They privilege structures that are supposedly more intimately connected to the *logos* and neglect all that reminds them that literature is made of flesh and blood. Moreover, by restricting characters to a corporeal, referential meaning, they discard the possibility that the "bodies" of characters are, in fact, as fictitious and ideologically marked as any other novelistic element, with their flesh and blood as speculatively grounded and as negotiated as a text's generic belonging or intertextuality.

What is important to my project, to be sure, is not to resuscitate the literal in order to discard the figural, or to focus on themes to the detriment of form, but rather to point out that both literal and figural meanings, both structure and reference, are intertwined, flexible, ambiguous, and constantly renegotiated and re-performed at the ideological level. Revising the way we approach characters does not mean moving against, or eliminating, a hermeneutic tradition; it means, more accurately, approaching the text with a linguistic and ideological awareness of the gendering of our own criticism.[8]

In terms of character conceptualization, Alex Woloch's *The One vs. the Many*, which I mentioned earlier, has brought the theoretical problems at stake up to date, as is cogently simplified in one of his opening questions: "[H]ow can many *people* be contained within a single narrative?" (1). Woloch devotes his lengthy text to an articulation of the relationship between protagonists and minor characters, including the "semiotics of asymmetries" (320) and the ideological significance of competition between different yet "potentially central characters" (245). He also introduces the notion of "character-space" as a "distributional matrix" (13), the intersection between the potentially infinite complexity of placing several human-beings-turned-characters into the necessarily limited room that can be found for them in a novel.

Woloch's analytical framework is cogent for me: "Characterization has been such a divisive question in twentieth century literary theory – and has created recurrent disputes between humanist and structural (or mimetic and formal) positions – because the literary character is itself divided, always emerging at the juncture between structure and reference" (17). Woloch is interested precisely in the intertwined existence of structure and reference, in the same parallelisms and conflicts between the two that I set out to explore. His work proposes fascinating and astute analyses of the novelistic objects of study, aiming at encompassing analyses that will account both for the plurality of characters inhabiting the novel and for the significance of the fields of force produced by different individualities.

Although in at least two cases – in chapters 2 and 5 – I illustrate the analytical interest that such an encompassing analysis can have, and although I also proceed to examine more than one character at a time, so as to articulate hypotheses about their interactions with one another, the scope of my work and the results of each of my analyses are substantially different from Woloch's. In each chapter, I focus mainly on the relationship entertained by a specific character with the narrative structure he or she (more often a she) inhabits – that is, with the ideological function carried out by that character – and on the ways in which the character's behaviour and narrative parable visibly affect the narrative and epistemological system in which the character is inserted.

Woloch's intriguing ambition to account for the overall fabric of the novel, woven as it is out of many different character-spaces, ultimately exhibits a blindness. Woloch writes that "[h]ow a novel finds new forms of representing individuals is connected ... to how a novel *distributes* significance across a group of characters" (51), yet he does not account for the asymmetries and specificities of significance that are to be ascribed to gendered attributions of meaning. That is, he does not take into direct account the impact of gender ideology on literature – either at the referential or at the structural level. This is Woloch's choice, of course, just as it is my choice to focus on this specific aspect and to preemptively concede that in doing so I will indulge in my own ideological blindnesses to, say, the importance of labour or regional idiolects to the fabric of a novel. A literary critique that is primarily oriented towards a recognition of gendered asymmetries and an analysis of the strategies adopted within literary texts to enforce or denounce a gendered system is useful, indeed essential, for understanding how novels work – and as such may, as any other critical approach, be blind to other aspects of the power relationships within a given society.

A number of productive analyses of character(s) attuned to the unpredictability of knowledge have emerged from new perspectives in recent years, especially from cognitive science – studies of empathy and the reader's response – and from scholars working within the theoretical framework of affect theory. Suzanne Keen's discussion of empathy, Blakey Vermeule's cognitively oriented analysis of readers' relationships with characters, and Sarah Ahmed's philosophical revisions of notions of subjectivity in view of the effects of affect – sticky subjects and wilful parts – all provide eloquent rewritings of traditional understandings of the business of writing (and reading) novels through an exploration of our relationship with characters. They offer approaches that do away with the gender dichotomy of traditional criticism and that open new ways of understanding stories. In particular, in several of my analyses, I shall call upon Ahmed's notion of "wilful" to clarify the category of the "problematic" character as it has been handed down to me by the Lukàcsian theoretical tradition concerning the novel.[9]

Characters, *Personaggi*, Performances

Insofar as the ideological production of characters in novels is concerned, we need to begin by asking what characters are, exactly, and what we are told by the words we use to define them. I borrow from Woloch to introduce the basics of characters and to foreground a few considerations vis-à-vis the double linguistic and cultural standard within which I find myself working. As I write "character," with the implied ambiguities of this English-language concept, I actually (also) mean the corresponding Italian term, *personaggio*, a concept that comes with its own set of fascinatingly unsettling conceptual ambiguities. In a section entitled "The Double Meaning of Character," Woloch rehearses the two "conceptions of character that exist in Jane Austen: character as social being (a person *is* a character) and character as inner quality (a person *has* a character)" (53), two conceptions that are bound in asymmetry. "Character" potentially evokes a substantially external concept of fictional agent while also encompassing the internal characteristics of an individual.[10]

"Character" is the lexeme I use throughout my work, although it does not entirely correspond to the Italian lexeme *personaggio*. The Italian term is derived from the French *personnage*, which in turn is derived from the Latin *persona*, a term that can designate an individual as well as, originally, the mask that actors wore onstage in Greek and Roman theatres. The *persona* was a wooden mask with exaggerated facial features and a voice-enhancing shape to embellish the audience's audiovisual experience. The original Latin etymological root *persona* thus carries with it a striking double meaning: *persona* is both the individual (the content) and the instrument that turns a person into an artistic medium (the form).[11] To fully grasp the centrality of the notion of character to the ideology of the novel, we need to acknowledge the conceptual importance of this etymological notion: characters are fictional individuals that I analyse as such, not in their referentiality (as social beings) but in their fictionality, in the complex ways in which they are ideologically woven by and in turn weave the novel they find themselves belonging to, the complex ways in which, although aspiring to be "persons," they are in fact never simply that. Characters are performative notions, events that exist as they take place. To appropriate one of

Judith Butler's terse definitions of gender, characters take form as "a practice of improvisation within a scene of constraint" (*Undoing Gender* 1).

Indeed, the modern Italian lexeme for character, *personaggio*, is a noun whose primary characteristic is that of being derived from *persona* by means of a suffix (*-aggio*) that turns it into a new noun, that is, into a notion clearly distinct from that of person. Grammatically speaking, "*-aggio*" is a deverbal suffix – a suffix that, attached to a verb of action, forms a name of that action. For example, in the case of the lexeme *atterraggio* ("landing"), the suffix transforms a word denoting a basic action, *atterrare* ("land") into a word denoting the act of landing. There is a clear temporality, and actionality, linked to the class of words formed with this suffix. Just as there is no such thing as a landing pre-existing or following the actual action of landing, there is no such thing as a character preceding or exceeding its own actions: character is a performance-based notion.

Within this perspective, the ambiguity of Austen's characters – *being a* character and / or *having a* character – remains significant to my project only when we understand it in its structural dimension, that is, when the difference between being a character and having a character results in a different textual treatment for the fictional subject involved. In the novels I analyse there are patterns of characters' behaviour that can be deemed coherent with the generic structure to which they belong and those that instead disrupt the narrative equilibrium. In most of the stories that I examine, the issue is that the character at the centre of the story refuses to become, in Sarah Ahmed's words, a secondary part of the scenery: "Willfulness for women in particular or as particulars might describe the costs of *not becoming background*" ("Willful Parts" 245). The ideological investment in these characters is mediated through their structural importance. The fact of not becoming background is a political action, coextensive with the awareness of injustice: "[T]he process of becoming conscious of harshness – the affective consequence of injustice – is described as willfulness" (247). In the best-case scenario, wilfulness becomes a narrative resistance, that is, an argument for a different distribution of ideological roles.[12]

The unsettling – indeed, unsettled – quality of the characters examined in this book is thus directly tied to their progressively "becoming conscious"; broadly speaking, it is tied to the theme of knowledge. How do characters come to know, and how do novels handle their "truth"? There are several ways in which each of my chapters tackles the issue of knowledge in novels and shows the arbitrariness of cognitive tools. My initial analysis of Manzoni's formation of the character of Gertrude allows me to bring into focus several analytical threads that re-emerge in different ways in the following chapters: the sexualization of knowledge, the ideologically ambiguous use of cognitive tools such as revelations, conversions, irony, and spectral "returns," and, more broadly speaking, the constitutive presence of gender dissonance in these narrative and cognitive projects.

Dissonance, Gender, and the Italian Context

The notion of "dissonance" in relation to a character is one I borrow from Ezio Raimondi's definition of Manzoni's "Anonimo" (the anonymous chronicler of *I promessi sposi*) in his *Il romanzo senza idillio*. Examining the "vecchio cronista del Seicento" (156; the old sixteenth-century chronicler) behind whom Manzoni hides his modern narrator, Raimondi is drawn to emphasize the anachronism and ideological incongruities into which the chronicler lapses: his voice is in such glaring contradiction with itself that the analytic reader must, in Raimondi's view, be convinced "che l'universo mentale dell'anonimo teorico del romanzo è costruito in virtù di una contaminazione anacronistica" (that the mental universe of the anonymous theoretician of the novel is built by virtue of an anachronistic contamination). This contamination turns him into "un mediatore non sincronizzato con il messaggio che comunica" (a mediator who is not synchronized with the message he is communicating), and the chronicler becomes a "veicolo dissonante della modernità" (156; dissonant vehicle of modernity), simultaneously proclaiming and denying his belonging to a specific ideological system, injecting his system of beliefs with dissonant directives.

The novels analysed in this book similarly stage characters as "dissonant" subjects, that is, novelistic figures at once subservient to and complicit with the ideological framework they inhabit. They are carrying two ideological messages at once, or, in some cases, one message that is however in such clear opposition to the structural context as to continuously create doubts about its validity for the bearer of the message. These dissonances are the problematic knot on which I focus. They become the centre of my analyses because they need to be understood as structural, as directly connected with the ideological negotiations at work at the narrative and epistemological levels in the novel. In contrast to Raimondi's analysis of Manzoni's opus, my book does not take anachronism as one of the main topics of scrutiny; the dissonances perceived in the novels it studies are not bound to enhance the conflicted status of modernity. Rather, my book is an investigation focusing on the dissonant configurations of gender within socially symbolic acts in the context of Italian modernity, as well as on the characters that complicate and oppose a hegemonic understanding of the relationship between narrative and gender.

The dominant gender ideology of nineteenth- and twentieth-century Italy, as it can be summarily drawn from the texts studied in this book, is the all-too-familiar ideology that hierarchically places the male sphere of agency above the female sphere and that assigns dominions of agency according to a highly patriarchal economic structure. To the father, husband, and son go the public domain of politics, of economic exchanges and commercial enterprises, of the sciences, engineering, and intellectual labour, and of war and international relationships. To the mother, wife, and daughter go the private domains of domestic economy, childbearing, and child raising, as well as an array of public yet subordinate positions as assistants, nurses, and low-wage members of the workforce. In the sphere of sexuality, the dividing line is very clear: male sexuality can – and, in fact, must – operate actively both within and outside of the boundaries of the family household, so much so that a male character's sexual failure at any level is often meant to be read as a clue about textual "problems" at the ideological level – as I will discuss in the case of Elsa Morante's *Aracoeli*. Conversely, female sexuality is confined to and defined by its reproductive value or by its exchange value as a source of pleasure for men; in both cases women's role is strictly confined within codified boundaries, within the conjugal house or the *casino* (brothel). When reproduction has been ruled out (or virginity is in danger), the female body is enclosed within the claustral confines of Catholic monasteries, as happens to Manzoni's Gertrude, or reduced to a "beast of burden" that produces (rather than reproduces), as Marchesa Colombi's Nanna in *In risaia*.

Traits of a more specifically Italian gender ideology can be found by taking into consideration, on one hand, the role that the Catholic Church played – and still plays – within the Italian context and, on the other, the gendered ideology of Fascism as developed during *Il Ventennio* (the twenty years of Fascist rule). In both instances women's maternal duties are emphasized above all others and are deemed essential to maintaining and improving the social structure. The Catholic Church has actively promoted the identification of women with the "fiction" of either the Virgin Mother or Magdalene the sinner, leaving no space for alternative representations of femininity that take into account women's individuality and desires. The Fascist regime progressively silenced all the emancipatory trends that emerged between the end of the nineteenth century and the first quarter of the twentieth (such as the call for women's suffrage and increased access to professions outside the house), sharing – indeed, surpassing – the Vatican's engagement in a gender politics based on the radical biologization of women's destiny. I discuss Morante's title character, Aracoeli, through her adherence and tragic submission to such gender politics, while I analyse the protagonist of Masino's novel, the *massaia*, through the combination of her dissonant submission to such ideological directives and her resistance to the biologizing politics of reproduction.

Although the ideological construct of masculinity clearly concedes more individual freedom, it is nevertheless similarly built into a rather constraining role, in this case the role of the public and belligerent (both socially and sexually) agent, always ready to take upon himself the celestial or imperialistic causes. This role is well exemplified by the figure of Egidio Orlandi, the protagonist's lover, in Neera's *Teresa*: his physical appearance evokes both Garibaldi and Christ. Masculinity, too, can be described as an extremely codified set of behavioural expectations that individuals endorse or reject in their attempts to come to terms with their narrative parable. In Neera's novel *Lydia*, for example, the gender confusion between the female protagonist and the male object of her desire brings the novel to its ideological and diegetic catastrophe: Lydia's desire to be a man is juxtaposed with the fraudulent seducer's pose as a feminine, weakened individual. Such a utopian exchange of gender roles is ultimately exposed as "monstrous" and impossible, and it determines the protagonist's deadly defeat.

An analysis of the relationship between power and gender and of the dynamics articulating gender ideology has been at the centre of feminist scholarship on Italian literature for almost half a century, although gender as an analytical concept was only introduced within the last three decades. The first revision of "neutral" notions of literature came from feminist scholars interested in giving women's voices more resonance and widespread attention, mainly focusing on bringing women back onto the creative and critical stage. Only in a second wave has gender become an important analytical tool, allowing for an analysis of the formation of subjectivity in both male and female individuals and thus answering the call for a revision of gender ideology that would unveil the ideological nature of femininity, masculinity, and everything in between.[13]

As JoAnn Cannon has written in her reflection on the overwhelmingly male diachronic canon in Italian literature, "[O]ne of the first acts of feminist literary criticism in all countries seems to be that of insinuating greater numbers of women writers into a male-dominated tradition" (17). The texts in Giuliana Morandini's classic anthology and Antonia Arslan's editions of late nineteenth-century women writers are representative contributions to this corrective, exemplifying the works of many scholars, mainly in Italy, who have set out to recover and spotlight the actual presence of women in the public sphere, thus contributing to a reassessment of Italian literary history.[14]

A different approach to feminist literary studies has come from gender studies scholars, with their emphasis on a critical attitude that does not focus exclusively on female authors. Elaine Showalter describes a shift in the Anglophone world from "gynocriticism" (feminist critiques focusing exclusively on women writers) to gender studies in the late 1970s: "[C]ritics have begun both to rethink literary theory in the light of gender, and to build gender theory into their critical practice" (8). The focus on gender is limited in the Italian context, as the distinction between sex and gender has only relatively recently been discussed in Italy – although there are several notable exceptions, such as the philosophers Adriana Cavarero and Teresa de Lauretis (de Lauretis's intellectual career is, however, tied more to American than to Italian academia).

In the Anglophone context, there is increasingly more interesting scholarship that, through an analysis of the intricate relationship between power and gender, engages with the representation of gender and sexuality in both female- and male-authored Italian texts.[15] For example, in *Decadent Genealogies*, her work on Baudelaire and D'Annunzio, Barbara Spackman has analysed the ideological import of the "feminine" for the works of decadent European authors, showing how critical rejections of D'Annunzio's work were motivated by his poetics – predicated, as it was, on a weakening of the male subject rather than on the traditional "full" masculine subjectivity, with the potential, as such, to open a different textual space. One of the most important thematic analyses of women's issues in recent years – one that also does not shy away from the ideological interrogation of male-authored texts – is Laura Benedetti's *The Tigress in the Snow*, a broad examination of the central thematic and ideological knot of motherhood in Italian literature from the Unification to the present day.

With *Gender, Narrative, and Dissonance*, I similarly aim to integrate the critical approach of women's studies, which holds that the sex of a work's author is a fundamental starting point, in that it calls attention to the material and ideological constraints shared by female subjects, with a broader commitment to understanding gender ideology as an analytical category that should not be restricted to women's texts (or to female characters). My work engages eight texts with the goal of bringing together narratives that are very different from one another, both thematically and chronologically, yet nonetheless share a common ideological concern. In focusing on one analytical trend – gender dissonance – I work within the tradition of gender scholars such as Barbara Spackman, JoAnn Cannon, and Lucia Re and cinema scholar Angela Dalle Vacche, all of whose works interrogate the way specific discursive and ideological notions shape a debate, a narrative genre, or the production and the reception of specific kinds of stories.

Compared to the Anglophone tradition of gender studies in English and American literature, remarkably few works (most of which are by the authors I mentioned above) have been devoted to the intersection of gender, narrative, and epistemology in Italian literature. None has directly focused on the novelistic character as a hinge between structure and reference or as a productive vehicle for understanding how gender works in novels. While entirely devoted to female writers, Stefania Lucamante's analysis of the production and reception of novels in contemporary Italy is useful in considering this connection. Whereas Lucamante identifies a new "epistemology of the novel" elaborated and proposed by such contemporary writers as Di Lascia, Ferrante, and Vinci, I argue that novels such as those I analyse in this book – Manzoni's *I promessi sposi*; Neera's *Teresa*, *Lydia*, and *L'indomani*; Marchesa Colombi's *In risaia*; Paola Masino's *Nascita e morte della massaia*; Elsa Morante's *Aracoeli*; and, more cursorily, Verga's novella "Le storie del castello di Trezza" – contribute to a reshaping and a reorganization of the notion and function of novels within the Italian context and simultaneously engage in the task of "unfixing identities," a task that, in Lucamante's view, "contemporary Italian women writers have chosen in their works" (21).

The specific contribution of my book to the assessment of Italian literature is an analysis of how writers who chronologically span almost two centuries, with very different formal and thematic ambitions – from Manzoni's Catholic enterprise to the "shabby"[16] Neera and experimental Masino, from the fantastic concerns of Marchesa Colombi and Verga to Morante's parodic modernity – share an approach to narrative and knowledge in which no one truth, no real absolute, can be univocally endorsed, particularly remarkable in the case of the first five authors, for they wrote when the (post)modern dismantling of grand narratives could only have been a glimpse into the future. The need that their problematic characters have to undermine the assumption of a single pathway to knowledge is driven by a greater, ontological urgency: the need to overcome the disciplining nature of traditional gender ideology and to affirm the possibility of being a subject – and a dissonant one at that.

Together with a notion of character that is structurally, not uniquely thematically, relevant to the ideology of the novel, gender dissonance is thus the common thread in my research. I explore dissonances as they take shape in the characters' journeys throughout their stories, at the level of the *fabula*, and I consider them by focusing on the narrative choices of each novel – the endorsement of specific generic requirements and the relationship between character and narrator. Finally, I discuss the epistemological choices endorsed by the problematic characters, that is, how their projects of "truth" unfold within – and inform – the story.

Organization of the Book

The attention of the following chapters is thus on the intersection of narrative and epistemological structures with specific characters. I choose to focus mainly on each novel's "problematic" character, that is, on the figure that exhibits the most visibly conflicted attitude towards the ideological context. The status of problematic character that I attribute to Manzoni's *monaca di Monza* in the first chapter is one I initially derived from a Manzoni scholar, Robert Dombroski. In one of several essays about this novel ("Alessandro Manzoni: The Cultural Transformation of Narrative"), Dombroski compellingly argues that the true problematic character of *I promessi sposi* is not, say, Renzo or fra Cristoforo or the Unnamed, but the tragic figure of Gertrude. In both Dombroski's case and mine, the adoption of this label bespeaks a debt to the Hungarian philosopher and theorist of the novel Georg Lukács.

To be a problematic character, according to Lukács, the character must first of all belong to the novelistic universe, as opposed to the epic one, for whereas epic texts have entire peoples at their centre and a transcendental timelessness for their unfolding, novels remedy their own lack of transcendence by setting themselves biographical limits and by putting at their centre an individual "significant only by his relationship to a world of ideals that stands above him" (77). In his words, "[t]he inner form of the novel has been understood as the process of the problematic individual's journeying towards himself, the road from dull captivity within a merely present reality – a reality that is heterogeneous in itself and meaningless to the individual – toward clear self-recognition" (80).[17]

Lukács's classic introduction to the formal and ideological problems posed by novels informs my work in its entirety, as does, necessarily, his emphasis on individuals and on the imperfection portrayed in these texts as one of the characters' necessary structural characteristics. All of the characters examined in these chapters are problematic in this sense, insofar as they cannot permanently reconcile their inner world with the world they live in (be it the novel itself or a phantasmatic referential universe). Nonetheless, it should not come as a surprise, after my gendered objections to the works of some of the previously mentioned literary theorists, that Lukács's (and Dombroski's) notion of the problematic character needs to be revised so that it acknowledges the ideological and structural "problems" pertaining to gender.

Lukács and Dombroski clearly have in mind a male, traditional (in the sense of positively virile) problematic individual, and Dombroski treats Gertrude as such: he fails to account for the fact that her problematic status is, in large part, to be ascribed to her gender, and to the gendering, as it were, of the epistemological structure of which she becomes the dissonant subject.[18] The concept of the problematic character can only be enriched by a discussion of problematic female characters as "wilful," where wilfulness, together with a definition of "inner" character, comprises a structural attribute: a desire not to become background to one's own story. On the one hand, the female characters examined here are problematic because they are wilful – they explicitly consider the option of not receding from their central roles in the story. Indeed, Beccaria Manzoni's letter briefly, almost spectrally, conveys to us precisely this peculiar status of the problematic character: the structural impermanence, the uncertainty of her narrative status. On the other hand, the last character that I analyse (in Morante's novel) is problematic because he is *not* wilful – as a male character, his problematic desire is precisely the opposite: he would like to renounce the centrality, the structural prominence, of his narrative role.

In chapter 1, the ideological function of Gertrude, the *monaca di Monza*, becomes the focal point to assess a series of key questions and concerns about the different ways in which gender structures stories. As I mentioned in the opening to this introduction, the figure of Geltrude was a dominant presence in the first draft of what would become *I promessi sposi*, in which Manzoni subsequently contained and "reduced" the character to more acceptable – although still extravagantly rich – standards. Gertrude is in many ways a figure for excess, and by analysing Manzoni's constraining strokes that drove the final version of the novel, I draw out the extent to which her presence unbalances thematic as well as structural systems, namely, the organization of heterosexual desire and of narrative authority.

Gertrude's textual evolution establishes the precedent of a female figure whose cloistering does not prevent her from acting upon her own environment, that is, from elaborating a narrative and epistemological alternative in stark opposition to the ideological framework of the novel. Through the example of Gertrude, several problematic modes are highlighted and analysed, modes that can be recognized as veritable strategies of ideological unruliness within Manzoni's novelistic project. In the chapters that follow I return to these same concerns as they are put in place, modified, or expanded upon by other problematic characters. In particular, I focus on the juxtapositions of different epistemological paradigms, the narrative strategies enacted to "survive" one's own story, against all odds, the compulsion to disobey and disavow the novel's directives (even post mortem), and, ultimately, the explicit mise en cause of the very desire to be in the story at all.

In chapter 2, the combination of two distinct epistemological and narrative paradigms, "analysis" and revelation, becomes central to my reading of the work of the fin-de-siècle writer Neera. Her three novels *Teresa* (1886), *Lydia* (1887), and *L'indomani* (1889), while devoted to the strikingly similar destinies of three young women, bring about poignantly individualized outcomes. When read in terms of the ideological management of gender dissonance, the open-ended outcome of the first novel, as opposed to the more restrictive outcomes of the second and third works, is to be ascribed to a successful combination of contradictory narrative models, as well as to a wise management of gender conflicts. Analysis and revelation, two opposite (and gendered) ways of knowing the world, are reconciled to the benefit of the protagonist only in *Teresa*, who can then access a body of knowledge about herself and her place in society from which she was initially barred.

In chapter 3, the juxtaposition of two texts that are only apparently very different – Verga's novella "Le storie del castello di Trezza" (1877) and Marchesa Colombi's *In risaia* (1878) – allows me to explore the convergences between their protagonists' strategies for narrative survival and their distinct uses of "disappearance." In both stories, the combination of dissonant generic spaces emphasizes the common ideological aim of making visible wilful characters who cannot exist within a realist space but who assert their presence within a fantastic, separate space. Their "absent presence" is an eerie reminder of the cruel optimism – to use the apt formulation entitling Lauren Berlant's book – that drives women's fates to subjection, but also of the optimistic revenge that sometimes finds its way to the (narrative) surface.

In chapter 4, I consider another strategy of ideological dissonance in the sophisticated and highly experimental work of Paola Masino's last novel, *Nascita e morte della massaia* (1945). The text explores and denounces the alienated condition of women from the standpoint of a fully formed, ascetic female philosopher protagonist who consciously accepts the role of bourgeois wife and *maîtresse de maison* as an intellectual experiment. In addition to highlighting the *massaia*'s use of irony to denounce her historical and cultural environment while she acknowledges her own complicity within it, I consider the *massaia*'s narrative presence powerfully innovative in that it constantly disavows the narratorial imperatives that dictate how her biographical parable should unfold. It is in this way that her critical, subversive posture destabilizes the narrative rhetoric of gendered conversion.

The final chapter introduces Elsa Morante's last novel, *Aracoeli*, by focusing mainly on its male protagonist, Manuele, and the figures of his parents: Aracoeli, the title character, and his father, Eugenio. In the hands of Manuele the narrator, *Aracoeli* becomes a liminal text, one that takes the strategic unruliness discussed in the earlier chapters to its ultimate consequences. The son's belated attempt to grasp his mother in all her complexity – as a little girl, as a mother, and as a prostitute – is doomed to failure because of his inability to go beyond those very epistemological and narrative (stereotyped) structures that dictated her life (and character) in the first place. At the same time, Manuele's refusal to endorse an active narrative and epistemological role parallels his refusal to endorse a positive virility and ultimately sanctions his refusal to exist within his own story.

The novel's failed attempt to narratively maintain traditional notions of the feminine and the masculine within the limits prescribed by society becomes, in Morante's universe, an outspoken illustration of a now structural impossibility of defending any aprioristic truth within a literary text. Morante's novel is the last point of the epistemological journey I propose in this book, one that focuses on emblematic dissonances and instances of ideological unruliness within the modern Italian novel and that highlights the shortcomings of narrative whenever it conceives of itself as ideologically univocal. In the conclusion, I reflect on the relationship between literature and reality as it emerges from these novels: characters are dissonant subjects whose "truth" is to be found less within their relationship to the real than in the dialogue they establish – perform – between the stories they tell and the structures that frame them, and that they themselves shape and inform.

1 "A Somewhat Unusual Nun":[1] Writing Gender in *I promessi sposi*

È meglio avere per madre Madame Bovary o Salomé [invece] di Cornelia o Lucia, che erano due grandi e presuntuose mediocrità.

It is better to have as a mother Madame Bovary or Salomé rather than Cornelia or Lucia, who were two huge and presumptuous mediocrities.

(Masino, *Io, Massimo* 66)

In a discussion of the pros and cons of "saying it all" when it comes to sex in erotic narratives, contemporary Italian author Alessandro Piperno returns to the roots of the modern Italian novel. He categorically states that Gertrude, Alessandro Manzoni's famous "nun from Monza," is "il personaggio più arrapante della letteratura italiana" (115; the most sexually arousing character in Italian literature) and that this is precisely because nothing is said of her anatomy or of her famously damning encounter with the criminal Egidio. The certainty with which Piperno offers Gertrude as a paragon of inspiring female sexuality is not surprising, given her renown as one of the most fascinating fictional characters in Italian literature. At the same time, Piperno's provocative judgment articulates a traditionally superficial appraisal of a character whose "problem" extends well beyond her transgressive sexual behaviour. Juxtaposed to the "modest beauty" (trans. Penman 57) of Lucia, the novel's supposed female protagonist, Gertrude's unruliness – in many senses: aesthetic, moral, sexual, and narrative – presents a model of femininity and of fictional characterization that was unheard of at the time. She is a very explicit instance of a "problematic" – that is to say, wilful – character.[2]

In his essay "Alessandro Manzoni: The Cultural Transformation of Narrative," Robert Dombroski analyses the ideological conflicts at work in Manzoni's *I promessi sposi* and argues that the only truly problematic character is Gertrude herself. Examining the dual directions that Manzoni imparted to his novel, Dombroski writes that on the one hand, *I promessi sposi* features a deeper "focus on human experience and ordinary life" than previous literary works, while on the other it strives for a "meaning that transcends the events and experiences it recounts" (2). Dombroski analyses two of the novel's most famous episodes in light of this dialectic: the story of the Innominato, the lawless aristocrat whose conversion constitutes the novel's turning point, and that of the "monaca di Monza," the daughter of a feudal lord who revolts against her father's decision to cloister her, but to no avail. Noting that both episodes feature what he calls, following Lukács, a "problematic individual" (18), Dombroski exposes in each case the author's need "to suppress and recode what may be potentially subversive in [the characters'] outlook and behavior" (2) in order to propose "an ideal of accommodation" (21) between individual initiatives and transcendental directions.

Dombroski also highlights the profound difference between the narrative paradigms of the two stories, and he discusses the unique problematic posed by the tale of the *monaca*. In the episode of the Unnamed, "the dialectic between providential necessity and free will is played out dramatically" (5) yet only to effect the character's salvation so that the episode can be recast within a hagiographic framework. Dombroski remarks that "in effect, the role of free will in the conversion process is more apparent than real" and is subservient to "a modern legend of conversion" (8). In contrast, he finds in Gertrude's story a character whose introspection and psychological depth cannot fully be captured by a parable of salvation, and this leads Dombroski to consider Gertrude the only "truly problematic individual" (18) in the novel, that is, the only character who does not subscribe to the ideological system that structures the novel and the world within which Gertrude lives.[3]

In this chapter I discuss the complexity of Gertrude's problematic status by examining the different facets of her character. Several elements conspire to construct Gertrude as a character who defies definitions – effectively crafting her as a site of ideological and narrative unruliness – a *dissonant* subject of gender and ideology, to use Ezio Raimondi's productive definition of the anonymous chronicler in the novel (*Il romanzo senza idillio* 156).[4] As far as the structural connection between the novel and the "problematic individual" is concerned, Georg Lukács has, admittedly, set the stage for Dombroski. In *The Theory of the Novel*, Lukács argues that the authentic novelistic protagonist is the problematic individual. "He" (because the protagonist is male for Lukács) is "significant only by his relationship to a world of ideals that stands above him" (77), and it is this conflicting, at times tragic, relationship between reality and ideals that – for both Lukács and Dombroski – engenders the quest at the core of each novel.[5]

To illustrate the problematic nature of the Signora, Dombroski compares Gertrude to her predecessor, Geltrude, the initial incarnation of the *monaca*'s character in Manzoni's first draft of the novel, now known as *Fermo e Lucia*.[6] Dombroski highlights the extent to which Gertrude, unlike Geltrude, "appear[s] much more a product of historical forces than a victim of evil" (13). He also argues that in the case of Gertrude (as opposed to the Innominato), the focus is not so much on one of the two terms of the ideological conflict, free will and necessity, as "on the dialectic itself" (15) and the fact that the terms are "equally true and operative" (16). The character of Gertrude appears to be endowed with a complexity that almost contradicts the ideological organization subtending the novel as a whole, where one term of the equation – personal initiative and responsibility – is ultimately rendered subservient to the necessity of transcendental organization and justice.

Gertrude's story, according to Dombroski, is inevitably contained by the textual organization: the novel rejects her self-sufficiency and enlists her as one of the function-bound characters serving the development of the plot. Yet the subversive nature of her character remains visible as a narrative paradigm that is contained but not denied by the author: "[A]lthough Manzoni's authorial viewpoint rejects Gertrude's individual choices and desires, it does not negate the narrative of self-discovery through which her story is conveyed but rather seeks to make it commensurate with the standpoint of final causes and metaphysical necessity." In even clearer terms (and beautifully put), he writes, "[T]he figure of Gertrude as a problematic individual contradicts the form of writing that ultimately determines that figure" (20).

Dombroski also concisely outlines Gertrude's evolutionary arc, which can be traced from the first draft of the novel to its second edition, showing the "process of secularization" (13) she undergoes. My discussion of the character of Gertrude also begins with the original figure of Geltrude in *Fermo e Lucia* and traces, through her parable, the extraordinary process of revision through which Manzoni finally succeeded in offering his readers "il primo romanzo leggibile che sia sorto in Italia" (Giordani 105; the first readable novel that was ever written in Italy).

From *Fermo e Lucia* to *I promessi sposi*: The Genesis of a Problematic Character

Manzoni completed *Fermo e Lucia*, the first, unpublished draft of his novel, in 1823. He published the first edition of *I promessi sposi* in 1826–7 and a second and final revised edition in 1840, also known as the "Quarantana" (the 1840 edition).[7] Dante Isella has written that the narrative structure of *Fermo e Lucia* is "nettamente diversa" (definitely different) from that of *I promessi sposi*, underscoring that in this sense, the novel is "perfettamente riconoscibile come un'idea di romanzo autonomo rispetto ai *Promessi sposi*" (perfectly recognizable as an idea of the novel independent of *The Betrothed*), even though the "processo elaborativo" (creative process) remains "unico, come un ponte a un solo arco, dalla pagina bianca all'edizione del '27" (30; a single one, like a single-arched bridge, from the blank page to the 1827 edition) and also, according to Salvatore Nigro, "nel passaggio alla Quarantana" (xlv; in the transition to the 1840s edition).[8] It is therefore possible to compare the first and final versions in terms of their different structures and also in terms of the evolution of the characters from one text to the next, as several scholars have already done. Here I shall focus on several changes that occurred between the first draft and the final edition, leaping across specific details that might be drawn from the first print version.[9]

The structure of *Fermo e Lucia* is radically different from that of *I promessi sposi* (1840; henceforth I shall omit the date). *Fermo e Lucia* was conceived in four *tomi* (volumes), each of them divided into chapters (8, 11, 9, and 9, in that order), whereas the final novel would compose one volume divided into 38 chapters. Initially, the novel was organized in narrative blocks that followed a chronological order, with few or no points of intersection between the subplots. The story of the *monaca*, called "Geltrude" in this first version, primarily occupies chapters 1 through 6 of the second *tome* and ends in chapter 9, where the narrator also tells the reader about "gli ultimi casi di questa sventurata" (339; the last cases of this unfortunate woman), that is, what happens to her beyond the chronological limits of the novel.[10]

The story of Gertrude (whose name took on an *r* by 1827) is divided into three separate segments in *I promessi sposi*, in contrast with the organic unity it exhibited in *Fermo e Lucia*. This discontinuity is a first indication of the more complex structure of the novel's final version; the fortunes of the different characters are not followed uninterruptedly from one end to the other, as they usually were in the first draft, but are brought in according to a certain chronological coherence, in an attempt to keep all the threads of the story in progress simultaneously.[11]

Geltrude's story in *Fermo e Lucia* is very explicitly framed as a tale of conversion: the narrator justifies its inclusion through direct interventions in chapters 2, 4, and 9 (at the beginning, in medias res, and at the end), precisely on the basis of its positively Christian ending. At the beginning of the second chapter, after the first encounter between Geltrude and the two fugitives, the narrator explains that "avremmo anche soppresso tutto il racconto, se non avessimo potuto anche raccontare in progresso un tale mutamento d'animo della Signora, che ... deve creare un'impressione ... consolante" (192; we would have eliminated all of this tale, if we had not been able to also relate as it happened such a change of mind in the Signora, which ... is bound to have a ... comforting effect). He would have left this story out, he continues, "per non offendere coloro ai quali il rimettere nella memoria degli uomini certe colpe già pubbliche, ma dimenticate, quando non sieno terminate con un grande esempio, o con un gran pentimento, sembra uno scandalo inutile, comunque uno le esponga" (192; in order not to offend those for whom the act of recalling certain crimes that were previously known but had been forgotten, when the stories do not conclude with a moral, or with great repentance, seems a useless scandal, no matter how one presents it).[12]

In *Fermo e Lucia*, then, the narrator tells us that no matter how the tale is told, it is immoral to tell it if it does not contain a lesson, if it does not adhere to a narrative paradigm aimed at underscoring the presence and meaning of the transcendental law within each individual's life. Retribution or punishment must be allotted within the temporal frame of a person's life, which then acquires meaning accordingly. The reader is thus already informed that the story must have a happy – that is, Christian – ending and that this happy ending will be recounted, even if it goes beyond the chronological space occupied by the novel itself.

In *I promessi sposi*, Manzoni suppresses much of this first intervention, reducing it to a short introduction explaining the need to reveal more about this mysterious character: "quel tanto cioè che basti a render ragione dell'insolito e del misterioso che abbiam veduto in lei, e a far comprendere i motivi della sua condotta, in quello che avvenne dopo" (125; "enough at least to explain the air of oddity and mystery which we have already noted, and to clarify the motives of her conduct at a later stage"; trans. Penman 175). This explanation is tied to an understanding of the plot and of this specific character; that is, it is an explanation that finds an internal, narrative justification as a necessary complement to the story. It is not aimed at framing Gertrude's story within the reassuring paradigm of a tale of repentance; the narrator no longer exhibits any apprehension about the reception of a tale that is not explicitly framed as exemplary.

Towards the end of chapter 4 of *Fermo e Lucia*, the exemplariness of Geltrude's story is reasserted. Following a paragraph in which Manzoni discusses one of the characteristics of Christian religion, "di potere in qualunque circostanza dare all'uomo che ricorra ad essa, un rimedio, una norma, e il riposo dell'anima" (242; that it can, in any situation, offer to the man who resorts to it a remedy, a norm, and the rest of the soul) – a passage that is retained, with some variations, in the final edition – the narrator refers to Geltrude's own destiny as one that belatedly confirms the consolatory power of religion: "Che dico? Geltrude stessa fu uno di questi esempj, e insigne; ma ben tardi e dopo aver commessi ben altri errori anzi delitti" (243; What am I saying? Geltrude herself was one of those examples, an eminent one; but very late, and after having committed many more mistakes, crimes in fact). The explicit allusion to the end of Gertrude's story is expunged from the final version.

Finally, at the end of chapter 9, Geltrude sends Lucia out of the monastery on a false pretext, thus allowing for her kidnap by Geltrude's lover, Egidio. Geltrude's function within the novel is now exhausted: "quivi l'abbandona il nostro autore" (338; here our author leaves her). The narrator nonetheless feels "[il] dovere ..., quando abbiamo raccontati i delitti, di non tacere il pentimento" (339; the duty ..., having told her crimes, not to keep silent about her repentance), and so he briefly informs the reader about Geltrude's final "pentimento" (341; repentance) and her years of "espiazione" (341; atonement). Geltrude's story, it appears, can exist within the novel only in virtue of what happens *outside of and above* the novel, that is, only if it is a story that conforms to the narrative paradigm constituted by the novel as a whole. The "metadiegetic" – to use Genette's terminology (228) – replicates and confirms the diegetic at the level of both the content (the romance of a character swerving from the correct path but finally being brought back to exemplary conduct) and the form (a righteous, conciliatory ending).

I promessi sposi introduces the reader to Gertrude's story in chapters 9 and 10. The account of Lucia's kidnapping occurs farther on, in chapter 20; and we are told the conclusion of her story only as the novel itself draws to an end. In the final pages of chapter 37 (the penultimate chapter), the narrator feels compelled to inform the reader about several things that happened during the last months of the plague, between Renzo's encounter with Lucia in the *lazzeretto* and Lucia's return to her hometown. The narrator briefly explains that, although he is willing to accommodate "la fretta del lettore" ("the reader's … haste"), there are "tre cose" ("three things") that he does not want to "passar sotto silenzio" ("pass over in silence"), and also because, for at least two of these, "il lettore stesso dirà che avremmo fatto male [a non raccontarle]" (524; "the reader will agree that it would be a mistake to leave them out"; trans. Penman 697).

One of the three things concerns the Signora: Lucia's widow friend shares with her "di costei cose che, dandole la chiave di molti misteri, le riempirono insieme l'animo d'una dolorosa e paurosa maraviglia" (524; "some information about the Signora which explained many things that had been puzzling Lucia, and which filled her with sorrow and timid astonishment"; trans. Penman 697). The widow tells Lucia about Gertrude's suspicious conduct, her subsequent transfer to a different monastery, and the self-accusation and reformation that followed after "molto infuriare e dibattersi" ("much fury and many struggles") as well as her present life of "supplizio volontario" (524; "voluntary penance"; trans. Penman 698). The epilogue of her story is a hasty summary that is justified more by internal coherence, by the need for closure that dominates these last chapters, than by an adherence to a paradigm of salvation. Moreover, the end of Gertrude's parable is now doubly framed: it is grouped with the epilogues of three other characters' stories – the deaths of padre Cristoforo and Lucia's two "benefactors" – and it is recounted by one of the novel's characters, the widow, rather than directly by the narrator. This has the effect of distancing the narrator from his material, and it emphasizes the need for closure, which is the uniquely functional contribution of these three epilogues. I add that the repeated use of such a generic and banal term as "cose" (things) in reference to these three events – Gertrude's reformation, fra Cristoforo's death, and donna Prassede and don Ferrante's deaths ("tre cose" [three things]; "venne a sapere di costei cose" [literally, she came to know things about her]; "avrebbe anche desiderato di saper qualcosa de' suoi antichi padroni" [literally, she would have wished to know something about her old protectors]; 524)[13] – similarly devaluates them, as if these "things" hold no importance beyond contributing to the reader's satisfaction with the narrative.

The end of the *monaca*'s story is thus partially divested of its ideological and hagiographical meaning and reduced to a piece of the narrative puzzle that is bound to fall into place because of structural concerns. Moreover, the events concerning the Signora and her "future" are now contained within the temporality of the novel. This means that there is no doubling of the salvific paradigm, one within the story (Fermo's) and one outside of it (Geltrude's), as found in *Fermo e Lucia*; the *monaca*'s story is contained *by* the novel. Rather than being a second plot that reinforces the first by stretching its temporality to encompass something that happens beyond the novel's chronological boundaries, this is a subplot contained within the main plot.

This framing of the parable makes clear the very strict rules according to which Manzoni organized his first novelistic attempt, *Fermo e Lucia*. The narrator's interventions betray an attitude intent on morally justifying his choices and defending them from possible criticisms. As Manzoni's writing progressed, the narrator withdrew his most fervent interventions, and the structure of the novel gained both sophistication and coherence: rather than contain Gertrude's story through an explicit insistence on its pedagogic possibilities and its "necessity," the final narrator left it to the novel itself to restrain the subversive possibilities connected with her character.

On the one hand, this different encapsulation of the story draws attention to the novelistic structure, to its heightened strength, to its ability to govern its material without needing to resort to the use of transcendental laws. On the other, it also opens up a space within the novel itself, a space where a story lacking a moral purpose is allowed to exist. This space allows an alternative (narrative) economy, one in which, as Dombroski has written, the "limitedness and relatedness" of the novel prevail over the "exemplary and overarching absolutes" of the romance ("Cultural Transformation" 20).

Similar observations can be made when the evolution from *Fermo e Lucia* to *I promessi sposi* is approached in terms of content: at this level, too, Manzoni reorganized the text with a weakening of drastic ontological oppositions between good and evil and between the seventeenth and the nineteenth centuries, eliminating the direct generic references to romance and Gothic novels. In parallel with the suppression of the hagiographic framing of the *monaca*'s story, the content of that episode, its *fabula*, is also substantially reduced, and arguably for the same reasons – for internal coherence and as a consequence of the substantial change in the generic space the story is made to occupy.

The basic plot remains the same in the two versions of the novel, at least as far as the tale of Gertrude's forced *monacazione* ("taking the veil") is concerned, that is, up to the time when the Signora actually becomes a nun. The young woman's formative years and the psychological scrutiny she is subjected to by the narrator as she vainly attempts to resist her father's will are substantially unchanged. The roles of Gertrude's mother and brother are diminished in order to focus on the dynamic between Gertrude and her father (whose personal thoughts are, nevertheless, also trimmed). This part of the story is also freed of several of the abundant direct interventions and comments by the narrator in *Fermo e Lucia,* which visibly changes the proportions allotted to Geltrude's introspection and the moral and religious considerations that the narrator draws from it.

Inserting his insights about the development of Geltrude's personality into the novel, the narrator of *Fermo e Lucia* tends to read them as both the symptoms and the symbols of an era and to use them to show how such a "guerra mentale" (197; mental war) could, in other circumstances, have been won by resorting to religious discipline that, properly used, would turn the young mind into "una mente tranquilla, saggia e forte contra i pericoli della giovinezza e di tutta la vita" (197; a peaceful mind, wise and strong against the dangers of youth and of an entire life). In contrast, the suppression of such commentaries in *I promessi sposi* magnifies the relevance of Gertrude's internal conflicts and her attempts to resist her father, amplifying the tension between compliance with her role as a subjugated daughter and an ambition for a power and independence unfettered by genealogy or a gendered seclusion. Gertrude thus becomes a more complex figure, less specifically bound to her times and the topos of the *monaca forzata.*

I promessi sposi's attenuation of the suggestions of Gothic and romance novels that appeared in *Fermo e Lucia* also points to a more dialectic organization of Gertrude's character.[14] There are radical differences in the accounts of Geltrude's/Gertrude's clandestine relationship with Egidio and her subsequent criminal deeds. Recall that Manzoni's mother, Giulia Beccaria Manzoni, wrote in her 1824 letter to Monsignor Tosi that the first two readers of *Fermo e Lucia,* Fauriel and Tosi himself, both suggested to Manzoni that the nun's episode be eliminated altogether. One of the reasons for this suggestion was that the episode exploited a set of themes – beautiful and unlucky woman, blasphemous relation, and hideous, haunting crimes – that strayed (especially in Tosi's opinion) from those of a serious Catholic enterprise and seemed rather to indulge the tastes of a scandal-hungry readership. Another reason – and this was more Fauriel's opinion – was that the length of the episode might compromise the readability of the novel and distract from the primary plot, Renzo's and Lucia's delayed marriage.

Colombo provides a quick summary of the critical interpretations of the changes in the story of Geltrude/Gertrude: "C'è chi accusa un inopportuno moralismo e c'è chi vede preminenti le ragioni estetiche: e c'è chi colloca la decisione del Manzoni – una decisione libera e sofferta – nell'armonia tra arte e morale, come Michele Barbi" ("La Monaca di Monza" 187; There are those who blame [the changes] on an inopportune moralism, and those who see aesthetic reasons as pre-eminent. And there are those who situate Manzoni's decision – a free and carefully thought-out decision – in service of harmony between art and morality, as Michele Barbi does). Like Barbi, Getto is conciliatory: "Il fatto che, a consigliare la revisione dell'episodio della Signora, accanto a Mons. Tosi, si trovi il Fauriel, riesce quanto mai significativo. Ancora una volta le ragioni della morale e quelle dell'arte si incontravano" (72; The fact that, in suggesting the revision of the Signora's tale there is Fauriel, together with Mons. Tosi, is all the more significant. Once more, moral reasons agree with artistic ones). On the other hand, Giancarlo Vigorelli takes sides – as do I: "si era arreso [alla riduzione dell'episodio] per le ragioni di economia artistica suggerite dal Fauriel più che dalle censure religiose del Tosi" ("La monaca di Monza" 95; he surrendered [to reducing the tale] for artistic economy, as suggested by Fauriel, rather than because of Tosi's religious censorship). As I mentioned in the introduction, what is most remarkable about the evolution of this character is that Manzoni followed the advice of his first readers only to a certain extent. He did so through an ideological revision of his novel, and of the figure of Gertrude, that only enhanced her importance within the whole.[15]

Manzoni conspicuously expunged the history of Egidio's upbringing and various crimes, the direct dialogues between the lovers, and the detailed account of the murder of one of the nuns by Geltrude's accomplices. A succinct example of Manzoni's abridgement of the more spectacular elements of this part of the tale is the manner in which he conveys Geltrude's frightful vision of the dead nun. In *Fermo e Lucia*, Geltrude describes it to Egidio: "l'ho veduta sempre, sempre; l'ho veduta smuovere a poco a poco il mucchio di sassi, e poi metter fuori il capo, e poi venir su" (327–8; I have been seeing her ever since; I've been seeing her move the pile of stones little by little, and then put her head out, and then come up). In the final edition, the episode is turned into a mediated piece of information offered by the narrator: "Quante volte al giorno l'immagine di quella donna veniva a cacciarsi all'improvviso nella sua mente, e si piantava lì, e non voleva moversi!" (151; "Many times a day the woman's image thrust itself unexpectedly into her mind, and planted itself there, and would not go away"; trans. Penman 208). The shift from a direct recounting of the ghostlike apparition of the dead nun to an indirect reference to Gertrude's troubled imagination and her "spectres" transforms the episode into yet another opportunity for focusing on Gertrude's internal drama.[16]

Overall, the romance between Egidio and Geltrude is explored in *I promessi sposi* only as much as is needed to intensify Gertrude's internal laceration before she gives in to her persecutor; the rest is subsumed by the famous phrase "La sventurata rispose" (150; "The poor wretch answered him"; trans. Penman 206), a masterpiece of discretion that cuts short any possibility of indulging in the temptations of romance. The detailed account of the murder of the *conversa* ("lay sister") is replaced by a short, covert reference to the place where her dead body could have been found (151). In addition to lessening the traces of Gothic and romance novels, the narrator inserts another intervention concerning his attitude towards his character. He lightens the most critical edges, which parallels his diminished emphasis on framing the episode in terms of morality – he suppresses several expressions and comparisons concerning Gertrude's character that, while not always unequivocally moralistic, nevertheless carried negative connotations. Manzoni frees Gertrude from an explicit characterization as a necessarily evil character, conferring upon her a more ambiguous conflictuality.

As an example, the description of Geltrude during her encounter with Agnese is filled with sinister qualifications: "Così dicendo il suo aspetto prendeva sempre più un non so che di sinistro, di feroce che quasi faceva scomparire ogni bellezza, o almeno la alterava di modo che chi avesse osservato quel volto in quel punto ne avrebbe conservata una imagine disgustosa per sempre" (188; While she said this, her appearance took on an increasingly sinister, ferocious quality that almost erased all her beauty, or at least altered it so much that whoever observed her face at that moment would have kept a disgusting image of it forever). In this visually dramatic passage, the dichotomy between beauty and ugliness corresponds literally to that between good and evil, so that Geltrude appears inhabited by an evil force that perverts her youthful beauty. This passage is replaced in the final version by a shorter, nuanced description: "interruppe la signora, con un atto altero e iracondo, che la fece quasi parer brutta" (124; "the Signora interrupted, with a gesture of angry pride, which made her look almost ugly"; trans. Penman 173). The newer passage is noncommittal as far as Gertrude's morality is concerned.[17]

The good/evil dichotomy is more apparent in *Fermo e Lucia*, and Geltrude's biography leans more obviously towards a tale of predestination and necessity. As with the framing of the encounter with Agnese, where the narrator's moralistic intentions give way to more narrative preoccupations, thus freeing the story of its more restrictively catechizing aims, the narrating voice at the thematic level takes on an allusiveness and distance that ultimately leaves the reader as the arbiter of her interpretation. The narrator himself retreats from judging the character and her surroundings, just as he has retreated from binding her story within the strict limits of a hagiographic tale. The dialectic between necessity and free will is enhanced by this retreat, and its tension is exploited for a more careful organization of the conflicts at work within the novel.

Far from eliminating her from the novel, then, as Tosi and Fauriel had suggested, Manzoni's revisions enhance Gertrude's role and importance. On the one hand, from a structural and stylistic point of view, the *monaca*'s story is finally better integrated within the novel: it is interwoven with the other subplots and freed of its darkest tones. On the other hand, from a narrative point of view, Gertrude's parable no longer reinforces the salvation paradigm offered by the novel as a whole. Instead, the novel hastily relegates her reformation to a cluster of epilogues that are structurally necessary for wrapping up the novel's subplots. From this textual evolution, Gertrude's dissonance emerges as a measure of the tentative modernity of Manzoni's novel, of the "room for maneuver" that Manzoni opens within his literary work by exploring the limits of transcendence.

In the second part of this chapter, to better understand the extent to which her character is innovative, I consider the terms of Gertrude's "difference" (i.e., of Gertrude's problem) as she comes to exist in *I promessi sposi*: her relation to literary topoi, her thematic and epistemological agency, and her establishment of a textual authority.

Gertrude's Literary Constraints

Briefly assessing whether the two most eminent feminine characters in *I promessi sposi*, Gertrude and Lucia, endorse the "canone che presiede alla rappresentazione della bellezza in letteratura" (92–3; canon that governs the representation of beauty in literature), Verina R. Jones writes that Lucia continues the line of "the home-maker, unexciting but steady and sweet" (94). Gertrude, in contrast, appears to be an embodiment of the classic "dark lady": "passionate, violent, mysterious, alluring, and untrustworthy" (94).[18] The initial lengthy portrayal of Gertrude in *I promessi sposi*, as she meets Agnese and Lucia in her parlour, provides a clear illustration of what her "dark-lady-ness" comprises. As the women look at her through "due grosse e fitte barre di ferro" (121; "two heavy, closed-barred gratings"; trans. Penman 170), Gertrude appears a figure of excess in both her femininity and her lack of it. Her display of femininity is more direct (and ominous) than Lucia's – as described in Lucia's first appearance, in chapter 2 (31–2) – but is complemented by traits that appear to explicitly connote masculinity. On the one hand, the movements of her lips are "subitanei, vivi, pieni d'espressione e di mistero" ("abrupt and lively, full of expression and mystery"); her dress is "attillat[o]" ("laced in") at the waist; and a "ciocchettina di capelli neri" ("curl of black hair") escapes from her veil to signify her secular vanity and, notwithstanding her religious status, a self-consciousness indicative of her (female) sensuality. On the other hand, her movements are described as "repentin[i], irregolari e troppo risolut[i] per una donna, non chè per una monaca" ("hasty, uneven and much too full of determination for a woman – let alone a nun"). Her glances appear to demand "affetto, corrispondenza e pietà" ("affection, understanding and compassion") in some moments and to reveal "un non so che di minaccioso e feroce" ("something strangely threatening and ferocious") – that is, a masculine aggressiveness – in others (122; trans. Penman 171). It is because of this combination of highly contradictory features that she is a dark lady: she is "una versione femminilizzata dell'uomo" (Jones 95; a feminine version of man), that is, a topos combining feminine and masculine elements.

Jones also discusses how, in the evolution from the first draft to the final version, Manzoni eliminated the elements that alluded to the more classic beauty of a "blonde woman": he purged the reference to "candido avorio" (snow-white ivory) for the bandage covering her forehead, a similitude allusive of a poetic code of visual conventions in effect since Petrarch. He also purged the mention of her lips as "regolarissime" (very regular), a comparison of her chin to "quello d'una statua greca" (that of a Greek statue), and the qualification of her person as "di alta e regolare proporzione" (of high and regular proportions), three descriptions that had also connected her to an ideal of classic beauty (183–4).[19] Jones plausibly explains that the purpose of these modifications was to strengthen the contrast between the two protagonists of this episode, Gertrude and Lucia; the result is that Gertrude's "darkness" and unreliability and Lucia's fairness, innocence, and naiveté are both enhanced. Gertrude's dangerousness is thus signalled, according to Jones, by the juxtaposition of feminine and masculine characteristics but is at the same time contained and structured by the literary representation: her mobility and mysteriousness are combined within the parameters and dictates of a specific code.

We can endorse Jones's conclusions, that the tension between the two gendered postures is "always already" contained by its canonicity and that, paradoxically enough, "è Gertrude, il personaggio ribelle, che si conforma al canone" (100; it is Gertrude, the rebel character, who conforms to the canon), although only if Gertrude's canonicity is understood as the first movement of a complex articulation of masculinity and femininity within this character, even in her relationship with literary models. Indeed, Manzoni's complex composition of literary echoes and epistemological positions in the novel was an explicit attempt to turn Gertrude into something different from simply a literary "given."

It is interesting to note that the elaboration of Gertrude's novelistic and epistemological roles continues with a "complication" introduced by Manzoni: a trace of another literary topos. I have already quoted, as an example of the dichotomous representation of Geltrude in *Fermo e Lucia*, a reference to Geltrude's duplicity in her encounter with Agnese, one that immediately follows the initial description analysed by Jones: "While she said this, her appearance took on an increasingly sinister, ferocious quality that almost erased all her beauty, or at least altered it so much that whoever observed her face at that moment would have kept a disgusting image of it forever" (188).[20] Here Manzoni resorted to the dichotomy between an appearance of beauty and an underlying truth of appalling ugliness to unveil the meanness beneath Gertrude's surface kindness – again, a reference to the implicitly evil nature of the dark lady.

As I noted, the image as such is eliminated in the final version of the novel, arguably because it reified good and evil. It is replaced by a more nuanced reference to ugliness as a consequence of Gertrude's acts: "interruppe la signora, con un atto altero e iracondo, che la fece quasi parer brutta" (124; "the Signora interrupted, with a gesture of angry pride, which made her look almost ugly"; trans. Penman 173). This is, to be sure, a revision that parallels the suppression of several other explicit references to Gertrude's beauty in *I promessi sposi*. But it is also a "complication" of the epistemological model of the enchantress-turned-hag, and as such, it reflects the extent to which Gertrude is turned into more than a canonical "object of knowledge" or of desire – which come to the same thing.

The sexualization of knowledge is, as Spackman has shown, indispensable to a conservative epistemological structure; that is, rather than following as a consequence, it is one of the conditions of that structure. Discussing the topos of the "enchantress-turned-hag," Spackman explains that "this particular embodiment and consequent gendering" of the hermeneutic process "is 'as essential' as what it presumably hides": such a model "gives us a structure of knowledge that positions the knower as male, and what is unknown or to be known as female" ("Monstrous Knowledge" 299). Spackman describes this recurrent figure as "that familiar topos in which it will be revealed that a seemingly beautiful, alluring young woman is a shrunken, usually toothless, and usually diseased old woman" (298).[21]

As Spackman makes clear, the traditional explanation of this topos does away with the letter of the text – the female body unveiled – and focuses instead on what it stands for: the hermeneutics of truth. But if we focus on what this metaphor literally means for the female body at its centre, it appears that the revelatory paradigm equates the female surface to an illusory projection and the hideous – monstrous – reality underneath to the gendered "truth" that can only be found beneath appearances, a truth that is not available to female subjects as such but can only be found by another (male) subject gazing at the female body. Manzoni's complication of this paradigm in the case of Gertrude is extraordinary and should not be underestimated. Rather than maintain the tie to an epistemological topos that bound Geltrude's body to a literary tradition of females (truths) unveiled, from Dante's "femina balba" to Ariosto's Alcina and Machiavelli's epistolary prostitute (Spackman, *Decadent Genealogies* 95), Manzoni consistently frees Gertrude from these literary and metaphorical echoes and instead grants her the ideological autonomy of realistic psychological introspection: the possibility to be a subject to herself and to her story.

Gertrude's Desire

The tension between necessity and free will that I have analysed along its literary, and gendered, dimension is always already linked to another fundamental opposition, that between female and male social and narrative roles. This is important and productive for Gertrude's problematic character, and it suggests an analytic approach that has generally been neglected by Manzoni scholars. Gertrude's status is in this sense more troublesome than is implied by either Lukács's or Dombroski's discussion of the typology of the problematic character. Lukács's "problematic individual" is, as I pointed out, a hero on a quest to find an immanent meaning for his life, a protagonist whose "mental attitude" is that of "virile maturity" (88) and whose story is characterized by a structural "discreteness, the separation between interiority and adventure" (88), that he struggles to accept.

Dombroski employs Lukács's label to designate Gertrude as a "truly problematic individual" ("Cultural Transformation" 18). Similarly to Lukács, who does not probe beyond the confines of a masculine imagery meant to encompass all human beings, Dombroski chooses to define Gertrude with this (falsely) neutral description, thus erasing the import of one of the economic and social forces that weigh her down. When Dombroski considers the *monaca*'s problematic role within the novel and the power relations between the characters, he writes that "her power is limited to her role within the confines of convent life" (18), but he goes no further in discussing this powerlessness. In fact, he contrasts the limitations of her role with those of other characters, namely the Unnamed, the Cardinal, and fra Cristoforo, but he fails to entertain the possibility that such powerlessness to influence the plot might also be connected to Gertrude's status as a woman, in contrast with the three noble male characters who populate the novel. Dombroski fails to consider "the gendering of epistemological structures" ("Monstrous Knowledge" 299) as Barbara Spackman puts it – that is, "the projection of male sexualized bodies onto the structure of knowledge" (298), a structure that is then proposed as neutral.

I detect this kind of projection in Lukács's and Dombroski's critical analyses; it has the effect of uncritically pointing to a narrative paradigm built by and for male subjects, explicitly so in the case of Lukács, and of neglecting the fact that the problematic individual might happen to be gendered as a woman, as Dombroski does. Needless to say, this is a problem that goes beyond Dombroski's and Lukács's specific (and fundamental) critical interventions and that reflects the general organization of the epistemological process at both the creative and the critical levels. A discussion of the connections between Gertrude's problem and her gendered presence can ultimately show how it is that this dialectic allows for some "room for maneuver" within her story: namely, the tension between what she "ought" to be and what she actually is allows her to represent a subversive figure within the novel, to open up a discursive space that is not necessarily precluded by her belonging to a specific sex or literary topos.

Chambers's focus on the oppositional narrative emphasizes its ability to exploit "that structure of power for purposes of its own." An oppositional narrative, or "behavior," "[cannot] change the structure of power in which it operates," just as the story of the *monaca* does not ultimately change the novelistic structure within which it occurs. Rather, the oppositional narrative "discovers a power ... to *change its other* (the 'narratee' if one will), through the achievement and maintenance of authority, in ways that are potentially radical" (11). Chambers points in the direction of the effect (indeed, the affect) that Gertrude's story can have on readers. I like to think that Gertrude's affect – the establishment of a different kind of authority over both the story and its readers – is what makes Gertrude such an innovative and everlastingly alluring character, rather than (to mention two possible critical extremes) the sexual *boutade* that Piperno proposes or some rigid allegorical reading of Gertrude as a fictional player bound to a Christian drama of redemption.[22] If, in *I promessi sposi* and, more specifically, in the story of the monaca di Monza, there is some "room for maneuver" at the level of the power structure constituting the text, this is due to the fact that we are confronted with a problematic individual who happens to be a woman and who therefore confounds the sexualization of knowledge and desire that characterizes traditional narrative structures. Gertrude's parable, when read in Chambers's oppositional terms, is relevant in its establishment of a different, and gendered (if textually short-lived), form of authority.

Gertrude's creation of authority can be viewed from two perspectives: thematically, as an active desire displayed and acted out by Gertrude towards another character, and ideologically, in the actively epistemological and self-referential stance that Gertrude takes as an ironic commentator on her frustrated attempts to "know." The contradictory position in which female characters find themselves within "masculine" narrative structures has been described by de Lauretis in *Alice Doesn't*: there appears to be a basic pattern constituting narrative, wherein "each reader – male or female – is constrained and defined within the two positions of a sexual difference thus conceived: male-hero-human, on the side of the subject; and female-obstacle-boundary-space, on the other" (121). This is due to what de Lauretis, following Russian semiotician Jurij

Lotman, understands as a "mythical structuration" of traditional narrative models (*Alice Doesn't* 118). In it, certain characters "are mobile" and "enjoy freedom with regard to plot-space," while others "are immobile, ... [and] represent, in fact, a function of this space" (Lotman 167).

Just as Spackman has done in her essay on monstrous knowledge, de Lauretis also underscores the primacy of sexual difference within the narrative structuring mechanism, yet focusing more specifically on the theme of desire: "[I]f the work of the mythical structuration is to establish distinction, the primary distinction on which all others depend is not, say, life and death, but rather sexual difference" (119). One of the dangers of this distinction lies, inevitably, in its "mythical" dimension: Frank Kermode has written (in a very different context) that "we have to distinguish between myths and fictions. Fictions can degenerate into myths whenever they are not consciously held to be fictive" (39). Although it founds the epistemological and narrative structures that define our apprehension of reality, the fictional hierarchy relating femininity and masculinity is most often obliterated or taken at face value.[23] It is thus crucial for projects such as mine to unearth the sexual economy and strict heterosexuality that the mythical structuration describes. On the one hand, a woman's position as obstacle, receptacle, and boundary allows for only a passive desire: her desire can only be a yearning to be discovered by the male hero, that is, a desire for objectification. On the other hand, an act of active desiring on the part of a woman will be read as a desire to act "as a man," to endorse a different role within the narrative structure.

In *I promessi sposi*, Gertrude is caught precisely in the tension between being an immobile character, a "personified obstacle" (de Lauretis 118) gendered as feminine, and being an individual subjectivity rebelling against objectification. She is both an object of desire and a subversively desiring subject (a subject, that is, whose desire is not only to be subjected). The unforeseen potential of such agency on her part resides, at the textual level, in the fact that her desire suspends the heterosexual economy within which she is contained. Gertrude's behaviour can be read as a redirection of desire towards an agency within her realm – a diversion of her ambitions from being desired by a male hero ("the active principle of culture"; de Lauretis 119) to desiring another function of the plot-space, that is, another woman. Her actions towards this other woman temporarily interrupt the flow of the story and create a different narrative economy. As such, it is perceived as subversive and contained by the textual organization.

Dombroski's observation that Gertrude's role appears to be limited by the convent's walls brings us back to one of the aspects of her narrative position: her role is limited because she is a function of the space she is enclosed within: "'a cave,' 'the grave,' 'a house,' 'woman'" (de Lauretis 118). But Dombroski argues that Gertrude's inability to act upon other characters' lives is also due to her ambiguous character. Gertrude, he writes, "being neither completely evil nor completely good, … is unable to act directly on the lives of Renzo and Lucia" ("Cultural Transformation" 18). She certainly cannot act upon Renzo's life, since she is, as Dombroski has pointed out, secluded in a (feminine) space. On the other hand, her relationship with Lucia provides a motif for disagreeing with the claim that Gertrude cannot act, for she does act directly on Lucia's life. Here I do not refer to her mediating role in handing Lucia over to her kidnappers (a behaviour that can be read within the parameters of a "negative" alternative economy, ultimately replicating and serving the patriarchal system). Rather, I have in mind the relationship that develops between the two characters while they are both within the monastery.

Once again, tracing the evolution from *Fermo e Lucia* to *I promessi sposi* will be very useful, for it makes clear the explicit choices Manzoni made when he revised this story. As he developed Geltrude's relation with the young fugitive from the first draft to the published novel, Manzoni eliminated most of their dialogues (probably because, as in the case of her dialogue with Agnese, Geltrude appeared to be establishing parallels too overtly between her own situation and Lucia's). Moreover, since he removed all of her dialogues with Egidio, he eliminated the one instance in which Geltrude discussed Lucia with her lover. Geltrude's own words had confirmed her as a character succumbing to the evil surrounding her. Even though she was still trying to resist involvement in Egidio's kidnapping project, Geltrude admitted to her intolerance for Lucia:

> [O] colei! non la posso soffrire, è una superba, non fa che parlare della sua innocenza … L'ho accolta, sapete, perchè bisogna nel nostro stato farsi più amici che si può: no ch'io non l'amo: ma lasciatemela per carità, questa lasciatemela, mi diventerà cara, e quando un altro pensiero verrà a tormentarmi, riposerò i miei occhi sopra di lei, e dirò fra di me: – ecco, anche questa l'avrei dovuta sagrificare; ed è qui. (331)
>
> Oh, that one! I can't stand her, she is haughty, she does nothing but talk about her innocence … I have welcomed her, you know, because we need,

> in our condition, to make as many friends as possible. No, I don't love her: but leave her to me, I beg you, she will become dear to me, and when another thought comes to torment me, I will rest my eyes on her, and will tell myself: here, this one I should have sacrificed; but she is here."

Her resistance to Egidio's project remains linked to Geltrude's hope to turn Lucia into a token of her good will, a living proof of her kindness that would counterbalance her sins. She subscribes to an external economy of retribution that, once again, reifies good and evil.

Manzoni subsequently reworked the relation between the two women into a more affectionate and reciprocal acquaintance. Their encounters in Gertrude's parlour are less interrogations filtered by the Signora's distorted perception of the world (as they had been in *Fermo e Lucia*) than actual conversations between two women, each finding solace in the other's company. They are "dissimili creature" (267; dissimilar creatures) in *Fermo e Lucia*; the *monaca*'s "confidenza" (confidence) and "carezze famigliari" (demonstrations of affection) in *I promessi sposi* actually comfort Lucia. Gertrude tells Lucia the "parte netta" (the more creditable part) of her life, and Lucia tells Gertrude the story of her missed marriage. Gertrude is taken with "la soavità di un pensiero che le tornava ogni momento, guardando Lucia: – a questa fo del bene" (251–2; "the sweetness of another thought that came to her every time she looked at Lucia: 'This is someone I can really help'"; trans. Penman 339–40). She knows that, in addition to protecting her from don Rodrigo's persecution, she is helping Lucia by offering her companionship, by comforting her in her solitude after Agnese's departure. It is a drastically different moment from her denial of any affection for Lucia in the earlier version; it is also a confirmation of the provisional opening of an alternative space, a positive economy of narration between two women. It is a moment that belies Dombroski's statement, one in which, despite the limitations of her power, Gertrude directly acts on her own life and on that of another woman.

This textual "interstice," in which the desire of each woman is redirected towards the other, challenges the heterosexual economy that feeds the novel: it is a glimpse of the possibility, evoked by de Lauretis, of "an interruption of the triple track by which narrative, meaning, and pleasure are constructed from his point of view" (*Alice Doesn't* 157). This is not to say that heterosexual desire – along with its consequent objectification of women – is denied or expunged from the tale: Lucia tells the *monaca* her story yet withholds the part connected most explicitly with "love," that is, her desire for Renzo, because she considers it improper to share this with others; and Gertrude will soon yield to Egidio's demands and reclaim her place as the object of male desire, turning both herself and Lucia back into commodities.[24]

Rather, "accidentally or unwisely" displayed in this encounter are "the terms of a divided or double desire," as de Lauretis puts it, in other words, a desire that can also be directed towards a subject other than the male hero of the story. Using examples from Alfred Hitchcock's movies, de Lauretis argues that this desire will be staged as "impossible or duplicitous, ... finally contradictory," and that it will be obliterated by "the massive destruction or the territorialization of women" (155). These two "solutions" apply literally in the cases of Lucia (territorialization) and Gertrude (destruction). Lucia will be expelled from this female space and reinserted within the economy of desire and exchange that constitutes the patriarchal society as much as the Manzonian novel. Gertrude's story, on the other hand, closes with her "supplizio" (524; "penance"; trans. Penman 698), a self-inflicted annihilation of her will. She is punished for her deviation from human and divine laws and forced into what Cardinal Borromeo historically promoted as women's *religio silentii*, a religion of silence (Prosperi 237), explicitly meant to burke women's aspirations to any active, autonomous contributions to religion.

The presence of a duplicitous desire is, then, the dangerous element within the story of the *monaca di Monza*. This unsettling component is to be perceived at the narrative level rather than at the moral one: Gertrude's desire for Egidio is dangerous in its transgression of the secular and religious rules existing in the society depicted in *I promessi sposi*, yet at the narrative level it is necessary, indeed indispensable, to the development of the plot. In contrast, Gertrude's desire for Lucia is not morally reproachable, insofar as it is represented as a desire for female friendship; but it is highly dangerous at the structural level of the novel, since its existence imperils the progression of the story. What is immediately important in my analysis is that this subversive instance will be contained at the narrative level, rather than at the moral level, by the author's careful reorganization and exertion of a stronger control over his material.

It is thus necessary to also consider how this display of desire on the part of the female subject remains important at the level of the novel's ideological organization and in the construction of a different narrative paradigm. To show this, and to better highlight the value of casting her stance as "oppositional," I shall discuss yet another aspect of Gertrude's problem: the coexistence of literal and ironic modes within her character and its dangerous connotations for a conservative (i.e., patriarchal) epistemological model.

Gertrude's Irony

There is, interestingly enough, only one occurrence in the entire novel of a lexeme connected to the semantic field of irony. As ironic as the novel's narrator has been shown to be, he does not evince a need to explicitly qualify any situation or character as ironic, other than the notable – and hence more significant – exception of Gertrude. In the ninth chapter of *I promessi sposi,* after the initial portrayal of the *monaca* and her agreement to shelter the two women, Gertrude's closing reply to the Father Superior reveals an explicitly ironic understanding of her position within the social organization, an understanding that stands in stark contrast to the literal meaning of her reply.[25]

Here again, I analyse this passage in light of its absence in the first version of the story. In *Fermo e Lucia,* there is a brief exchange between Geltrude and the *padre guardiano* who accompanies the two fugitives, Lucia and Agnese, as he introduces them to her and asks her to help by sheltering them. In reply, the *monaca* refers to her happiness at being able to put her family's name and prestige to good use and her good luck in "potere render servizio a' nostri buoni amici i padri cappuccini" (being able to help our good friends the Capuchin fathers). Her words are accompanied by "un sorriso che ad altri avrebbe potuto parere di compiacenza, ad altri di scherno" (185; a smile that might have made some think of complacency, others of scorn). The passage, as I have noted of many other passages in *Fermo e Lucia,* stresses Geltrude's duplicity as well as her arrogance.

In *I promessi sposi,* this scene of reciprocated gratitude is moved to the end of the first encounter, so as to seal the nun's decision to help Lucia and Agnese. When Gertrude returns the Father Superior's thanks, she explains "non occorron cerimonie" (125; "there's no need for too much ceremonious gratitude"; trans. Penman 174); "'[a]lla fine' continuò con un sorriso, nel quale traspariva *un non so che d'ironico e d'amaro,* 'alla fine, non siam noi fratelli e sorelle?'" (125; "'[a]nd in any case,' she went on, with a smile that had *something bitter and ironical about it,* 'in any case, are we not brothers and sisters?'"; trans. Penman 174, emphasis mine).[26] The tone of Gertrude's assertion is radically changed; the reference to her family is eliminated and her reflection appears less a cruel joke than an interrogation of her own condition. This time, her smile is not capable of two distinct interpretations. Rather, it has a double meaning: irony and bitterness. She is neither lying to nor scornfully mocking the *padre guardiano*; her reply hints of longing for a world, or a time, in which she could have believed in such spiritual kinship.

This passage occurs only two pages after the initial portrait of the *monaca* and also belongs to the preliminary phase of the novel's acquainting its readers with Gertrude. Yet, as the reader can sense from the allusiveness of the portrayal and will later be given to fully realize, the passage is an expression of an advanced stage in Gertrude's parable, the result of the "lenta estenuazione" (slow exhaustion) to which she has been subjected. Gertrude's smile is to be understood as a display of her increased understanding of the complexity of the world, and as a self-reflexive acknowledgment of the difference between personal aspirations and reality, "the unbridgeable chasm between the reality that is and the ideal that should be," as one of Lukács's definitions of irony goes (198). Irony is the result of the thwarting of knowledge that defines Gertrude's character, and as such it is one of the most visible marks of the "monstrousness" of her subjectivity and of her role within the novel.

Notably, the ironic stance establishes a connection between Gertrude and the narrator, one that is built on both analogy and difference. On one hand – and this is, in part, what Ross Chambers refers to when he insists that "there must also be ... a relation between the ironizing ideology and the ironized ideology to mediate the 'split'" (239) – their shared employment of irony is for each of them the endorsement of an authoritative role. The narrator's irony reminds the reader of his (the narrator's) powerful role as organizer of the tale, and Gertrude's irony claims for herself, that is, for her character, an authoritative role insofar as it signifies her detachment from her own story.

On the other hand, there is a clear difference between the irony of a narrator dissociating himself from an event, a statement, or the beliefs of one of his characters, as so often happens with the narrator of *I promessi sposi*, and the irony of a (female) character dissociating herself from what should constitute her understanding of reality. The narrator combines a participatory attitude – "colui che conduce il racconto sa bene di essere uomo anche lui" (the narrator knows very well that he is human, too), as Spinazzola puts it – with a vertical standpoint: "il punto di vista dell'io narrante ... è di chi osserva e giudica, dall'esterno e dall'alto" (615; the point of view of the narrator ... is of the beholder and of the judge, from outside and above). The ideological dissociation serves to place the character's individuality back within the proper perspective and to reinforce the ideological coherence of the text. Conversely, Gertrude's character's dissent from the status quo prompts a "horizontal" revision of the ideology regulating her destiny. Gertrude's protest is completely subjective and autonomous (i.e., it has no vertical power), and it is not answered with compensation for the injustice of her destiny. Her protest fails to be legitimized by any authority other than herself and her experience of life; it serves, to the contrary, as an attempt to forge herself as authority within the text and to signal her subversive desire to survive her own disciplining.

Gertrude's ironic stance can be understood as the modern signifier of a text's dissociation from itself. In Chambers's discussion of oppositional practices, irony is oppositional in that it undermines the literal meaning of a text, its "narrative function," and in so doing reveals a different, often contradictory meaning that precludes the possibility of there being a univocal, authorized textual message. Irony becomes an index of what Chambers calls "the textual function" (16), a textual self-consciousness that dismantles the authoritative power of the story in its literality. Gertrude is subversive both in her display of an autonomous desire within her story and in the slippage that she authorizes between the letter of her story and her own understanding of it. She establishes an oppositional narrative within the novelistic structure and establishes herself as an alternative authority, a self-conscious presence that prevents her tale from merely closing around and fully containing her.

It is all the more fitting, then, that Gertrude's ironic smile is addressed to the supposed kinship, literally the fraternity, between males and females, between monks and nuns. She ironizes the possibilities of reciprocity between representatives of the opposite sex and in so doing subtly underlines the fundamental (and hierarchical) contradictions inherent in her own character and in the narrative structure in general, the contradiction between female passivity and male agency, and the contradictions in the hypocritical obliteration of this sexual hierarchy into a supposedly egalitarian structure ("alla fine, non siam noi fratelli e sorelle?").

Gertrude simultaneously exhibits two opposite postures: the structural subjection that is constitutive of characters and the authoritative role that is proper to the novel's narrator. The monstrousness (or, say, the irony) of Gertrude's irony is, once again, that this self-reflexive attitude is allotted to a woman: the ironic posture de-objectifies her and entrusts to her the role of "knower," of a subject ready to assume a critical position vis-à-vis herself and the world. Her smile displays her active commitment to an epistemological process from which she should, theoretically, be excluded, and it signifies her as "a female knower [in] a metaphorical structure that positions the knower as male" (Spackman, "Monstrous Knowledge" 301). Her ironic posture is another function of the tension between necessity and free will that I have analysed at different levels and in its different manifestations, a tension that, as I have shown, is to be scrutinized in its gendered origins. Gertrude subversively embodies both terms of this tension so as to challenge their "neutrality": the necessity inscribed within Gertrude's body – the submission and passivity that are "mythical" givens of her femininity – coexists with a self-awareness that allows her a "masculine" epistemological autonomy – that is, free will.

Let me put this in even clearer terms: if the tension between necessity and free will were not gendered, Gertrude's double stance within the novel as both subject and object of knowledge would not be perceived as problematic in the first place. Gertrude's subversion, as Dombroski indicates, is certainly to be understood at the level of her endorsement of a secular paradigm that does not seek to make her choices commensurate with the transcendental order. But it is also, most importantly, the infraction of a narrative and epistemological structure founded on the primary distinction that is sexual difference. Gertrude is a problematic character, then, not uniquely in the Lukácsian sense of being a subject conflicted between real and ideal, caught in the "unbridgeable chasm between the reality that is and the ideal that should be" (78), or in Dombroski's sense as a character caught between the world of men and the world of God. She poses an ideological problem for the narrative structure that disciplines her because she refuses to yield to self-renunciation and sacrifice and because she exhibits an awareness of the gendering process that has brought her to this dissonant epistemological position.

"The process of becoming conscious of harshness – the affective consequence of injustice," writes Sarah Ahmed in her reflection on "problem characters," "is described as willfulness." Ahmed's reflection on wilfulness is prompted by instances in which the label "willful" is issued as a "negative evaluation of character" ("Willful Parts" 247). Such negative evaluation, she remarks, is too often associated with the character's gender: "The judgment of willfulness is made when girls do not willingly occupy the place assigned to them by the gender order" (248). From being a demeaning, constrictive label, "willful" evolves, then, within the frame of a feminist theory of the novel, into an important operative notion: "even if willfulness leads only – in narrative terms – to renewed acts of submission ... [w]e can read in willfulness the very potential to deviate from well-trodden paths, to wander, to err, to stray" (249). Problematic and wilful, problematic because wilful, Gertrude displays her desire for change, and her determination not to become background, right to the end of the story. Her wilfulness is the trace of her subversive agency that remains and cannot be completely erased from the text. The *monaca*'s final "supplizio volontario" (524; "voluntary penance"; trans. Penman 698) is in this respect a fitting symbol of the impossibility of a full female agency that does not end up acting against itself. Reading this image as a final self-figuration, that is, for what it tells the reader about the *monaca*'s tale, we can interpret her self-torture as a symbol of Gertrude's desire to survive its reformation (or, at least, to enforce it with the aim of finding a perverted pleasure in her own annihilation).

"Supplizio volontario": How to Survive One's Own Story

The wilful coexistence of (male) agency and (female) passivity within a single character grants this very character space for resistance; indeed, it constitutes her as *the* resistance.[27] The last lines the novel devotes to her once again show that Gertrude's activism is never fully discarded within her story, even though her character is ultimately subjected to and contained within a broader narrative paradigm. Her narrative parable closes with the "supplizio volontario" in which she exerts her will through self-inflicted torturous gestures. Gertrude "writes" on her body as the one space that does not preclude her creativity: she is still using her imagination, even though against herself.

A final scrutiny of the few lines specifically devoted to the closure of her story is especially instructive. In chapter 37, after her friend the widow has informed Lucia of Gertrude's fate, Manzoni refers the reader to his main historical source, Ripamonti's *Historiae Patriae*, to learn more details about this "trista storia" (524; "tragic story"; trans. Penman 698) and about Gertrude's repentance. This is because the narrator relates only the essential lines of the widow's account: Gertrude "s'era ravveduta, s'era accusata" (524; "had finally come to her senses and confessed her crimes"; trans. Penman 698) – she has recognized her crimes and the gravity of her actions. She has repented and her life, the narrator concludes, is now one of expiation. In this account,

Gertrude's recognition of her sins remains confined within the framework of the self-accusation and is immediately re-signified as a bodily and spiritual mortification that points, again, to the theme of impossible self-determination.

Textually, the news of her reformation is followed by the explanation that "la sua vita attuale era supplizio volontario tale, che nessuno, a meno di non togliergliela, ne avrebbe potuto trovare un più severo" (524; "she had now chosen so agonizing a course of voluntary penance that no one could have devised anything harsher without endangering her life"; trans. Penman 698). The sole emphasis here is on her "supplizio." Her story ends with the recognizable iconography of a nun punishing herself with all available means of expiation. It is an image that perfectly resituates this tale within its century of origin, where ascetic and mystic women endangered their own survival through expiatory practices (in accord with the directives of the Council of Trent), while it also calls attention to the anachronistic (dissonant) need that Gertrude still has to act and to decide her own destiny, even in a self-destructive manner.[28]

From the very beginning of our acquaintance with Gertrude, Manzoni pointed to the importance of her body as an "inscribed surface of events" (Foucault, "Nietzsche, Genealogy, History" 83). He exploited Gertrude's body as a text that he could read, "literally written on, inscribed, by desire and signification" (Grosz, *Volatile Bodies* 60), that is, as a body that was shaped by the social (and literary) conditioning it was subjected to from its conception and that was completely interconnected with her interiority in a relation of mutual influence. He deciphered her body for what it could tell about this mysterious woman, thus hinting at the long story of struggle and attrition that would subsequently require two full chapters to be told in its entirety.[29] He also, as I have emphasized, refused to turn her body into a signifier for a gendered ideology of truth in which she would eventually be revealed as a monstrous, hideous hag and objectified as a mediator, rather than a subject, of truth.

If, from what is told, it is clear that Gertrude's character tells a story written against her will, in this closing image Manzoni presents us once more with the significant activation of Gertrude with respect to her own body, an activation justified, in this case, by repentance. Here again, critically speaking, both the narrative and the thematic approaches are needed. It is important to emphasize, as many have already done, that Manzoni explicitly chose to disassociate himself from the hagiographic paradigm adopted by his primary historical source, Ripamonti's *Historiae Patriae*. In his introduction to the edition of the archival documents relative to the trial of "Virginia Maria de Leyva, Monaca di Monza" (documents that Manzoni was able to consult only during the final phases of his rewriting and that therefore did not have a direct impact on his characterization), Giancarlo Vigorelli explains that in Ripamonti's account, "le pagine sulla Signora più che un racconto sono un abbozzo, che si estende quasi più sulla sua redenzione che non sulle sue colpe" ("Presentazione" xviii; the pages about the Signora are more a sketch than a full account, detailing her redemption almost more than her crimes). This supports the suggestion of a narrative evolution from an originary, paradigmatic tale of necessary salvation, where what counts is the final vision of a "*Signora* più spettabile per santità, ... curva vecchiarella, scarna, macilente [*sic*], venerabile" (Vigorelli quoting Ripamonti, xviii; a lady highly esteemed for her holiness, ... a hunched old woman, gaunt, emaciated, venerable), to a secular biography articulated around this woman's irresoluteness, her "extenuated" beauty, and her attempts to intervene in her own destiny. In shaping Gertrude's story, Manzoni forged his own path, endowing his character with unprecedented narrative and ideological latitude.[30]

What the text hands to us as the final image of Gertrude's life is "so agonizing a course of voluntary penance that no one could have devised anything harsher without endangering her life" (trans. Penman 698). The disciplining intervention that Gertrude displays is the final measure of her subjectivity. But the text here tells us even more: this self-annihilation is juxtaposed to an alternative punishment, death, which is discarded. The novel does not kill Gertrude – literally, it does not "take her life away from her"[31] – just as it chooses not to frame her, as Ripamonti did, with the available iconography of the old and venerable saint-on-earth. Rather, it channels her subversion into a literal figure for self-awareness: Gertrude is left to choose the means, degree, and intensity of her annihilation.

The fictional space Manzoni allotted to his character in *I promessi sposi* opened up room for her to manoeuvre between necessity and free will, between female objectification and male subjectivity, and to wilfully problematize the gendered structuration within which she found herself existing. Whether she is erasing her "blasphemous" masculinity with this final movement of annihilation, so as to endorse her feminine powerlessness, or actively obliterating her sinful womanliness, so as to be awarded a "neutral" subjectivity, we do not know. It is with this final uncertainty that the story of Gertrude is brought to a closure, or, rather, not closed at all.

2 The Epistemology of the Young Woman: Analysis and Revelation in Three Fin-de-siècle Novels[1]

Ma tutte queste quistioni di paragone tra l'un sesso e l'altro, non saranno mai messe in chiaro, e ne' pure ben poste fin che gli uomini soli ne tratteranno ex professo negli scritti: giacchè essi peccano tutti verso le donne o di galanteria adulatoria, o di ostilità grossolana. Con questa osservazione non s'intende già di sprezzare temerariamente tante opere profonde che sono state scritte sul merito comparativo del bel sesso, e le riflessioni infinite e bellissime su questo argomento che sono sparse in tante altre opere; ma per quanto una materia sia stata egregiamente trattata, è sempre lecito di desiderare qualche cosa di più.

But all these issues of comparing one sex to the other will never be made clear, nor well put, as long as only men write about it ex professo: given that they all sin against women of either adulatory gallantry, or coarse hostility. This observation is not meant to recklessly disdain many deep works that have been written on the comparative merits of the fair sex, or the endless and beautiful reflections on this topic that are scattered in many other works. But however much a certain topic has already been brilliantly covered, it is always legitimate to desire something more.

(Manzoni, *Fermo e Lucia* 236)

In chapter 1, I explained that the textual confusion created by the character of the *monaca di Monza* arises mainly from her status as a wilful female character occupying the dissonant position of both object and subject of knowledge. This chapter takes this finding as its starting point. At the centre of Neera's three novels – *Teresa* (1886), *Lydia* (1887), and *L'indomani* (1889) – we find three young women who, although they occupy different social and contextual positions, are engaged in a similar quest: to discover their role within society. If, to a certain extent, Gertrude's problematic status lay in the tension between her role as the protagonist of her own story and that of a secondary character within a much larger project, Neera's trilogy removes such ambiguity from the start: Teresa, Lydia, and Marta are the leading characters of the three novels, and the account of the contradictory, problematic status of each of these women is the story itself.

The novelty represented by female writers emerging during the second half of the eighteenth century did not lie solely in the fact that the *gentil sesso* was at last producing a public abundance of artistic talent. It also consisted in their thorough analyses of the condition of women and in the shift of perspective that placed female characters at the centre of their texts, as protagonists. This is not to say that gender alone, whether of the author or the text's protagonist, was responsible for shifting the ideological engagement of these novels. In many of these women's novels the subversive tale remained confined, as it had in Manzoni's *I promessi sposi*, within a narrative structure that was far from innovative, let alone subversive, as far as gender was concerned. The fictional roles typically allotted to women were those of obedient daughter and sister and then wife and mother raising her many offspring to respect secular and divine laws.

Yet women's literary production during these years would not proceed quietly: their active arrival on the public scene, along with their production of subjective discourses, had the potential for dissenting from the dominant ideology and for opening up dissonant spaces whose implications at times could not be fully grasped, not even by the writers themselves. In addition, the acceptance of women as writers was in itself indicative of the social and cultural changes taking place in Italian society by the end of the nineteenth century. The Milanese writer Neera exemplifies both the degree of notoriety these women achieved and the ambivalence they themselves continued to feel about the public visibility and creativity of females.[2]

Between 1886 and 1889, Neera published three novels so structurally and thematically coherent that they came to be considered a "trittico della fanciulla" (triptych of the young woman), as Antonia Arslan defines the trio (*Dame* 128).[3] *Teresa*, *Lydia*, and *L'indomani* examine the destinies of three young women striving to discover and affirm their role in society. Their similar quests soon configure them as paradoxical, split as they are between their intellectual attempts to understand their place in the world, the social subjection that binds them to their biological destinies as women, and the sudden revelations that shed light on their female condition. The novels enact three different solutions (or non-solutions) to resolve this dissonance: Teresa autonomously sets off on her quest for a happier life; Lydia is humiliated in her romantic hopes and kills herself; and, in *L'indomani*, Marta reinserts herself within the ranks of a traditional female genealogy, endorsing the very order that has defeated her cognitive ambitions.

These texts can be defined as quests that in fact have as their very objective the possibility of a free-will quest. The heroines attempt to achieve the status of "seekers," a role that is traditionally granted to male protagonists from the very start of a novel.[4] For Neera's protagonists, this status is not bestowed at the beginning of the story but is, in the best-case scenario, the final outcome of the text.[5] My analysis here follows in the footsteps of scholars such as Elizabeth Abel, Marianne Hirsch, and Elizabeth Langland, who offered the first gendered critiques of the Bildungsroman genre. In a collection they edited in 1983 they underscore the extent to which "gender … has not been assimilated as a pertinent category [in literary theory and analysis], despite the fact that the sex of the protagonist modifies every aspect of a particular Bildungsroman: its narrative structure, its implied psychology, its representation of social pressures" (5). Their analyses of nineteenth- and twentieth-century Anglo-American novels, ranging from Charlotte Brontë's to Toni Morrison's, provide cogent reflections on the variations in and original patterns devised by female novels about women's formation. Similarly, within the Italian context, Neera's novels are extremely compelling examples of "voyages in" and of the gendered nature of quests.[6]

Several literary scholars have suggested that Neera's writing provides an interesting example of conflicting representations of women within the work of a single author.[7] While her essayistic production elaborates very conservative and anti-feminist stances, some of her novels provide important material for a critical approach to the female condition and clearly combine ideologically conflicting discourses on women's role in society. Luigi Baldacci, for example, points out that "[f]emminista convinta ed efficace quando narra, e soprattutto in *Teresa* … Neera s'impone di rivedere le proprie idee, come saggista, dall'interno del sistema dominante, quando affronta espressamente il problema della donna" (Neera, *Le idee di una donna* xviii; a confident and effective feminist when she writes fiction, and especially in *Teresa* …, Neera forces herself to revise her ideas as an essayist within the dominant system when she specifically addresses the problem of woman).[8] This convergence of two different discourses, one complicit and one subversive, is undoubtedly the most striking feature of Neera's works. On the one hand, as Baldacci points out, Neera sometimes adopts protocols from within the dominating system that relegate women to the domestic sphere, but at other times, she conveys a different reality – or at least portrays women's condition exactly as it is – from a space that Baldacci implicitly characterizes as "outside." We can collapse this distinction between inside and outside if we think of the system within which Neera inserts herself as the very space that grants her and her writings their existence, that is, an all-encompassing system of social power.

The notion of a Foucaultian discursive system in which resistance to a dominant discourse can only exist and be enacted from within that discourse reveals the extent to which power is not a unified, centralized structure emanating from a governing will but is rather multiple and relational. Wherever there is power, there is always, already, resistance: "Il n'y a donc pas par rapport au pouvoir *un* lieu du grand Refus ... : mais *des* résistances qui sont des cas d'éspèces ... par définition, elles ne peuvent exister que dans le champ stratégique des relations de pouvoir" (Foucault, *Histoire de la sexualité I* 125–6; "Hence there is no single locus of great Refusal ... Instead there is a plurality of resistances, each of them a special case ... by definition, they can only exist in the strategic field of power relations"; trans. Hurley 95–6). Although it is not without its own blindness to gender asymmetries, Foucault's perspective is essential to an understanding of how every act performed by a subject is already inscribed with the relations of power that define and limit it. Foucault's concept of resistance is also a famously productive one in that it does not deny the possibility of change but rather situates that possibility in a systemic relation with the power that determines its existence.

Drawing on Foucault's analysis of society and of power relations, but focusing more specifically on gender, Judith Butler has emphasized the importance of "rethinking subversive possibilities for sexuality and identity within the terms of power itself" (*Gender Trouble* 40). One of the most important insights provided by Butler's critique of conservative notions of power is this: "[T]o operate within the matrix of power is not the same as to replicate uncritically relations of domination. It offers the possibility of a repetition of the law which is not its consolidation, but its displacement" (40). The performativity that she identifies as key to such displacements corresponds to "that power of discourse to produce effects through reiteration" (*Bodies That Matter* 20). The very act of telling – or retelling – one's story opens the possibility of creating a different message or of unchaining one's audience so as to allow a different reaction.

The narrative "matrix of power" – the ideological framework – displayed in Neera's three novels is the univocal parable, prescribed to and expected of women, that takes them from virgin daughter and sister to married woman and then to mother. Neera never explicitly dismantles the validity of this parable, but her texts demonstrate very clearly that a narrative enterprise setting out to exemplify the parable is, more often than not, bound to encounter a profusion of obstacles standing in the way of smoothly endorsing this basic narrative (and social) paradigm. Neera's works are, in this sense, highly performative: while telling (or retelling) stories with quite linear and traditional female trajectories, they succeed in negotiating new spaces for characters and readers alike, spaces that make it possible to measure the distance between the ideological framework of the text and the subjective aspirations of the characters inhabiting it. These are spaces in which revelations do not always work as they should and in which, by the end of her journey, a protagonist can affect an ironic stance vis-à-vis her own life – an attitude that would have been unthinkable at the outset. These three novels also neatly exemplify the extent to which the very categories of subversiveness and complicity, although useful analytically, need to be understood as codetermining factors, mutually dependent variables that are never mutually exclusive. The ideological tensions at work in these novels can be aptly defined as the expression of gendered dissonances, of the coexistence of different, contradictory ideological positions that will, more often than not, fail to find a peaceful coexistence.

Teresa, or the Successful Revelation

The first novel of the triptych, *Teresa*, offers the most apt example of the displacement of which Butler writes and an optimistic, if ambiguous, solution to the problematic status of a female seeker. Published in 1886, *Teresa* is Neera's most famous work, and it has been reprinted and republished quite regularly throughout the twentieth century and in the beginning of the twenty-first. In her introduction to the 1995 edition of the novel, Arslan notes, "*Teresa* è un romanzo speciale. Una storia coraggiosa, audace persino" (5; *Teresa* is a special novel. A courageous story, bold even), a "documento essenziale della presa di coscienza femminile dell'epoca" (8; essential document of women's consciousness raising). If Sibilla Aleramo's *Una donna* (1906) can be considered the first explicitly feminist Italian novel, *Teresa* should be placed among the most important fin-de-siècle statements and indictments of the female condition and as such should be considered one of the indispensable predecessors of Aleramo's fictionalized memoir.

Teresa, the daughter of a tax collector, is introduced to the reader at the pivotal moment when she turns her back on her childhood to take on a woman's role. At fifteen, she has just obtained her middle school diploma and is now staying at home to help her mother. She has grown up "lontana da tutte le emozioni" (*Teresa* 31; far from all emotions).[9] She is chaste, obedient, and devout. Her passage into adulthood is discursively sanctioned through the sudden investiture (a first, failed, revelation in fact) that her mother dispenses to her before giving birth to her sister: "Questa notte avrai un altro fratellino ... ma già sei la maggiore tu, *devi pur saperlo*" (31; "tonight you'll have another little baby brother ... but you're the oldest, *you should know about it*"; trans. King 14, emphasis mine).[10] The theme of knowledge versus ignorance is central to the development of this novel, as it is, in different ways, to the entire trilogy. Teresa's mother presupposes in her daughter a knowledge that she does not have, and Teresa apprehends her mother's revelation as a sudden but temporary ripping of a veil that had separated her from reality, a veil that immediately falls back to hide her future ("come fosse ricaduto il lembo di velo che le aveva squarciato il futuro," 32; "as though the rent veil disclosing her future fell back again"; trans. King 15). Images of obstructed vision recur throughout the novel to thematize the protagonist's hampered access to truth.

Neera characterizes Teresa as the passive recipient of a select piece of information to which her destiny is now tied, since she has been asked to take over some of her mother's responsibilities in the household. The episode also clearly contrasts her ignorance with the omniscience of males. Teresa tells her younger brother of the birth only to learn that he already knows about it: " – Ah! Sí? – fece Carlino – lo sapevo che doveva nascere ... Teresina rimase immobile, colpita dalle parole del fratello. *Come mai egli lo sapeva*?" (34; "Oh, really? I knew it was going to happen ... Teresina remained stock-still, struck by her brother's last words. *How did he know*?"; trans. King 17, emphasis mine). Teresa's surprise introduces the reader to the gendered disparity that regulates her life. The young girl has been informed of the impending event only because her help is needed, and throughout the novel, she is offered only those pieces of information that are deemed appropriate, so that her vision of life is shaped in accordance with a socially acceptable protocol that precludes her autonomous understanding of the world. In contrast, her brother's matter-of-fact answer attests to both his free access to knowledge and the way his experience is already, at such a young age, much more encompassing than his sister's.

As a consequence, this first episode, coupled with her sudden interest in her body, provokes in Teresa a more generalized "curiosità viva" (15; sharp curiosity). *Teresa* is the story of the multiple ways in which her keen curiosity is thwarted and mystified. As she tries to understand her role in society, the mystery of love, and the mystery of female and male bodies, Teresa is fed a set of preconceived notions of womanhood, love, and marriage. The narrator's realistic stance shies away from the rhetoric of heroism and indicates very clearly the impossibility of a girl as normal as Teresa explicitly revolting. The passive submission that is a gendered given of her life from the outset, and that casts her in the role of obedient daughter until the very end, is juxtaposed to her curiosity, so that *Teresa* progressively reveals the impossible coexistence of these opposite epistemological stances, of the subject and of the object of knowledge, and explicitly connects this impossibility to the social role assigned to women. As Teresa realizes later in the novel, she is not free to decide her own fate because of her gender: "la sua condizione di donna le imponeva anzitutto la rassegnazione al suo destino" (195; "her state as a woman required resignation to her destiny"; trans. King 168).

The novel incorporates the few sanctioned means available to young girls for educating themselves about life and systematically highlights the extent to which such methods are only discursive elaborations with very little connection to reality: the paintings of Telemaco's adventures hanging in the home of Teresa's aunt, or the performance of *Rigoletto* that she attends with her friend *la pretora* (the judge's wife), or the romances she reads under her mother's indulgent gaze. In fact, Teresa's mother, who had married for love and provided a conspicuous dowry for a socially inferior man, has directly experienced the unbridgeable gap between the rhetoric of love and the reality. Yet she sustains Teresa's mystification by refusing to explain to her daughter the full extent of the radical difference between romances and real life: " – Non c'è nulla di vero, sai? – diceva languidamente la signora Soave [as Teresa reads her novels] – la vita non è come la descrivono nei libri; ma alla tua età leggevo volentieri anch'io. Cose di gioventù!" (77; "'It's not all true, you know' – Signora Soave said languidly. 'Life isn't like it's described in books. But I read them, too, at your age. Things of youth'"; trans. King 56).[11] The mother fails to fulfil her role as mediator of the truth; she does not transmit her acquired knowledge about life and social roles to her daughter but rather leaves her in the dark about what awaits her as a grown woman.

The only other model of femininity available to girls such as Teresa, one that is conflated with the model offered by the passive heroines of romances, is the Catholic icon of motherhood and virginity, the Virgin Mary. Teresa dreams of devoting herself to love "come le vergini, chiuse nei chiostri, sognano di unirsi al Signore" (148; "like cloistered virgins dream of union with their Lord"; trans. King 123). She desires a submission that is perfectly consistent with the patriarchal order: women can be "schiave dell'uomo o schiave di Dio" (148; "slaves of God or man"; trans. King 123). Her yearning to sacrifice is complemented by her complete ignorance of what, socially (and anatomically), love is: she wonders "senza amore, a che cosa si riduce la vita di una donna?" (151; "without love, what would a woman's life be?"; trans. King 126), but she cannot grasp that, to be approved, love has to be socially useful and productive, not to mention legally sanctioned.

After the first episode, the novel soon focuses on the love story between Teresa and Egidio Orlandi, an impetuous college student. He initially appears in the novel as a brave young man sailing down a swollen river with a newborn he has saved from the water. The first time Teresa and Egidio cross paths (but without meeting), he is driving his sulky too fast and one of its wheels makes contact with and breaks one of the wheels of Teresa's aunt's carriage. Mobility, both literal and symbolic, is Egidio's most conspicuous attribute. He is presented as a heroic, fearless young man, and the first actual encounter between Egidio and Teresa highlights the specific gendered roles assigned to each of them. Teresa is visiting the chapel of a church with Egidio's aunt when she catches sight of Egidio climbing the bars outside of the window: "Teresina, nella penombra calma e pura della cappella, *come una santa vergine* staccata dal muro; egli, ardito, in attitudine aggressiva, col volto irradiato dalla porpora del tramonto" (110; "Teresina, in the pure and calm dim light of the chapel *like a saintly virgin* statue detached from the wall; he, bold, with an aggressive attitude, with his handsome face suffused by the purple twilight"; trans. King 88, emphasis mine). Teresa, the saintly virgin, is the object of the male gaze, guarded within a chaste space. Orlandi, the small-town hero – whose physical appearance evokes both Garibaldi and Christ with his "bei capelli neri" ("beautiful black hair") and a "barba morbida" (204; "soft beard"; trans. King 176) – is a subject who is deliberately choosing the object of his desire. Egidio and Teresa are explicitly cast in the two archetypal positions of "the 'mobile' man versus the 'immobile' woman" (Parati 7). The interior of the church replicates the domestic realm to which Teresa is confined and in which she will spend the ensuing years waiting until her love can be publicly expressed, while the outside world remains the domain of Egidio and men in general.

The romance develops through a clandestine exchange of letters. When Egidio, with a law diploma in his pocket, asks Teresa's father for her hand, the father refuses because of the young man's precarious economic situation and because he is not willing to provide Teresa with a dowry – the family money is all being channelled towards her brother's degree. Egidio continually promises to find a regular position and thus be able to marry Teresa, but he also continues to follow his personal ambitions in journalism, a profession that does not confer financial stability. The idealized love that ties Teresa to Egidio looks like a perfect storybook romance in the beginning, sanctioning a correspondence between novels and reality, but it quickly turns into an endless, embittering waiting period that transforms the vital naive girl into a hysterical woman – and what initially appeared to Teresa to be a fairy tale changes into an untold parable, a story that she does not recognize and cannot fully understand.

It is emphatically clear in the novel that no single character is to be condemned for this waste. Teresa's brother and father are selfish and tyrannical, but they are depicted as the product of their education and social customs; and although Egidio Orlandi is not as financially reliable as Teresa's father would like his son-in-law to be, he is in fact a good young man, smart and loving. The novel explicitly points to the unilateral advantages allotted to men, to society's "dominio assoluto del sesso forte" (106; "absolute dominion of the stronger sex"; trans. King 84), and to the contradictions inherent in nurturing in women a fable of never-ending, absolute love when in fact their sole societal role is procreation.

When her father forbids her to continue a romance that he has deliberately prevented from being legitimized, Teresa ends up spending her days in "nella inenarrabile monotonia della vita femminile" (180; "the unspeakable monotony of female life"; trans. King 154). She gradually realizes the lack of alternatives: "Che cosa poteva fare? ... mancare ai doveri di figlia ubbidiente e sottomessa? La schiavitù la cingeva da ogni lato. Affetto, consuetudini, religione, società, esempi, ciascuno le imponeva il proprio laccio ... Una fanciulla non è mai libera, non le si concede nemmeno la libertà di mostrare le sue sofferenze" (181; "What could she do? Rebel against her father, make that angel of a mother die of worry, break with all the family traditions, neglect the duties of an obedient and submissive daughter?"; trans. King 154). The novel powerfully depicts the gradual transformation of a serene young woman into a neurotic spinster. As she feels her youth coming to an end, the pathological symptoms of her impossible acceptance of her destiny appear: "[e]bbe un accesso di vera disperazione, durante il quale sentì agitarsi nel fondo delle viscere un torrente d'odio" (198; "she was overwhelmed with despair, her body rocked with torrents of hate"; trans. King 171). This is followed by regular crises of convulsions, which the family doctor hastily diagnoses as "isterismo nervoso" (198; "nervous hysterics"; trans. King 171).

The medical discourse that surfaces in the novel is immediately accompanied by a symbolic displacement: the old doctor is unable to handle the modernity of his own diagnosis. He prescribes tranquillizers, iron pills, and some physical activity. Then, unwilling to accept responsibility for Teresa's worsening "malattia nervosa" (213; "nervous malady"; trans. King 185), he suggests calling a younger physician "addottorato nelle teorie moderne, versato nella patologia come nella psichiatria" (214; "instructed in modern theories, and versed in pathology as well as psychiatry"; trans. King 185). The generational shift brings with it a new approach to understanding female pathologies, one that makes use of modern scientific discourses and that prefigures Freud's questions about the riddle of femininity. The shift (re)introduces sexuality, both within the medical discourse and in the relationship between male doctor and female patient. At the prospect of being visited in bed by a young man, Teresa prepares herself as for a love encounter and is then both terrified and subjugated by the physical attraction she feels for the man.[12]

According to Foucault, the elaborations of power that brought eighteenth- and nineteenth-century Western Europe to construct sexuality as a disciplining discourse also succeeded in founding sexuality as identity and, in the case of women, in investing the classic reduction of woman's essence to her body with a new social meaning. In Foucault's view, the modern discourse of sexuality is a different, more scientific, yet still fundamentally conservative way to explain women's conditions and pathologies from the standpoint of their biological functions. Along the same lines, Cristina Mazzoni has written that the medical intervention on women's bodies at the end of the nineteenth century was one of "appropriation and ventriloquism of that very body by an increasingly powerful discipline" (348). It is nonetheless striking that the introduction of this discourse in Neera's fiction has potentially subversive implications: the character of the doctor in her novels stands for a (positive) modernity, for empathic rationality, and, at times, for an original standpoint on society and on women's role within it.[13]

In *Teresa*, the doctor facilitates Teresa's discovery of physical desire and of the fact that her senses can have an autonomous life, "indipendente dal cuore e dalla volontà" (217; "independent of her heart and will"; trans. King 189). Her relationship with the young man constitutes a fundamental step towards her understanding the social laws separating men and women and a more realistic apprehension of love. Moreover, if there is initially a clear distinction between the knowledge accessed through Teresa's irrational idealism and that accessed through the doctor's scientific discourse, the two are ultimately reconciled and shared by the characters: Teresa's knowledge shifts towards an understanding of human encounters that is, if not scientific, certainly more "graphic" than before, while the doctor gradually reveals a romantic side that betrays his interest in non-scientific matters.

The narrator explains that during the same period, Teresa educates herself by chance as she leafs through the pages of a crumpled booklet, a text that she discovers is a "libro osceno" (291; "filthy book"; trans. King 190) detailing the modalities of heterosexual intercourse. It is a book that literally gives her "la chiave del mistero ch'ella aveva ricercato invano" (219; "the key to the mystery she had sought in vain"; trans. King 190). Reading this booklet is the shocking culmination of her apprenticeship, of a sentimental education that began with the heights and perfection of an ideal love and gradually descended to its originary depths. Although "non aveva mai udito né immaginato niente di simile" (218; "[n]ever had she heard or imagined anything like it"; trans. King 189), she soon realizes that "quelle spiegazioni crudeli erano la sola risposta ch'ella trovava alla sua lunga, insoddisfatta curiosità" (218; "[t]hose cruel explanations were the only answer she had found to her long unsatisfied curiosity"; trans. King 190). These explanations are a veritable revelation, the missing piece of her epistemological puzzle, the secret that explains everything else. They unveil the ugly truth of human misery and prompt her to finally see her womanhood through the eyes of society and to grasp the reasons why she has been ridiculed for endorsing a Platonic romance for so long. Coincidentally (but not by chance), it is a knowledge that tastes like a "medicina che torni a gola" (218; "medicine that won't go down"; trans. King 190), a revelation that narratively consolidates in this novel the connection between medicine and truth, reaffirming the contribution of the young doctor's presence to Teresa's successful epistemological initiation. It is a squalid revelation, yet a healthy one, insofar as it prompts Teresa to reread her life and her love for Egidio through this new epistemological filter and to understand her place in the world.

In a specular progression, the personality of the doctor gradually develops beyond his merely scientific role. In their last conversation, the young doctor is in fact configured as a male alter ego for Teresa. He is shown to be wrestling with the same phantasmatic constructs as she, equally torn between the realities of the body and the longings of the imagination: "il dottore provava forse qualcosa di simile; presente col corpo, aveva l'immaginazione lontana" (223; "[p]erhaps the doctor was feeling something similar: bodily present, his thoughts were far away"; trans. King 194). He criticizes the romantic ideal of love, stressing the importance of daily, prosaic proximity for the consistency of love: "Nei drammi e nei romanzi di una volta incontriamo spesso questa situazione: una donna cade nell'acqua, un uomo la salva, essi si amano. Ma come? Che ne sanno essi? … Sanno solamente come mangiano, come dormono? … [L]'amore, il vero, nasce da un complesso di circostanze, di affinità intime e continue" (223; "In plays and novels of the past we often meet this situation: a woman falls in a pond, a man saves her, they fall in love. Why? What do they know of each other? … Do they only know how they eat and sleep? … True love is born from a whole set of circumstances, of infinite and continuous affinities"; trans. King 194). Teresa comes to share his insistence on the importance of combining the ideal with a healthy appraisal of reality, which she will enforce with her final choice.

By the end of the novel Teresa has thus pieced together the scattered pieces of the mystery that she has puzzled over throughout the story: "che cos'era dunque quel mistero che le sfuggiva continuamente, sul quale sembrava concentrarsi l'attenzione di tutti?" (197; "[w]hat was the mystery that had constantly eluded her, which seemed to command everyone's attention?"; trans. King 170). She is transformed from an object of medical scrutiny to a friendly presence for the doctor as he visits her ailing father every evening. She wishes she could "ricominciare la vita ora che la conosceva meglio" (226; "start her life over now that she understood more"; trans. King 196), although she remains bound to her social duties as a daughter (and accepts these) as she takes care of her dying parent. But there will be one last surprise: the ending of *Teresa,* unlike that of the two novels that follow, reopens social possibilities for the aging young woman and engenders the metamorphosis of an existence that had been consecrated to stillness and waiting.

After her father's death, Teresa receives a desperate letter from her faraway lover, Egidio; his political and career ambitions have turned out not to be as productive as he believed they would be. She decides to leave her home and join him. When her friend the *pretora* asks her what other people will think, Teresa replies with an unfinished sentence, "Oh! la gente poi ..." ("Oh! The people ..."), and a melancholic smile "al quale si aggiunse una punta di ironia" (228; "traced with irony"; trans. King 199). In what is still a dichotomous partitioning of their roles, the once restless and mobile Egidio is now bedridden, his health failing, and it is Teresa's turn to mobilize, to abandon her home and hometown to look after her lover. The female protagonist of *Teresa* has finally accrued enough knowledge about herself and about the world to become a seeker and a mobile subject. The mystery of the connection between men and women is now completely unveiled, and Teresa departs, fully aware of the price she has paid for her freedom.

Scholars have read Teresa's departure in different ways: is she leaving to be Egidio's nurse, as the *pretora* sarcastically comments – that is, is the potential subversion of her departure downplayed by the prospect of chastity and the feminine task of caring for a bedridden patient, or is she actually joining her lover for the first time?[14] In either case, the daring novelty of Teresa's autonomous decision and departure cannot be overemphasized – just as her sister Ida's departure to fill a new assignment as a schoolteacher in the south of Italy is a symbol of the changing position of women.[15] It should be clear that while the *pretora*'s reading of her departure foresees chasteness, Teresa's does not. As Teresa leaves her home, she is described as "già impressionata dei misteri del futuro" (229; "all too aware of the mysteries of the future"; trans. King 199), struck by the possibilities inherent in her new understanding of life. Indeed, throughout the novel, the word "mistero" is employed in connection with the inaccessibility of the sphere of sexuality and then with the sudden revelation of the "despicable secret." Together with the novel's regular figural references to veils, fog, and blindness – for example, "sentiva di trovarsi isolata, attaccata al mondo solamente per il tramite della famiglia, e che intorno ci fosse una gran nebbia" (181–2; "she felt isolated, connected to the world only through her family, with a great fog surrounding everything"; trans. King 155); "Sì, di tutto ciò era convinta, ma anche un cieco è convinto che non può pretendere di vedere, e tuttavia chiede al mondo dei veggenti, perché egli solo debba essere la vittima" (195; "Yes, she was convinced of all that. A blind man, convinced that he can no longer expect to see, might still ask the seeing world why he must be the victim"; trans. King 168) – the rhetoric of mystery makes it clear that the unveiling of the truth of her sexuality can be the beginning of a different story for Teresa, one in which Teresa mobilizes herself.

The role reversal at the novel's close, while necessary for Teresa's mobilization, also alludes to the weakening of male supremacy. Egidio embodies a less monolithic and authoritarian male figure than Teresa's father and brother; he is a man who has chosen individual realization over social status and as such ends up defenceless against society's harsh realities. As Teresa turns into the one who knows, that is, into an alternative figure to a doctor (or, as the *pretora* puts it, in more gendered terms, of a nurse), Egidio's illness reflects the failure of his epistemological and social project. His attempt to combine an idealistic, but not very profitable, career with a simultaneous traditional venture into the conjugal economy is thus shown to be a failure.[16] It is also important to notice that the new Teresa, now ready to leave, seals her fate by answering the *pretora*'s questions with a smile "traced with irony" (trans. King 199). As I have discussed in the case of Gertrude in *I promessi sposi*, when an ironic posture surfaces in a female character, it is an index of an oppositional stance, of a status as knower, as exemplified by both Gertrude and Teresa by the end of their parables.

Teresa's journey is an important example of the ideological dissonance that female characters bring to narrative projects when they become active characters. *Teresa* has been read as a feminist novel precisely because the contradictions at work within the text are not contained by its formal structure and because its open-ended closing manages to be an optimistic statement regarding the displacements that can be performatively achieved by a narrative. The critical dissonances at work in Neera's fictional writings, however, are powerfully present even within texts that "redeem" themselves by more traditional, or more tragic, endings. They still maintain an unsettling status vis-à-vis the dissonant performances of gender that they propose, and as such they are equally powerful socially symbolic acts.

Lydia, or the Tragic Revelation

Lydia, the protagonist of her eponymous novel, is a young aristocratic heiress who is rich enough not to have to rush into marriage. Her financial freedom seems to place her in a more independent position than Teresa, providing her with the leisure to have fun (this is Lydia's motto: *divertirsi*, "to have fun," 27). However, as Lydia acts out, one after another, every fashionable role proposed to women as possible identities, this freedom does not open any possibility of learning about life or of independently choosing her way. Lydia's personal projects, whether they are an investment in social life or her mourning her mother's death, charitable missions to the poor or a passion for interior decorating, never last longer than a couple of months.

Lydia's financial assets lead her to believe that her social status is not entirely dependent on her connection to men, and she is persuaded that she can behave like a married woman without being one. But her views are not shared in her social milieu: "La sua posizione in società era bizzarra. Indipendente e non maritata; vergine e già passata attraverso le corruzioni della fantasia; non avendo mai concesso un bacio, eppure vituperata dalla fama" (93; Her position in society was bizarre. Independent and unmarried, virgin and having passed through the corruptions of fantasy, having never given a kiss, but berated in virtue of her fame), Lydia easily accesses a discursive knowledge that she then exhibits as experience, so much so that she is considered a "lost" woman. She is convinced she has learned all there is to know, but her assumed omniscience is unintentionally ironic, since she has only managed to access a collection of conventions, of social roles and rules that, although they apparently constitute a body of knowledge, do not provide her with any understanding of her specific role and its boundaries within such a system.

Over the years, Lydia refuses several marriage proposals, and the inexorable passage of time – yet again – turns the young woman into a lonely spinster. Lydia keeps awaiting the realization of an ideal, romantic love while outwardly, through her display of masculine detachment and sarcasm, denying any hint of an emotional investment. Teresa's narrator had written that "la sua condizione di donna le imponeva soprattutto la rassegnazione al suo destino" (195; "her state as a woman required resignation to her destiny"; trans. King 168), and in this sense Lydia is Teresa's opposite, because the one thing she does not want to do is to resign herself to her fate. However, Lydia does share with Teresa an ignorance of how, and against what, she should rebel. Her quest is an attempt to replace this ignorance with a knowledge that she can use to craft her own formation. Lydia's rebellious attitude is thus a provocation that remains confined within very restricted boundaries and that endangers only her because it isolates her socially.

Lydia tries to position herself as an active seeker but within the socially preordained role of being an object. This encapsulation of activity within passivity precludes any legitimate discovery and cuts short the subversiveness of Lydia's autonomy: she mimics the epistemological autonomy of males without ever achieving it. For example, she elaborates an original epistemological grid to classify the people she encounters, but the grid is "alchemic" at best: she distinguishes "cinque categorie ben distinte di persone: i *caldi*, i *freddi*, i *tiepidi*, i *morbidi*, i *pungenti*" (151; five different categories of individuals: the *hot*, the *cold*, the *lukewarm*, the *soft*, the *pungent* ones). Her friend Calmi, as the epitome of male intellectualism, is "freddo e pungente" (151; cold and pungent), a label that is meant to convey his cold, ironic rationality. The classification attests to her attempt to access some kind of autonomous intellectual knowledge but is also, later on in the novel, patently revealed as insufficient for decoding the world.[17]

While maintaining all of her feminine traits, Lydia assumes "un'affettazione di mascolinità" (111; an affectation of masculinity) as a way to rebel against convention. As time passes, in fact, alongside her desire to be seduced by a worthy man there surfaces an equally strong, if not stronger, desire to *be* a man herself. The narrator explicitly emphasizes the gender dissonance that Lydia's character provokes, outlining Lydia's double bind: on the one hand, she is deserted by her female peers because she too intimately frequents the company of men (117); on the other, she is misunderstood as easy prey when she tries to enjoy their company by behaving just like one of them – and is thus cast back into the role of the object of desire. To explain the absurdity of Lydia's social position, and the reason for her isolation, the narrator writes that "la donna sola ... nella condizione di Lydia è un *ermafrodita*" (118; a single woman ... in Lydia's condition is a *hermaphrodite*, emphasis mine). The narrator explicitly connects Lydia's violation of a social proscription with an image of sexual monstrosity, a combination of female and male sexual attributes. Her gender confusion is thus explained by her peers with a sexual diagnosis that once again ties women's social roles to their bodies: her dissonant behaviour is read as the trace of a bodily abnormality.[18]

The presence of such a secondary character as the lawyer Calmi serves to highlight Lydia's aspirations to masculinity. Years after she has ruled out any possibility of a heterosexual relationship with him, they become friends. The similarities of their behaviour and thinking are, in fact, so strong that they cannot help but clash. Their relationship is, at least with respect to intellectual exchanges, one of equals: "[A]vevano lo spirito fatto per comprendersi; solo si somigliavano troppo, e da questa somiglianza nasceva … un urto" (121–2; [T]hey were spiritually very close, made to understand each other; only they were too similar, and from such a similarity there arose … a clash). Whereas Calmi's behaviour is socially accepted, Lydia's re-gendering has a negative reception: her affectation of masculinity "ad alcuni riusciva ripugnante, ad altri incomprensibile, ai più ridicola" (111; to some appeared repulsive, to others incomprehensible, to most ridiculous). This paves the way for the tragedy that follows: Lydia's desire to be a man cannot be endorsed and is turned against her by the plot.

The reversal of her fate is orchestrated by Lydia's new friend, the baroness Won Stern, and her cousin Keptsky, with whom Lydia falls passionately in love. The gender confusion associated with Lydia is mirrored in her first, photographic, encounter with the man she will fall for. When the baroness shows Lydia a series of portraits of Viennese aristocrats, Lydia comments, "A me piacciono le donne … – Ecco l'imperatrice. – Stupenda creatura! … – E questa? – esclamò, sollevandone una alla fiamma … – Non è una donna, ti prego – ghignò la baronessa … – È mio cugino Keptsky" (134–5; I like women … – Here is the empress. – Wonderful creature! … – And this one? – she exclaimed, raising one to the flame … – It's not a woman, I beg you – the baroness sneered … – It's my cousin Keptsky). It is not an accident that Lydia thinks that the handsome lieutenant Keptsky is a woman. Even after this first misunderstanding is dispelled, the narration plays with the ambiguity of his gender role and with the uncanny correspondence that Lydia finds between her ideal of romantic love and her beloved Keptsky. Lydia uses her personal grid to attribute to Keptsky "il miglior amalgama: era tiepido e morbido" (151; the best mixture: he was warm and soft), in clear contrast to Calmi's cold, male rationality.

The lieutenant serves both as a perfect complement to Lydia's soul and as her emotional double. He is presented as an object that Lydia can finally grasp to her satisfaction but also as an unhappy soul with a history of misunderstandings and social rejections similar to hers. When first warned of Keptsky's financial problems, Lydia chooses not to face the truth but rather turns his story into yet another clue confirming their similar destiny: "[L]a storia di Keptsky non era la sua? Incompreso, viziato[,] solitario in mezzo alla gente, troppo nobile ..., indipendente, temerario, fiero, sdegnoso" (175; [W]asn't Keptsky's story her own? Misunderstood, spoiled, lonely in a crowd, too noble ..., independent, fearless, proud, disdainful). Lydia reflects that the lieutenant "le si era presentato sul tramonto della sua giovinezza, come il finale grandioso di un'opera sciupata, ... il tratto di genio di un autore incompreso" (155; has appeared on the evening of his youth, as the grand finale of a wasted work, ... the stroke of genius of a misunderstood author), deftly comparing her own life to a wasted work of art saved by Keptsky as the grand finale and herself to the very author of such a work, thus underscoring her dual status as both object and subject of creation.

Keptsky is, indeed, a work of art, as perfectly plotted as the romance he builds around her while he continues his secret liaison with his cousin, the baroness. His position as an object of desire within Lydia's revised epistemology is an index of his ability to exploit Lydia's rebelliousness. His goal is to constrain her within a very traditional heterosexual contract that would give him legal and social control over the aristocratic heiress and her financial assets and thus reposition him as a full subject. It is only after her engagement that Lydia realizes that the young man is fraudulently staging to his advantage the discursive ideal of perfect love that she seeks, and she realizes it only because of the intervention of her old friend, the lawyer Calmi, who ultimately destroys the spell.[19]

Calmi accompanies Lydia to the hotel where Keptsky secretly meets his lover every afternoon. This provides Lydia with a tragic revelation, one that cannot be disavowed precisely because of Calmi's presence at her side. From a room adjacent to Keptsky's, Lydia hears him exhorting the baroness to be patient (until, the reader infers, he succeeds in marrying Lydia and gets his hands on her money) – along with the other sounds characteristic of sexual encounters. Lydia "avrebbe voluto vedere, ma non ebbe bisogno di questo ... nessuna realtà impudicamente ostentata poteva essere più terribile di quella realtà che si credeva al sicuro e che aveva gettato ogni velo" (185; wanted to see, but did not need this ... no shamelessly flaunted reality could be more terrible than the reality that had believed itself safe and that had removed every veil). With the unveiling of reality, Lydia's illusion of finding a compromise between the activity of masculinity and the objectification of femininity tragically fails. The novel falls short of a re-gendering that cannot happen: she can never be a man (like Calmi), just as Keptsky's sensitive femininity is only a screen erected to defraud her. The novel's outcome is determined by the exploitation of Lydia's financial strengths and epistemological weaknesses to the advantage of others.

The lawyer Calmi occupies a fundamental position in this complex gendered structure, as he embodies both the impossible object with whom Lydia desires to identify and the enforcer of reality, whose attempt to save her from a disastrous marriage ends up provoking her suicide. In her introduction to this novel, Paola Azzolini emphasizes the purpose served by the presence of a male friend such as Calmi: "ironico, razionale, apparentemente freddo, … accanto a Lydia rappresenta la lucidità della mente maschile in confronto ai sussulti scomposti dell'animo femminile" (8; ironic, rational, and seemingly cold … next to Lydia he represents the lucidity of the male mind in contrast to the broken gasps of the female spirit). The lawyer is undoubtedly the voice of reason, the one friend Lydia can count on: in terms of her categorization of human beings, Calmi's cold and pungent qualities appear to be the defining traits of his personality.

It should be pointed out, however, that the relationship between Calmi and Lydia is not based on a contrast between male rationality and female irrationality alone: they clearly share an intellectual complicity that makes Lydia something more than an object of his speculations. As Lydia's alchemic epistemology illustrates, she is engaged in a personal attempt to intellectualize her understanding of the world, to decode the elements at the disposal of her intelligence. What separates Calmi and Lydia is a gendered difference that, although she disavows it, is ultimately the reason for Lydia's ruin. The connection between these two characters is thus a strict polarity not between reason and feelings or between knowledge and ignorance, but rather between a predominantly abstract position, Calmi's, and a dissonant position, Lydia's – characterized by a constant shift between active intellectual reflection and passive social objectification.

Azzolini also detects, in the inclusion of the character Calmi, a trace of Neera's debt to Luigi Capuana's novel *Giacinta,* first published in 1879. She writes, "Giacinta … aveva vicino l'autorevole dottor Follini che … rappresenta la scienza con la sua obiettività indiscutibile" (8; Giacinta … had close to her the authoritative doctor Follini, who … represents science with his unquestionable objectivity). I have explained, and I will also show in my analysis of the trilogy's third novel, that the presence of male secondary figures as representatives of rationality and science is endemic to these novels, as in fact it is to many Italian and European novels written at the end of the nineteenth and the beginning of the twentieth centuries. This similarity arguably owes more to the positivistic climate of fin-de-siècle Italy and, in general, to the increased medicalization of life in post-Unification Italy than to a direct debt between two authors. It is also a defining figure of the realist novel tout court: the novelistic figure of the doctor, according to Philippe Hamon, embodies an example of the "destinateur" (receiver) of the "discours réaliste" (realist discourse). Like "l'ingénieur (voir J. Verne), le spécialiste, l'érudit, l'autochtone, … [et] le professeur" (the engineer (see J. Verne), the professional, the erudite, the native, … [and] the professor), the doctor is, in Hamon's analysis, the "*fonctionnaire* délégué de l'énonciation réaliste" (141–2; *officer* in charge of the realistic utterance).[20]

As I have discussed in the case of *Teresa*, the presence of the doctor, and the shift in that novel from an older to a younger physician, is highly significant not only for the introduction of the discourse of science, but also for Teresa's ultimate understanding that sexual desire is autonomous from love. In *Lydia*, the role of the lawyer Calmi is that of an enforcer of reality, a reality that Lydia arguably already knows but fails to acknowledge as long as possible because such a recognition would also bring about her ruin. Calmi is also, nonetheless, Lydia's alter ego, a masculine version of the protagonist whose similarly disillusioned outlook on reality and distancing from heterosexual relations do not cast on him the social stigma that befalls Lydia.[21]

The revelation of the betrayal does not prompt Lydia to reclaim her active role; rather, it serves to sanction the impossibility of her re-gendering project. Earlier in the novel, when she encounters Keptsky in the street and asks him about his cousin, Lydia deliberately chooses not to remember that she almost caught them together during her visit to the baroness's villa: "una rimembranza molesta era passata qual lampo nella mente di Lydia, ma la cacciò via subito. La realtà era lì, bella, affascinante" (163; a bothersome memory had passed like a flash in Lydia's mind, but she drove it away immediately. The reality was there, beautiful, charming). The beautiful reality of Keptsky at her side will turn out to be, proverbially, too good to be true (a metaphor, I might add, that indulges in the same revelatory paradigm exploited in these novels). As in *Teresa*, Neera resorts to the traditional rhetoric of revelation by presenting a beautiful, romantic reality that is ultimately unmasked as a disguise for the shocking truth of human sexuality. Unlike Teresa, Lydia does not choose to mobilize herself. She cannot envision a destiny outside of the social circle that will now ridicule her for letting herself be deceived by a fraud.

Lydia turns against herself the rebellion that she could not carry forward: she commits suicide with a "grazioso *revolver*, un ninnolo elegante" (118; a pretty *revolver*, an elegant trinket) that she has won at a raffle. The irony of winning a deadly weapon at a charity lottery is coupled with the assertion of a social – and existential – defeat symbolically executed by a decorative object that recalls Lydia in her accessoriness. Extrapolating from one of the final paragraphs of Judith Butler's essay on Nella Larsen's novel *Passing*, a paragraph in which she discusses the "interpellation of the *white* norm," it can be said that this novel "displays in all its painfulness the ways in which the interpellation of the [*gender*] norm is reiterated and executed by those whom it would – and does – vanquish" (*Bodies That Matter* 185; emphasis mine). The "ninnolo" (knickknack) is the appropriate materialization of a gender norm that vanquishes the protagonist, just as Lydia is the ultimate example of a victim who spontaneously enforces the executioner's will to eliminate her. Frivolous and innocuous as the revolver appears, resembling a jewel more than a weapon – "sembrava un gioiello" (187; it looked like a jewel) – it eventually manifests its deadly properties.

The gender norm denies Lydia the possibility of self-realization and brings her to the (self-)destruction it envisages for women who aspire to realize their own desires. It is important to notice, also, that Lydia's quest – like Teresa's – is clearly hampered by a structural and epistemological bias that preludes women's access to experience and knowledge in all their fullness. Their gendered condition, carrying the social prescriptions and expectations that go with being a woman, constantly impedes their attempts to analyse and decode their social and existential environment. In the two novels, Teresa's and Lydia's rational efforts to singlehandedly gather the scattered elements they have gleaned through the years into a coherent and significant picture is structurally doomed to fail. They have no access to the social reality of the heterosexual relationship and its hierarchical organization, and thus they have no understanding of their own position within it.

On the one hand, their attempts at analysis fall short of recognizing that the gender imperative prescribes their ignorance and submission. On the other hand, both novels respond to the hampered quests with a revelatory paradigm that complements the analytical one: a sudden glimpse of meaning successfully fills the gaps left by their previous attempts at analysis, illuminating and conferring meaning to the entire picture. In addition, in both novels the inclusion of male professional characters such as the doctor and the lawyer – which seems at first to point to a programmatic distinction between educated, rationalizing male subjects and uneducated, emotional, and passive females – in fact facilitates these revelatory moments, thus upsetting traditional gendered prerogatives and implicitly campaigning for a non-separatist ideology of gender.

These revelations configure themselves as thefts of a sort, as unexpected (by both subject and environment) accesses on the part of the female protagonists to a knowledge or experience of which they are supposed to be unaware. These are voyeuristic – or eavesdropper's – experiences, and they are invariably accompanied by the vocabulary of unveiling. As philosopher Adriana Cavarero has argued in *Nonostante Platone* (*In Spite of Plato*), female (and feminist) seekers can profit from an approach to knowledge that configures itself as a theft, that is, as a counter-reading of classic epistemology that can find a different, alternative truth: they can investigate "l'ordine patriarcale … nelle *tracce* che esso conserva di ciò sulla cui cancellazione si è costruito e continua a dispiegarsi. Precisamente questa è la mia tecnica di furto: rubare figure femminili al contesto lasciando che il tessuto lacerato lasci intravvedere i nodi su cui si regge la sua trama concettuale occultante" (6–7; "the traces of the original act of erasure contained in the patriarchal order, the act upon which this order was first constructed and then continued to display itself. This is how my technique of theft works: I will steal feminine figures from their context, allowing the torn-up fabric to show the knots that hold together the conceptual canvas that hides the original crime"; trans. Anderlini-D'Onofrio and O'Healy 5). Cavarero's model of theft is one that, rather than calling for a different epistemological model, specifically argues for exploiting analytical tools in different, subversive ways. The intentionality of such theft is not something that the protagonists of Neera's novels can aspire to; but they do share with this more explicitly subversive approach the violent disruption of barriers placed between women and knowledge.

In other words, these novels clearly stage the absolute necessity of a juxtaposition, a combination of epistemological paradigms and characters' perspectives. It is only through combining multiple cognitive approaches and perspectives that women can rip the veil of mystifications, of romantic and social narratives that curtail their ability to wilfully inhabit their stories. They need both analysis and revelation, solitary quests and "professional" help, to defy the ever-present risk of becoming background to their own story. Within this multiplication of narrative and cognitive routes, revelation is a pivotal element.

What Teresa and Lydia find through revelation is a reality that, while negating many of their previous discoveries, also helps them put those experiences into context, giving these characters a more coherent picture of the world in which they are situated. Their formation, in both cases, is thus characterized by their attempts to fully attain the status of a seeker, that is, to achieve a freedom of movement that would also confer upon them the authority of free will. For Teresa, as we know, the revelation is the obscene booklet; for Lydia, it is the moment when she finally listens to her fiancé's encounter with his lover. For Marta, in *L'indomani*, it will be her witnessing a sensual encounter between a farmer husband and wife. However, the way that the last novel exploits the revelatory model differs substantially from how it is used to dispel mystifications in the first two, and it needs to be analysed in light of its surprising ideological outcome.

Marta, or the Phantasmatic Revelation(s)

As fond as Neera was of *signorine* (unmarried women), the "trittico della fanciulla" finally turns to consider what historically happened to 80 per cent of Italian urban women, that is, the experience of marriage.[22] *L'indomani* is the story of a young middle-class woman newly married to Alberto, a landowner fourteen years older than she. Marta is presented as a naive, well-meaning young woman who leaves her hometown and her widowed mother for the first time in her life to move with her husband to his country estate. Marta is engrossed in her new role as wife; specifically, she is eager to detect in her relationship with her husband the signs of that ideal, romantic love she read and heard about as a young girl. As a married woman, she is factually knowledgeable from the beginning of the novel about the sexual connection between men and women (the novel opens the morning after her marriage). What she sets out to find is the connection between the physical union and the spiritual affinity, the passion she has read about in books and thinks she and her husband should be feeling for each other.

As she fails to detect signs of such an ideal passion in her home, she also investigates the reality of conjugal life around her. In visits with her husband's friends, as well as through her conversations with her husband, she learns more and more of the prosaic realities of marriage. Merelli, Alberto's high school friend, annually impregnates his wife while involved in an affair with the maid. Toniolo, the pharmacist, agrees to remarry only when he is satisfied with the dowry his future wife will bring. Toniolo tells Marta that upon his marriage, he will relinquish his regular visits to the prostitute Giuditta just as, he informs her, Alberto relinquished them when he married her. The secluded couple living at the edge of the town, the Gavazzinis, initially appear to Marta to be the ideal example of love since, she is told, they eloped together as a young couple and spent their honeymoon carving their names on trees. But when she finally visits them she is faced with an unhappy, secluded wife and a husband who does not hide his lust for Marta.

Thus the young bride fully acquaints herself with the constraints placed on women, such as faithfulness and motherhood, and the liberties allotted to men, such as their premarital sexual experiences, their homosocial connections, and their extra-conjugal relations. These discoveries completely dismantle the ideal of romance nurtured in Marta when she was young. Her husband is conspicuously uninterested in helping her and does not engage in following the script of love that she expects of him. Yet, despite her progressive disillusionment, she strives to keep up the discursive illusion of love in the letters she writes to her mother:

> Si esaltava scrivendo dell'amore che Alberto aveva per lei, e si diceva il suo tesoro, la sua vita; ... rileggeva poi quegli aggettivi che le davano una dolce commozione, una specie dei piaceri immaginari che gustano i bevitori d'oppio ... Molte volte, dopo d'aver scritto a sua madre che "si adoravano," Alberto entrava e non si scambiavano neppure un bacio; lui serenamente freddo, lei distratta, paralizzata nella realtà dalle false sensazioni subite prima. (51–2)

> She was exalted when writing about the love that Alberto felt for her. She called herself his treasure, his life; ... she then reread those adjectives that gave her a sweet emotion, the same kind of imaginary pleasures that opium drinkers enjoy ... Many times, after she had written to her mother that they "worshipped each other," Alberto entered the room and they did not exchange even a kiss. He was calmly cold, she distracted, paralysed in reality by the false sensations she had experienced earlier.

In these letters, Marta mimics a discourse of love that reproduces the very illusions she has just dissipated, going so far as to provoke in her those *sensazioni* that she has futilely sought in actual interactions with her husband. It is through this portrayal that Neera captures with great precision Marta's disavowal of the reality of her marriage: the young woman invokes a discursive illusion of marital bliss in order to produce those bodily sensations that she cannot otherwise feel. Marta's adoption of the strategy of disavowal is extremely interesting because, as I discuss below, far from serving as a mere coping mechanism briefly adopted by a novelistic character, the strategy becomes by the end of the novel the very ideological process on which the novel relies.

The narrator subsequently dwells – in quite explicit terms – on the solitary pleasures Marta discovers at night, while waiting for her husband's return: "incapace di reggersi piegava il capo sopra un guanciale, su una spalliera di poltrona, su tutto ciò che poteva darle l'illusione di una carezza ... finché l'eccitazione, illanguidendosi, la lasciava sfinita, con le membra rotte" (60; unable to resist, she would bend her head over a pillow, over the back of an armchair, over anything that could give her the illusion of a gentle touch ... until the excitement, weakening, left her exhausted, with spent limbs). Just as she discursively produces the feelings she thinks she should have, she physically arouses in herself the sensations she would like to feel from her husband's embrace. In both cases, she eliminates reality – her husband – from the picture because his presence would bring her back to a conjugal situation in which, even when she is in his arms, she does not feel "la più lieve ebbrezza" (56; the slightest thrill).

Alberto's friends do not understand why "la sposina non fiorisse di quel rigoglio pieno ed espansivo che accompagna generalmente il passaggio dalla fanciulla alla donna" (34; the new bride did not flourish with the full and expansive bloom that generally accompanies the transition from girl to woman). The only one who guesses (in part) what is occurring in Marta's mind, and who makes a sustained effort to help her cope with the anxieties of her new situation, is another of Alberto's childhood friends, the *dottorone* (the "big doctor"), a non-practising physician. As the third example of a professional man in Neera's triptych, the *dottorone* is a captivatingly dissonant voice within the fabric of an otherwise quite claustrophobic narrative.

Marta's husband describes the *dottorone* to her as "un originale, un essere squilibrato. A volte parla troppo, a volte tace dei giorni interi" (16; an original, an unbalanced being. Sometimes he talks too much, sometimes he is silent for whole days). He appears to denigrate in his friend precisely what he does not like in his wife: her feminine instability, her inability to be unfailingly serene and practically oriented. The narrator characterizes the *dottorone* as very intelligent and passionate about both earthly and spiritual fares (gastronomy and poetry); his face is described in a way that confirms the impression of a tension between the ideal and the real, between sensuality – "[una] faccia dai lineamenti volgari, sensuali" (39; a coarse-featured, sensual face) – and intelligence – "una fronte larga, dove gli occhi brillavano con tutto il fuoco dell' intelligenza" (39; a broad forehead where eyes glowed with all the fire of intelligence) – a tension that he undoubtedly shares with Marta. While the other men amuse themselves by denigrating women as constitutionally unfaithful, treacherous, and fake, the *dottorone*'s opinions range from an idealistic vision, such as "La donna [è] … creatura delicata, gentile, anima sensibile" (48; Woman [is] … a gentle, delicate creature, a sensitive soul), to an exceptionally realistic one that is completely extraneous to misogynistic simplifications.

The irony of Neera's project in this novel is that a truly feminist voice would come from the mouth of this eccentric male doctor. In several encounters with Marta, he shares his view about "la mostruosa ingiustizia dell'amore civile coi suoi milioni di isteriche, coi suoi miliardi di adultere" (47; the monstrous injustice of civilized love, with its millions of hysterical women, with its billions of adulteresses) and offers Marta a counterpoint to her romantic vision of marriage: "allevate nell'idea fissa del matrimonio, … ognuna accetta quel marito che il caso, gl'interessi, la mamma o gli amici le pongono davanti: è un *lotto*, una *roulette*, bazza a chi tocca, e chi le piglia se le tiene" (47; raised with the fixed idea of marriage … each woman accepts the husband that chance, interest, the mother, or her friends put in front of her: it's a lotto, a *roulette*, spoiled for choice,[23] and whoever seizes the woman keeps her). The *dottorone* is, in fact, the sole unmarried male character in the novel; he has intentionally avoided any heterosexual relationship because, in his view, such a relationship cannot ensure the happiness of the two parties. His theories constitute the exact antidote to the discourse of love with which Marta was raised. With his explanations, she comes to understand that her union with her husband was not the fruit of a fervent and reciprocal passion but that of economic and practical considerations.

The *dottorone*'s expositions of his theories to Marta represent the most advanced stances taken by any character in Neera's novels with respect to the condition of women. His exceptionally critical analysis of marriage exposes it as a social contract hypocritically masked under the illusory drapings of love. He describes women as being seduced from the youngest age into adopting a set of behaviours that fill expectations promoted by men to their practical and economic advantage: "[e] fin da bambine, all'età degli zuccherini, vi si fa balenare davanti agli occhi quest'altro zuccherino, ammonendovi 'se ve lo meriterete con la docilità, la modestia, la pazienza, l'abnegazione'" (39; And ever since you are young girls, at the age of sugary treats, they flash before your eyes that other sweet treat [marriage], admonishing "you have to earn it with docility, modesty, patience, self-sacrifice"). This forceful defence of women and of the pathological consequences of a social order built to preclude them from any choice other than marriage is astonishingly radical. It is also narratively functional, up to this point, for ratifying Marta's doubts and feeding her search for a different model, for an alternative to the way of life she was taught to embrace since her childhood. The problem the novel will ultimately face concerns the very possibility of such an alternative, that is, the ideological dangers inherent in undermining the importance of marriage and drawing attention to its purely reproductive function.

Just when the *dottorone*'s theories imperil the myth of marriage, Marta finds her way through the idealization of maternity. The news of her pregnancy does not placate her anxieties but, rather, it enhances her dismay. Indeed, Marta perceives her new condition as possibly just as ideologically "manipulated" as she has discovered love and marriage to be: "le grandi cose che aveva udito sulla maternità dovevano essere, come quelle udite sull'amore, esageratissime" (96; the great things she had heard about motherhood had to be, just like those she had heard about love, greatly exaggerated). Her doubts underline the extent to which the reproductive prerogative of women is, in fact, defined by a social discourse that offers it as the one and only meaningful experience in their lives. Even her body reacts negatively to such a "natural," glorifying condition: "le ... membra sembravano spersonirsi, la pelle perdeva la lucentezza della gioventù; accanto alle labbra si disegnava in permanenza una piega triste e gli occhi s'incavavano, velati, e i muscoli apparivano meno elastici, meno pronti all'appello di una volontà che sonnecchiava; un tutto insieme di lampada a cui l'olio manchi, di macchina guasta ne' suoi più delicati congegni" (98; her ... limbs seemed to lose life, her skin was losing the lustre of youth; near her lips there was a permanent crease; her eyes, veiled, were hollowed, and the muscles seemed less elastic ... overall, [she was] like a lamp without oil, a machine with its most delicate devices broken). Pregnancy is a mechanical process that has taken over her body and veiled her eyes.[24]

Marta's reflections on her condition carry the reader to the final stages of this short novel. One afternoon, surprised by rain while walking to meet her husband, Marta finds shelter in the farmer's house, where his wife awaits his return and tends to their newborn son. Marta is surprised at the woman's attachment to her baby and wonders about herself: "Ella dunque avrebbe fatto allo stesso modo? E quello era l'amor materno?" (101; Was she going to behave in the same way? And was that maternal love?). When the farmer finally arrives, he runs to his wife and embraces her passionately. Unintentionally, Marta witnesses their sensual and wordless reunion, and she experiences the young couple's bodily contact as an authentic, veil-parting revelation about the existence of love.

Like Teresa and Lydia before her, Marta is fortuitously granted a piece of knowledge that shocks her, forcing her to reconsider her understanding of reality. Unlike Teresa's and Lydia's revelations, however, this one is articulated in two moments. With the revelation about passion at the sight of the couple, Marta experiences an internal movement: shocked by the vision, she holds back a scream, feels her womb rise, and realizes that a being is moving inside her – the revelation that passionate love actually exists has provoked, in turn, the revelation of her maternity. Then, in a narrative movement that reinforces the identification of womanhood with motherhood, the text emphasizes the constitutive significance of this double epiphany: "ogni velo era tolto, … la sua virginità cadeva in quel punto, ella era fatta donna" (102; all veils were withdrawn, … her virginity fell right there, she was now a woman). The first revelation merely prepares her to become, through the second revelation, a mother, thus reversing the symbolic (although, of course, not literal) failure of her husband's actual impregnation. Marta's passive witnessing of the love displayed by others instantly transforms her into a devoted parent, and the fact of her motherhood, in turn, transforms her – indeed, converts her – into a real woman, with her very virginity "falling" at the sight of the farmers' embrace.

This double movement, of revelation and conversion, is far from being logically and narratively justified. Witnessing the sensual embrace between the farmer and his wife has confirmed for her the possibility of a coexistence of ideal love and sexual desire. One of the most logical consequences of such a revelation would seem, in fact, to be Marta's overt criticism of her own passionless marriage and, as a consequence, of the institution of marriage tout court. Such an outcome would have her endorse the view of the *dottorone* and would give the novel a subversive orientation. But instead, the second revelation appears to swerve the novel away from such an ideological path and to bring it back to the much more conservative identification of womanhood with motherhood. Rather than confirming her disillusioned appraisal of women's condition in society, Marta's revelation about passion and sexual desire arises from a narrative and ideological displacement that obliterates her previous discoveries and exploits the revelatory model as a means to enforce a phantasmatic structure.

The revelatory model, as we have seen, had enabled an epistemological theft in the two previous novels precisely because of its improvisational structure; the narrative employed it as an ideal complement to the quests of Teresa and Lydia, a way to dismantle the phantasmatic workings of gender ideology and allow the protagonists to confront the harsh reality of the male/female relationship. In this last novel, however, the text exploits the revelatory model against itself. It uses the revelations to have the protagonist surrender to the gender ideology she has tried to analyse and understand. Once Marta is "fatta donna," the text goes on to explain that she now understands, feels, and desires everything: "comprendeva ... tutto" (102; she understood ... everything). It thus suggests that the revelation has broadened her horizons and her understanding of the world. But her understanding everything is, in fact, rather phantasmatic itself.

What does it mean, exactly, to "be made" a woman by the (non-)act of witnessing? As Teresa de Lauretis reminds us in her analysis of the technologies of gender, gender can be understood to function in the same way that, according to Althusser, ideology functions: as an "imaginary relation of ... individuals to the real relations in which they live" (Althusser 125). De Lauretis's borrowed understanding of gender emphasizes that it is an imaginary, rather than a real, construct, but nonetheless one that has a direct impact on social and cultural realities. She takes this insight even further, ultimately integrating Althusser's philosophical discussion of the formation of individuals with a concrete description of how these individuals are actually constituted as sexed beings: "Gender has the function (which defines it) of constituting concrete individuals as men and women" (*Technologies of Gender* 6). Marta's gender ideology thus unveils its imaginary construction as well as its consequences: she is *fatta donna,* concretely constituted as a woman, by virtue of her subscription to a specific phantasmatic order that seamlessly connects romantic passion, loss of virginity, motherhood, and womanhood.

Earlier in the novel, as we saw, Marta semiconsciously recreated the conventions of conjugal passion in her letters to her mother, and this provoked in her body those sensations she could not feel in her husband's arms. These solitary remedies to her own unsatisfactory conjugal situation should be understood as clear signals, early in the novel, that the narrator is aware of the distance between reality and imagination and of the gendered conventions that fool young women such as Marta into unrealistic expectations – conventions, I might add, whose fictionality Neera appears to be directly deconstructing. The unexpected (and unexplained) displacement carried out by the final double revelation suggests that the behavioural model that the novel first presented as a mere reality-filler enacted by the naive protagonist has, in the end, become the very paradigm on which the narration relies. The novel ends up employing the same phantasmatic technique that Marta had initially endorsed as a way of coping with an unsatisfactory reality: both *L'indomani* and Marta remain within the province of a discursive (yet formally sanctioned) romance and recreate it as necessary at the expense of reality.[25]

The novel thus concludes that the alternative embodied by the *dottorone*, that is, a prosaic understanding of the coexistence of real and ideal (an understanding that has brought him to seclude himself from the heterosexual pact and its hypocrisies), cannot be endorsed by its female protagonist; Marta is socially needed as a reproductive force. The earlier progression that had Marta envisage, with the help of the *dottorone*, a different picture of marriage and maternity, one that might have eventually led her to "reveal" it as deceptive and constraining, is discarded in these later pages. This is arguably because such a dissonant imaginary relation to the real relations in which Marta lived would have turned her into a critical and subversive agent: the novel is not willing to endorse such an alternative role for its protagonist. Neera resorted to using a leap of faith, that is, the supposedly natural connection between the perfection of a passionate marriage and the perfection of maternal duty, to purge such a subversive alternative from the novel. No wonder, then, that the writer would subsequently express utter amazement upon learning that some readers, notwithstanding the twist at the end of the novel, still read it as critical of marriage: "vi fu infatti ... chi ebbe l'impressione che tutto il romanzo tendesse a scuotere la vecchia istituzione del matrimonio – nientemeno!" (*L'indomani*; there were indeed those ... who thought that the entire novel aimed at unsettling the old institution of marriage – nothing less!).[26]

As the novel draws to a close, the *dottorone* is eliminated and promptly replaced by another secondary character, Marta's mother, who is called to her side to endorse the ideal of motherhood. The final chapter of *L'indomani* is conceived as an essayistic conversation between the two women: their dialogue is fundamental in confirming the ideological shift that occurred in Marta's revelation(s), framing it within a rigorously moral endorsement of traditional roles. Although Marta resists her mother's argument that love is an illusion, she salvages her ideal by transferring it from the romantic to the reproductive realm. The displacement is sealed by a little hand knocking from within Marta's womb, saying, "Io sono l'amore e la verità" (110; I am love and truth), a fetal deus ex machina summoned by the novel to sanction the ideal economy of love between mother and child.

As George Hérelle had written to Neera in one of the letters they exchanged as he worked on a French translation of *L'indomani*, this last chapter reads less as "un 'hymne à la maternité' qu'une dissertation écrite dans une langue abstraite, un article de journal mis en dialogue" (Folli, "Le arpe Eolie" 104; an "anthem to maternity" than a dissertation written in an abstract language, a newspaper article put into dialogue). The tone of the chapter is certainly closer to an entry in Neera and Mantegazza's *Dizionario d'igiene* than to a poetic coda or, for that matter, to the rest of the novel. The difference in style indicates the need for closure Neera feels after the revelatory scene: the coherence of the analogy between ideal and maternal love is endorsed in the last pages, thus erasing any doubts about the meaning of the revelation itself. In the end, Hérelle's translation was not published, precisely because Hérelle and his publisher, Brunetière, deemed it necessary to eliminate this chapter from the novel, whereas Neera considered it absolutely fundamental to the economy of her text.[27]

With the last chapter drawing to a close, the final paragraphs sanction the view that the progress made throughout the novel is in fact ineffectual, hinting at a circularity connecting the end with the very beginning of this failed quest. *L'indomani* opened with Marta's awakening, the day after her wedding, to the uncertainties of her new status, waiting for something to happen, feeling like "uno che va a tentoni con gli occhi bendati, ... udendo la voce dei compagni che gridano: *Avanti, niente paura*!" (2, emphasis mine; one who advances gropingly, blindfolded, ... and hears the voice of companions who cry: *Come on, do not worry*!). The image of hampered vision is by now a familiar device in Neera's trilogy, an allusion to the obstacles that lie between the protagonists' aspirations to understand and the actual achievement of knowledge. Strikingly, *L'indomani* closes with an exhortation very similar to this opening. Lying in her bed, Marta has a vision of humanity brought together in a common, unrewarding effort to continue while a voice encourages each one of them: "Avanti, coraggio!" (111; Come on, courage!).

The interpellation recurs basically unchanged: it is the signal of a narrative movement that has brought the protagonist back to where she started, of a structure that has allowed only for a conservative maturation of the protagonist. The negotiation of her position within the gendered structure of subjectivity has failed to open up a subversive space within it. If a change between the initial and the final image can be detected, it is in Marta's passage from object of interpellation to interpellator herself: she has accepted her destiny as natural, reoccupying her place within the human chain so as to endorse the gender norm that has just vanquished her and that vanquished Lydia before her.

On Gender Norms and Cruel Optimism

As we have seen, the three protagonists experience a similar epistemological trajectory. They all embark on a quest for knowledge, and their initial attempts at analysis, at intellectually understanding what is happening around them, are thwarted. Each then experiences a revelatory moment, the exposure to a painful truth that, realistically or not, fills in the picture and connects their imaginary understanding of the world with the reality of their position within it. These revelations are all, in fact, primal scenes, scenes concerning a sexual encounter between a man and a woman, witnessed from the outside by these women (in Freud's analysis, it is the child's witnessing a sexual act between his parents).[28]

The use of the primal scene appears to be fundamental to the development of the three protagonists' subjectivity. In each case it is the crowning moment of an apprenticeship that had been led through scattered analytical attempts that could only be reviewed and understood for what they were retrospectively. The primal scene represents the moment in which these women finally face reality – and its dissonances – as it is and understand the relations of domination and exploitation to which they have been, and still are, subjected. Through their experience of the primal scene, they are provided with a broader understanding of the gendered world, an understanding that might, in its most optimistic version (in *Teresa*), be the basis for an autonomous decision as well as the starting point of a new process of self-determination.

These scenes thus constitute the culminations of the protagonist's quests. They heavily condition the outcomes of the plots in the three novels, but, although the revelations configure themselves in terms of a factual, graphic truth that needs to be acknowledged in *Teresa* and *Lydia*, the revelation in the last work ends up being contained and exploited by the novel's disavowing technique, modelled on Marta's own phantasmatic attempts to come to terms with reality in a non-confrontational way. Interestingly enough, in this last example of revelatory structure – unlike in the first two novels – the revelation itself is completely detached from the figure of the professional man, the *dottorone*, serving rather to disavow his views as well as Marta's discoveries about gendered life and marriage. As it is, the different intersections of the protagonists' epistemological projects with the role of the male professionals are also directly connected to the different outcomes of the ideological projects carried out by the novels.

What is more, these revelations – these primal scenes – are, unlike in the Freudian model, not understood retrospectively (after the occurrence of a second, similar scene) but instead serve to reorganize the previous information the protagonists had collected. Nonetheless, as in the Freudian model, they are characterized with a traumatic charge. They represent unmediated encounters with reality, moments in which the ugly truths of gender and sex force the characters to reshape and reread their previous understandings of gender roles and social possibilities in the context of the realities of their lives.

It is important, therefore, to stress the extent to which the same epistemological model has been bent to serve very different purposes in the novels, in ideological as much as in generic terms, the extent to which the very notions of truth, and of trauma, are subjected to the discursive manipulations of different narrative paths. Lydia's tragedy and the quasi-feminist novel about Teresa contrast starkly with the peremptoriness of the patriarchal message and trajectory proposed in *L'indomani*, where Marta's final conversion is as much a veritable prescriptive moment for the protagonist as it was meant to be for Neera's readers. In this sense, Marta's epistemological parable, from her critical analysis to her revelation and (especially) to her final, phantasmatic conversion, can be better defined as belonging within the ideological narrative of "cruel optimism" – to use Lauren Berlant's compelling formulation – that is, an affective investment in an existential project that never satisfies but rather actually works against one's well-being.

Whereas in the cases of Teresa and Lydia, the revelatory paradigm functions as a dissociating technique, as a way to educate these women about the perils and inconsistencies of their own misplaced gender optimism, Marta's revelation serves to strengthen her fantasy of "that moral-intimate-economic thing called 'the good life'" – "[f]antasy is the means by which people hoard idealizing theories and tableaux about how they and the world 'add up to something'" (Berlant 2). Marta's fantasy places her squarely back within an ideological world that allows her no mobility, not even at the intellectual level: remarkably, unlike Teresa's thoughtful final mobilization, there is nothing ironic in Marta's closing emphatic exhortation to keep going, no matter what. Marta has failed to become the author(ity) of her own life.

It is also true that, in the case of Marta, our first glimpse of the protagonist is at the beginning of her journey as a wife and mother. As readers and critics, we are not allowed to see the evolution of her optimistic attachment to that which defeats her. In the next chapter, we shall see that Marchesa Colombi allows us to do just that. Using the same post-Unification framework as that of Neera's novels, Marchesa Colombi proposes a very different reflection on social narratives and individual desires, one that ultimately engages with the ideological import of narrative genres and that questions the validity of the novel as a genre for women writers – and for wilful characters.

3 The Mule and the Ghost: Gender, Realism, and the Fantastic in Giovanni Verga and Marchesa Colombi

Per [le ragazze] non c'era la speranza di poter diventare, crescendo, un bello e grande eroe. La loro sola speranza era di diventare le spose d'un eroe: di servirlo, di stemmarsi del suo nome, di essere la sua proprietà indivisa, che tutti rispettano.

For [the girls] there wasn't the hope to become, upon growing up, a beautiful and great hero. Their only hope was to become the wife of a hero: to serve him, to crest themselves with his name, to be his undivided property, which everybody respects.

(Morante, *L'isola di Arturo, Opere* vol. 1, 998)[1]

The novelty of Neera's trilogy resides in its realistic focus on dissonant female characters and their novel quests for knowledge. Its structural interest lies in the way each novel exploits the same epistemological route to reach very different ends. In this chapter, I consider two texts of the same period that, in contrast, engage in testing the possibilities and the versatility of the novel by juxtaposing different genres. Although very different in content and structure, Giovanni Verga's novella "Le storie del castello di Trezza" (1877) and Marchesa Colombi's novel *In risaia* (1878) are texts in which the dissonant coexistence – the simultaneous presence and absence of bodies as well as genres – is the constitutive principle. The distinct generic domains, realism and fantasy, bear distinct ideological messages, and female characters that must submit – or perish – within one of these domains have a different kind of permanence, and power, within the other.

I begin with a long detour through Giovanni Verga's "Le storie del castello di Trezza" because of the uncanny connections that I find between the text – as playful and cruel as it is – and Marchesa Colombi's *verista* Christmas tale, and also because Verga presents a clear and illuminating example of the generic dissonance that Marchesa Colombi's novel subsequently adopts as a way to highlight economic and sexual disparities. Both stories are told in realistic terms, and both position the realist tale against a contrasting epistemological dimension: a fantastic one. The fantastic is always already folkloric (more markedly so for Marchesa Colombi), in that it belongs within a narrative space organized by a lower-class, oral collective of voices that transmit knowledge. Folkloric knowledge needs not submit to the same kind of reality checks, or truth requirements, that bind realist narratives, and as such it is characterized by an interest in absence, that is, an interest in all that which realist stories do not fully reveal and explain.

Since the 1870s, both Giovanni Verga and Marchesa Colombi (like Neera) have been visibly associated with *verismo*, Verga as its most formidable representative and spokesperson, and Marchesa Colombi as a minor female epigone whose work never fully fulfils its dictates and expectations. Yet their attachment to realism, their investment in presenting reality in the most objective way possible, can be problematized if we look at the contrasting epistemological commitments inscribed in their stories. Their writing is, at least in the works studied here, a reflection on the relationship between fantasy and reality and on the suggestion that a distinction between these two realms might not be as clear-cut and productive as *verismo*, among other movements, made it out to be.

Several recent works dwell on the line drawn between the realistic and the fantastic to show the inconsistencies of boundaries that are too rigid. In her monograph on the politics of the body in nineteenth-century Gothic and fantastic tales, Deborah Harter argues that the concern of the fantastic narrative is "to read the world quite plainly, a concern that ultimately betrays this form's surprising affinities with its contemporary, the realist novel" (1). Harter's argument is that the "partialness" (2) with which Gothic and fantastic tales evoke the world is just as realistic as the totality to which realist novels aspire, if not more so. Within the field of Italian studies, a recent collection of essays by Francesca Billiani and Gigliola Sulis discusses the political implications of the Italian fantastic narrative within the ideologically conservative landscape of liberal Italy. Most of the contributions in this collection analyse the choice of a genre that is alternative to the realist novel as an index of the author's subversive agenda and of the innovative gender politics at work. For the studies in Billiani and Sulis's collection as well as my own analyses, the most productive meaning of "fantastic" is the one enunciated by Todorov in his 1970 study *The Fantastic – A Structural Approach to a Literary Genre*: Todorov sees the fantastic not as something tied to fantasy or the Gothic as precisely delimited fields, but rather as a narrative genre characterized by a moment of hesitation ("uncertainty") between different epistemological paths (the "uncanny" and the "marvelous").[2]

The two tales I discuss here, Verga's "Le storie del castello di Trezza" and Marchesa Colombi's *In risaia*, are especially fascinating because, rather than belonging to a specific genre, they appear to linger between two literary approaches: both tales contain aspects of the two realms, the realist and the folkloric, and it is this coexistence that marks the novelty of the texts. The coexistence is to be understood as a gendered dissonance and read as a specific ideological strategy on the part of the authors. The recourse to oral storytelling and folklore to explain unexplainable events in these stories adds a dissonant epistemological layer to the modern-realist layer, undermining univocal notions of reality.

Fantastic Presence: Verga's "Le storie del castello di Trezza"

Verga published his collection of stories, *Primavera e altri racconti*, in 1876 (it was reprinted in 1877 as *Le novelle*).[3] The stories in this collection briefly reverted to the elegant and mundane society of early novels such as *Eros* but also include the novella "Le storie del castello di Trezza," a formidable hybrid of the entertainment literature of his early years and his burgeoning interest in local folklore and regional realism. It is likely, in fact, that "Le storie" and such a proto-verist story as Verga's *Nedda* were written at about the same time. "Le storie" concludes the collection with an allusion to itself as "vagabonde fantasticherie" (130; wandering reveries), a choice of terminology that obviously alludes to the title ("Fantasticheria") of the opening story in his next collection, *Vita dei campi* (1880). "Fantasticheria" explicitly thematizes the shift from Verga's interest in bourgeois lives and dramas to the reality of poor Southern villagers and fishermen's lives – a sort of prelude to the politics of *I Malavoglia*. Although not yet imbued with verist concerns, there is no doubt that "Le storie del castello di Trezza" participates in the contemporaneous reflection on finding new approaches to recondition the way literature represented (or created) reality.

In "Le storie," a framing subplot about bourgeois visitors to the Sicilian castle gives way to the legend that one of them, young Luciano, recounts to Luciana, the object of his love interest, and her morose husband. The twelfth-century story of don Garzia, baron d'Arvelo, is a gruesome tale of marital revenge lifted straight out of the island lore. After discovering the interest that his first wife has taken in a young valet, the brutal baron d'Arvelo believes his problem is solved when his wife throws herself out of a window. He leaves the castle for a period, and it is only when he returns home with a second wife that he is forced to face the truth. The new wife, donna Isabella, a strong no-nonsense woman – "La seconda moglie del barone d'Arvelo era una Monforte, nobile come il re e povera come Giobbe, forte come un uomo d'arme e tagliata in modo da rispondere per le rime alla galanteria un po' manesca di don Garzia" (89; Baron d'Arvelo's second wife was a Monforte, noble like the king and poor like Job, strong like a warrior and cut to answer in kind to don Garzia's somewhat aggressive gallantry) – realizes that strange sightings and noises inhabit the long-deserted castle. The young bride gathers information from the servants and is soon familiar with the main events: the baron's first wife, donna Violante, disappeared one night, and they believed her to have thrown herself into the sea below the terrace of the conjugal bedroom. Soon thereafter, fishermen at sea began to report sighting the dead baroness's soul strolling up and down the ruined and almost invisible steps leading to the castle roof, where an ancient surveillance tower still stands.

The barely visible steps recur in the story as the objective correlative of the uncertainty that readers will have about the direction their reading should take: "e gli avanzi della scalinata, cadenti, smantellati, senza parapetto, sospesi in aria a quattrocento piedi dal precipizio sembravano un addentellato per qualche costruzione fantastica" (97; and the staircase's ruins, crumbling, collapsed, without rail, dangling four hundred feet from the abyss, seemed a connecting link for some fantastic construction).[4] The ruined remains literally function as a bridge between the reality of life in the castle and the "fantastic construction" that the novella slowly reveals. Nocturnal sightings are regularly reported by servants in the house, and the cook realizes that "gli spiriti fa[n]no man bassa sulla credenza" (92; the spirits [are] pillaging the kitchen supplies). As unwilling as donna Isabella is to believe in a ghost stealing the kitchen reserves, she is nevertheless slowly brought to acknowledge that something is, indeed, going on. After yet another sleepless night, she warns her husband, "Io credo che fareste meglio a ordinare delle messe per l'anima della vostra donna Violante" (103; I believe that it would be best if you'd arrange a few masses for the soul of your Lady Violante) – words that the baron remembers when he fails, that same night, to catch a white figure swiftly making her way up the crumbling steps to the roof: "Egli correva come un forsennato, seguito da Bruno, inseguendo il fantasma che fuggiva come un uccello, sull'orlo del parapetto rovinato; entrambi, coi capelli irti sul capo, *videro al certo, non fu illusione,* la bianca figura arrampicarsi leggermente pei sassi che sporgevano ancora dalla cortina, al posto dov'era stata la scala, e sparire nel buio" (105; He ran like a madman, followed by Bruno, chasing the ghost that fled like a bird, on the edge of the ruined parapet; both, with their hair standing on end, *saw for sure, it wasn't an illusion,* the white figure lightly climbing the stones that were still jutting from the wall where the steps once were, and disappearing in the darkness). The narrator's insistence on the authenticity of the men's vision encourages the reader to lean towards the realm of the uncanny, to use Todorov's distinction (25), rather than that of the marvellous. The baron has seen something lightly climbing the stones, and so the ghost "really" exists – although, of course, for a ghost to really exist it would have to not, realistically speaking, exist at all.

The presence of the ghost is predicated upon the absence of a body, in this case, the body of donna Violante. To be sure, the subtly ironic reference to the kitchen expeditions allows the reader to anticipate a resolution that is more realistic (uncanny) than fantastic – but yet, at this point of the tale, nothing is certain. The presence of the ghost – the presence of a first wife, in whatever form – creates a rift between the newly married husband and wife. When asked about the cause of his first wife's death, don Garzia answers, "mal caduco" (106; epilepsy). The baroness knows very well, from what she heard from the servants, that donna Violante met a different ending. From that point on, the burden of the quest to uncover the truth about donna Violante – as well as the burden of re-establishing marital harmony – falls on don Garzia, while donna Isabella retreats into a different part of the castle.

The baron keeps watch night after night, and on the fourth night, among the many frightening noises and movements in the house, he finally perceives a presence in the darkness in front of him. Donna Violante is invisible and unreachable until a flash of lightning illuminates her, staring at him "con occhi lucenti e terribili" (107; with eyes that are shining and terrible). As he delivers a sharp strike with his sword, once again in the dark, he hits "something," he hears a deathly scream, and he withdraws his sword. Moments later, as his huntsman Bruno is admitted entrance to the room, we learn what the baron has struck. Bruno mediates for the reader the revelatory "spettacolo orribile" (108; horrible sight) of donna Violante's corpse, dressed in the white bathrobe she was wearing when she disappeared, starved and unkempt and wildly terrifying even in death. The lore is revealed to be more truthful – more real – than anyone could imagine: the baron and the huntsman experience the brutal revelation of a truth they had tried to deny.

Fully aware of what he has just done, baron d'Arvelo verbally orchestrates a perfect epistemological reversal. He states to Bruno, "[N]on volevo crederci ai fantasmi; le credevo sciocchezze di femminucce; ma adesso ci credo anch'io" (108; I didn't want to believe in ghosts; I thought they were old wives' tales; but now I believe it too). His statement is tragically ironic, predicated as it is on a rhetorical disavowal. His strategic conversion to a gendered knowledge, to the wisdom of "old wives' tales," allows him to programmatically enforce a different truth, one that he plans to exploit to his advantage. He quickly disposes of the corpse and threateningly commits Bruno to silence. But rumours about this other truth are not as easy to silence: as the village commemorates the anniversary of donna Violante's (first) death, people both within and outside of the castle begin to murmur "che *la cosa fosse proprio avvenuta come sembrava*, e come don Garzia non voleva che sembrasse" (109; that *it really did happen as it appeared*, and as don Garzia didn't want it to appear). Appearances (or, in this case, the ensuing lack of *apparitions*), clearly, do not deceive, and the baron's belated attempt to hide his crime behind the veil of a ghost story fails. Because of the rumours, fearing that his master might blame them on him, Bruno "fortuitously" kills the baron during a hunting trip. Donna Isabella has in the meantime left the castle, never to return.

The ghostly tale is revealed as, first, an attempt of the people to make sense of an otherwise unexplainable presence and, then, as a shrewd artifice endorsed by the baron to hide an actual uxoricide. In both instances, it is a discursive elaboration meant to explain or disguise a material truth: the body of a woman. The baron ultimately succeeds in turning donna Violante into a "thing": "egli rimase in mezzo a quel buio, vicino a quella *cosa* che la sua spada aveva toccato" (108; he stood in the midst of that darkness, close to that *thing* that his sword had touched). Yet "Le storie" is also the tale of the transformation of donna Violante from the woman described in the first pages as "debole, sola, timida, tremante al fiero cipiglio del suo signore" (85; weak, lonely, timid, trembling at her master's fierce scowl) to an uncontrollable force that holds the castle hostage day and night with her ghostly escapades.

The legend that is passed on from generation to generation, from the baron d'Arvelo's epoch down to the nineteenth century, is an uncannily realistic tale of female submission, female subversion, and a haunting struggle for power. The body of the baron's first wife is physically eliminated by her husband only after she has made a profound and lasting impact on the imaginations of the inhabitants of her former domicile. Her ghostly presence is predicated on her supposed absence, just as her definitive absence is tied to and dependent on the text's avowal of her actual presence. The encounter between realist concerns (to be understood as an interest in presence) and a fascination with the marvellous (i.e., a curiosity about that which is absent) produces an unexpected clash in "Le storie" that undermines traditional narrative patterns and opens up a space for negotiation in terms of gender, as well as genre, politics.

The sadistic, homicidal tendency in this text could not be more explicit or more accomplished. The literal transformation of donna Violante into an object – the baron alone in the dark with the *cosa* – is the culminating moment of the patriarchal fantasy, the literalization of its sadistic desire to annihilate the other.[5] At the same time, the female fantasy of surviving one's own death, of escaping one's destiny as an abused wife (the second part of the "storie" adds much detail about the unhappy conjugal relationship between the baron and donna Violante before her disappearance) is alive and well in Verga's tale. Donna Violante's terrible eyes and white shape are a veritable ideological spectre: they signify the emergence of a desire for subjectivity that this story validates even as it recognizes its demise.[6] As becomes strikingly clear at the very end of the story, the female subject has a chance of surviving only in the marvellous realm, the realm mediated by the tradition of folklore – a realm that is also, in the baron's case, explicitly gendered as feminine.

The contemporary setting in which the legend of baron d'Arvola is retold closes with the bourgeois triangle par excellence and its tragic demise: the husband (signor Giordano), the wife (signora Matilde), and her young paramour Luciano have returned to the ruins of the castle for a second visit. Luciano, the narrator of the legend in the opening sequences of the tale, listens as the legend is now being collectively retold by the other visitors while he and Matilde pretend not to notice each other. The husband is watching them, and they are increasingly uneasy about his gaze. Matilde knows that her husband suspects her of being unfaithful and is afraid. After the tale has been completely retold, the three are the last to leave the ruins. As the husband crosses the wooden board that now serves as a makeshift "ponte levatoio sull'abisso spaventoso" (130; drawbridge over the terrifying abyss), his wife and her lover follow him, holding hands in the dark. Signor Giordano, who has probably seen this – "li vide forse nell'ombra, lo indovinò, aveva calcolato su di ciò" (130; maybe he saw them in the shadows, he guessed it, he had planned on it) – abruptly turns around and calls his wife's name. Startled, Matilde vacillates, and then falls, with Luciano, into the abyss.

The closing tragedy echoes the tragedy of the love triangle at the centre of the legend and ideologically sanctions the patriarchal "indifference," the substantial immutability of gender relations, and the punishment of infractions of the conjugal rule. Be it in the context of twelfth-century aristocracy or of fin-de-siècle gallant bourgeoisie, the fate that awaits women who contravene their wifely duty is – despite all appearances of social progress – the same. "Le storie" closes with a strong affirmation of the conjugal pact as the only legitimate alliance and relationship allotted to women through its emphatic endorsement of the fate reserved for unruly subjects.[7]

Yet the very last words in the text belong to a narrator who conveys the popular wisdom: "A Trezza si dice che nelle notti di temporale si odano di nuovo dei gemiti, e si vedano dei fantasmi fra le rovine del castello" (130; At Trezza people say that during stormy nights one can once again hear the wailing, and see ghosts among the castle's ruins). These final words not only sanction the similar fate shared by the two unfortunate couples; they also serve a more important purpose, allowing the narration to swerve one final time away from the realm of reality and towards that of the fantastic, sagely suggesting an entanglement of the two epistemologies. As Harter reminds us, "[I]n the end the 'imaginary' of fantastic narrative is uncannily close to the 'real' of the novel, its fascination with the realist's world quite striking" (8). In Verga's case, the closing emphasis on the very real punishment awaiting those who fail to obey the law of the father – and the conjugal pact – gives way to a moment of ideological incertitude about the relationship between reality and fantasy. The bourgeois tragedy closes the book, yet the narrator insists one last time that the Gothic part of the tale might be worthy of another (retrospective) look. Reality, Verga is saying quite explicitly, is bound to be understood only if we connect two mutually dissonant ways of reading it.[8]

Cruel Narratives: Narrative Revenge in Marchesa Colombi's *In risaia* and "Il folletto – sei anni dopo"

Marchesa Colombi's *In risaia* is equally interesting in its upsetting of gender and genre boundaries. When Maria Antonietta Torriani, writing under the pseudonym Marchesa Colombi, published her novel *In risaia* in 1877, she was one of the most respected and innovative female authors of her generation.[9] Although written before the properly *verista* wave of Verga's *Vita dei campi* (1880) and his *I Malavoglia* (1881; as Giuseppe Zaccaria puts it, "spartiacque verghiano" [93; Verga's watershed]), her novel bespoke an explicit interest in the lives and customs of regional, *laissez-pour-compte* lower-class individuals, with the added novelty of being entirely focused on a female protagonist.

In risaia details the adolescence and adult years of Nanna Lavatelli, a young woman of very modest means in rural Piedmont. Her personal aspirations are juxtaposed to her economic needs; she needs to earn a dowry in order to be desirable on the marriage market, and by age seventeen she has naively identified Gaudenzio, the local "Don Giovanni rusticano" (21; rustic Don Juan), as the object of her desire. She goes to work in the rice fields with her younger brother, Pietro, to earn the 72 lire she needs for her dowry. Because of the unhealthy living and working conditions in the rice fields, she becomes ill with malarial fever on her first stint. The second time she goes, during the *mondatura* (weeding), she again falls sick. Her older female companions take matters into their hands: they diagnose her with *cefalite* (49; encephalitis) and propose to cure her with traditional remedies.

In an often quoted scene, the oldest woman among the rice workers, who is nicknamed the *medichessa* (49; female doctor), places a slaughtered black hen on Nanna's head and lets the blood and intestines drip on her:

> Sta pronta, rizzati, disse la medichessa impugnando arditamente un gran coltello da cucina. S'udì un gracidare alto e disperato, e tosto la povera bestia, squartata dal collo in giù, fu applicata al capo indolorito della Nanna, che si sentì scorrere sul volto, sul collo, sugli abiti, una pioggia calda di sangue, d'umori, di liquidi viscerali d'ogni tinta ed odore, mentre il collo della bestia, palpitante ancora, le si agitava dinanzi gli occhi inondati, nello spasimo dell'agonia. (50)

> Be ready, stand up, said the female doctor, bravely grasping a large kitchen knife. A loud and desperate squawk was heard, and quickly the poor animal, ripped open from the neck down, was placed on the aching head of Nanna, who felt pouring down her face, neck, and clothes a warm rain of blood, of humours, of visceral liquids of all kinds of colours and smells, while the animal's neck, still pulsating, was flailing in front of her flooded eyes, in the throes of agony.

The crude realism of the scene facilitates an ethnographically accurate description of a folkloric practice in use among the peasants in the Novara countryside. The narrative point of view here is that of an dispassionate observer. The folkloric remedy is inserted within the fabric of the novel and quickly juxtaposed to the more reliable domain of male science, of modern medicine.

The black hen cure, in fact, worsens Nanna's condition. When she arrives at the hospital, doctors diagnose her with typhus instead and are barely able to save her life. In addition, as a result of the folkloric medicine, she has lost all outward signs of health and beauty: she loses weight along with her hair and the overall healthy, promising complexion that she had hoped would make her marketable and desirable, especially in Gaudenzio's eyes. What follows is a very realistic – and chilling – account of Nanna's slow metamorphosis from a hopeful, merry young woman to an embittered spinster.

As years go by, she fails to find a husband, witnessing instead Gaudenzio's explicit displays of interest in other women, particularly Nanna's new sister-in-law Rosetta. After observing their flirtations, Nanna sets out to thwart Gaudenzio's plans to seduce Rosetta and to expose him and her brother's wife as reckless. But as the final denouement and Christmas draw closer, the story takes a different turn. On Christmas Eve, Nanna abruptly changes course, intervening to save Pietro and Rosetta's marriage. She also redirects Gaudenzio's desire, somewhat unwillingly, towards young Lucia, Rosetta's sister. As they gather for their Christmas meal the following day, everyone celebrates a new beginning – even Nanna, who has finally (overnight) found a fiancé in the person of her neighbour Pacifico.

The most striking feature of this tale is its structural determinism: it is a tale bound to turn from tragedy to comedy with the advent of Christmas, a tale that cannot escape its happy ending. Nanna has a considerable responsibility for this turn of events, as it is literally around her role as observer, bitterly excluded from the different paths of desire that cross beneath her gaze (her brother, Pietro, cannot express his love for his wife, Rosetta; Rosetta, frustrated, is about to give in to Gaudenzio's courtship; and Lucia, Rosetta's sister, is in love with Gaudenzio), that the whole tale functions.

The abrupt change of course brought about on Christmas Eve was eloquently scrutinized by some of the book's first readers. In 1878, an anonymous reviewer wrote in *La rassegna settimanale* that "la preoccupazione di fare un racconto di Natale, cioè a dire di dargli uno svolgimento convenzionale, le ha fatto dimenticare la parte grandiosa e tragica del suo argomento" (Benatti 136; the preoccupation with writing a Christmas tale, that is to say, with giving it a conventional development, made her forget the grandiose and tragic part of her argument). Similarly, in his 1879 appraisal of the book for the *Dizionario biografico degli scrittori,* Angelo De Gubernatis remarked on the discrepancy between the stark verism, the novel's commitment to objectively recounting in great detail the peasants' lives in the first part, and the sentimental tale of rewarded good deeds into which it evolves at the very end:

> Questo libro ci dà, nella prima parte, una viva pittura, fatta con linee semplici e sicure, della misera vita che i contadini conducono nelle risaie. Peccato soltanto che poi, forse per timore di allontanarsi troppo della via battuta, o per seguire il consiglio di chi mirava piuttosto all'opportunità del tempo in cui doveva uscire il libro, ella non si sia accontentata della tragica nudità del soggetto vero, e abbia concesso troppo alla favola. (303)

> This book gives us, in the first part, a lively painting, sketched with simple and confident lines, of the miserable life that peasants lead in the rice fields. It is only too bad, then, that – perhaps for fear of going too far off the beaten track, or in order to follow the advice of those who sought to profit from the season during which the book would be published – she was not content to limit herself to the tragic nakedness of the actual subject but conceded too much to fable.

In her article "Un genere di occasione: I 'racconti di Natale' della Marchesa Colombi," Patrizia Zambon reminds us that "nell'editoria degli ultimi decenni dell'Ottocento ... anche in Italia il racconto di Natale appare un'abitudine consolidata" (121; in the publishing industry of the nineteenth century's last decades ... in Italy, too, the Christmas tale appears to be a consolidated habit). It is a habit born of a market opportunity but also of a special interest in literature as a "gesto sociale" (122; social gesture) that becomes a veritable "tipologia narrativa" (121; narrative typology). It was so consolidated a gesture, in fact, that between 1875 and 1885 Marchesa Colombi alone wrote nine *racconti di Natale* (*In risaia* included). To my knowledge, though, *In risaia* is her only Christmas tale (her only text tout court) whose ending was superseded by a later textual addition. We should turn to the ideological value of this Christmas tale as social gesture, then, to better understand this novel and the motivations behind its short sequel. Why would Marchesa Colombi move beyond her own original conclusion, if the socially appeasing final gesture (its happy ending) was the reason for her choice of genre and indicative of the relationship she aimed to establish with her readers?[10]

As the novel works its way towards its ending, Nanna reflects on how despised and humiliated she is and expresses very clearly her resolve to take revenge against those who do not notice her. While kneading the Christmas cake in the kitchen on Christmas Eve, she ponders, "Che Natale, mio Dio! ... Non ho mai avuto tanto veleno nel cuore. Che cosa ho fatto per essere disprezzata, avvilita, come sono? Ma è venuta la mia volta. Li avvilirò anche loro e resterò io padrona di casa" (100; What a Christmas, my God! ... I have never had so much venom in my heart. What have I done to be so despised, so debased, as I am? But my time has come. I will debase them, too, and I will remain the master of the house). This is, as clear as it can be, Nanna's desire: to take her revenge against those who do not notice her unhappiness and to return to her place as mistress of the Lavatelli household. As Silvia Benatti writes when describing the difference between this novel's heroine and typical *verista* characters such as Verga's Nedda, "non c'è rassegnazione in Nanna, c'è invece la volontà di incidere sul proprio destino" (139; there is no resignation in Nanna, instead there is the will to influence her destiny). Even as a solitary, embittered spinster, Nanna is determined to exert her will and to not become background to her own story.[11]

Only two pages later, however, a revelation abruptly changes the course of events. The women (Nanna, Rosetta, and Lucia) have placed their clogs outside the window for Santa to deposit presents. Nanna knows that Gaudenzio will give a costly brooch to Rosetta to encourage her into an adulterous relationship. Pietro, Rosetta's husband, also suspects this will happen and is bringing his own costly brooch to show his wife his love. While presiding over the comings and goings in the kitchen, Nanna is ready to reveal to Pietro that Gaudenzio has already given his present to Rosetta. But a sudden vision steers her away from this act and its tragic consequences. In her mind, she sees a "scena di sangue" (bloody scene) that she had heard about a few months earlier in the story of a husband who, "geloso del proprio fratello, l'aveva ucciso, poi aveva ucciso la moglie" (102; jealous of his own brother, killed him, and then killed his wife); she suddenly realizes that Pietro would be unable to kill Rosetta or Gaudenzio but would kill himself instead. At that moment, "tutte le passioni ignobili che l'avevano eccitata si dileguarono dinanzi a quella paura" (102; all the vile passions that had excited her vanished in light of that fear), and a deep repentance falls upon her: "era ridivenuta buona, e sentiva orrore de' suoi sentimenti malevoli" (107; she became good again, and was horrified by her evil feelings).

This revelation – a revelation of the violence lurking behind the conjugal pact – acts as a catalyst for Nanna's conversion. Her change of heart brings a Christian framing to the story, shaping it along very traditional ideological lines. Nanna explicitly reflects on the effect that Christmas has on her: "[A]vevo il demonio nel cuore. Se gli avessi dato retta, che Natale d'inferno si sarebbe fatto in casa! Ma il Signore mi ha toccato il cuore" (107; I had a demon in my heart. If I had followed his advice, what a hellish Christmas it would have been in this house! But the Lord touched my heart). As I discussed in the previous chapter in reference to Neera's novels, a revelation can be a textual strategy through which a specific "truth," one that was previously foreclosed to the female character, is finally made available. But it can also be textually exploited, as happened to Marta in *L'indomani* and – in different measure – in Verga's *Le storie*, to encourage a character (or a community) to accommodate to an ideological perspective that appeared previously unlikely. In this case, Nanna's revelation helps to swerve the Lavatellis' tale from a potential family drama to a conservative happy ending, in which everyone gets their reward (or at least so it seems).

Nanna's good deed prompts retribution. Immediately after she prays to the Lord to give her "una buona ispirazione" (108; a good inspiration), she visits her neighbour Pacifico, who, upon finding her in his house, explains that he has loved her all along. The bald, aged Nanna thus receives the consolation prize of a widower husband who also brings to the house his "*bastarda*" (110; *bastard*) child, as Nanna initially puts it, before she "converts" to a more Christian attitude of acceptance: the generic constraints have brought her to a deep repentance and purged the demon from her heart. The final scene amounts to a cinematic zooming out, moving from the individual story of Nanna to a collective view of the newly formed couples gathered in the Lavatelli household. Nanna disappears behind Pacifico, who lovingly asks her, "[Q]uand'è che comincerete a scodellare la minestra a casa mia?" (111; [W]hen are you going to ladle the soup in my house?), and the last words of the novel are devoted to Gaudenzio's contentment and Lucia's happiness.

As the novel closes with a Christmassy happily-ever-after for everyone involved, one cannot but wonder about the reasons for such a change of tone and the abrupt narrative shift that successfully did away, quite literally, with Nanna's destructive desires.

In writing about the nature of happy endings, Ray Fleming emphasizes that the act of "happily ending" a story represents a narrative decision that needs to be read from a certain standpoint, one that seldom encompasses the desires and contentment of all the characters. As he writes, "what may at first glance appear to belong to a specifically literary taxonomy reveals itself ... as an ideological category ... [A]pparently serene and happy endings" – and here he is specifically referring to *Decameron*, Day 5, stories 8 and 9, which, although very distant in time, share similar structural concerns about happy endings – "can only be termed as such in light of masculine priorities and values that ... exclude the implicit and explicit wishes or priorities of the resisting female characters in the texts" (30). This specific happy ending undoubtedly presents a similar shift of narrative attention, an implicit disavowal of Nanna's resistance and wilfulness.

The conclusion of *In risaia* serves to appease while steering clear of any alternative outcomes for women, that is, any outcomes other than marriage. Whereas the compromises made by this conclusion have been thoroughly discussed from the narrative point of view – as being "convenzionale" (anonymous, quoted by Benatti 136) and as having "concesso troppo alla favola" (De Gubernatis 303; conceded too much to fairy tales), to quote a few interpretations from the reviews mentioned earlier – I want to focus more directly on its ideological significance, that is, the ideological dissatisfaction that it fails to dispel.

Several scholars have argued for a more optimistic reading of this conclusion, asserting that it *can* be read in ideologically "happy" terms for Nanna as well. Pierobon contends that Nanna's final settling down with Pacifico should be understood as a moment of growth for the protagonist, as the acceptance of a different, less superficial, kind of "beauty": "se prima dipendeva dai valori esteriori e dall'ambiente e perciò era incapace di decidere per se stessa ... ora dà prova di lucidità mentale e indipendenza" ("Per la conquista della bellezza" 108; if she had earlier relied on exterior values in the environment and therefore was unable to decide for herself ... she now shows mental lucidity and independence). Zambon considers this tale a "percors[o] di maturazione" ("Un genere di occasione" 127; maturation process) for the protagonist.[12] My reading of this novel does not ignore the personal growth potentially inscribed in Nanna's narrative parable, but rather it emphasizes the extent to which this genre-mandated happy ending endorses an uneven distribution of "Christmas presents," or narrative rewards, to its protagonists. This "asymmetry," the ideological conundrum left unresolved by the ending, can in fact be read through the lens of Nanna's frustrated desire, the affective remnant that the novel leaves aside and that eventually comes back to haunt the story in its surprising, and surprisingly understudied, fantastic coda.

It is important to underscore that, whereas Nanna's final change of heart is relatively realistic, that is, explainable in terms of her revelation about what happens to women who break the conjugal pact and about her brother's tragic state of mind – "tutto questo le passò come un lampo nella mente e nel cuore" (102; all this ran through like lightning in her mind and heart) – Gaudenzio, the object of her own desire, is described in the end as obtaining exactly what he wanted all along: sexual and economic satisfaction acquired through marriage to a busty, hardworking woman. The fact that he ends up marrying a different woman from the one he initially wanted does not seem to matter; "la Rosetta" easily persuades him to choose her younger sister, Lucia, assuring him that she will soon grow to be just as buxom, good-natured, and productive as herself. In only a few minutes, "l'idea di sposare quel gioiello di bimba, ed innamorata poi, che lo lasciava trasparire da tutti i pori, gli andò a sangue; e fu un affare concluso" (111; the idea of marrying that jewel of a girl, who on top of everything was in love with him, and bursting with it, was to his liking; it was a done deal).

Women, as long as they correspond to his productive and reproductive criteria, are interchangeable for Gaudenzio. He ends the novel just as self-absorbed and confident about himself and his sexual future as he was at the beginning, and with a "donna da lavoro" (46), as he once referred to his ideal companion, a "woman of burden" at his side who will obediently produce and reproduce for him. Indeed, the crux of the novel, its main final unresolved dissonance, lies precisely in the extent to which this single character, unlike all the other main characters, fails to change and be changed by the impact of social conditions and other people's needs. There will be no ghosts in Marchesa Colombi's handling of Gaudenzio's unjust reward, at least not in the same way that donna Violante reappears to her husband to unsettle his new conjugal arrangements and reveal her own dissonant truth. But Nanna's desire is a force that can, indeed, survive a revelatory "swerving" of the novel's priorities. It is a desire that transcends the novel's ending and that will eerily reappear, a few years later, within a friendlier narrative frame.

In fact, the folkloric imaginary of Novara peasants becomes fertile ground for telling a different part of the story, one in which animals and fantastic creatures can haunt the impossible object of Nanna's desire. As Lauren Berlant puts it, "when we talk about an object of desire, we are really talking about a cluster of promises we want someone or something to make to us and make possible for us" (23). When considered in terms of its main character and her expectations, *In risaia* is, indeed, the story of Nanna's frustrated optimism about her own "cluster of promises," the tragedy of an imaginary connection between a damaged subject (the bald Nanna) and the most prized male object of desire to be found in the countryside between Novara and Trecate. It is for him that Nanna goes off to earn her *argento*, the set of silver pins with which she will decorate her hair and display her wealth. It is for him that Nanna decides to return to the rice fields even after her first bout of malarial fever, a decision that will turn out to be catastrophic for her beauty and her health. She does this even as Gaudenzio, who has noticed her new *argento*, rudely points out that her chest has been flattened by the fever – that is, even as he points out, very early on in the novel, that she is definitely not attractive to him (37).

Berlant says, "'[C]ruel optimism' names a relation of attachment to compromised conditions of possibility whose realization is discovered either to be *im*possible, sheer fantasy, or *too* possible, and toxic" (24). Nanna's optimistic desire is impossible almost from the very beginning, because she had never fit Gaudenzio's ideal of a tireless and unbreakable woman of burden – she is initially described as "magrina ma aggraziata" (18; thin but graceful) and as having a "bellezza delicata" (21; delicate beauty) – and because her attempt to improve her sexual and economic status through her work in the rice fields became the very cause of her complete social defeat, so that she was "worn out by the labor of disappointment and the disappointment of labor" (Berlant 45).[13] Berlant's book navigates very different waters than mine, and her conjugation of cruel optimism is tied to contemporary texts and movies that discuss the sexual and racial marginalization that exist in everyday, market-driven Europe and America. Yet the substantial ideological reflection that her notion facilitates allows me to focus productively on what happens within a nineteenth-century Italian novel when its author – or its protagonist – decides that the novel, as it stands, is not enough.

As we move from the story and its frustrated optimism to its surprising textual afterthought, then, it should come as no surprise that six years after the first appearance of *In risaia*, in 1883, when Marchesa Colombi published a second, revised edition of her *racconto di Natale*, she appended a seven-page sequel entitled "Il folletto – sei anni dopo" entirely devoted to, of all people, Gaudenzio himself. In the sequel, Nanna does not even appear as a character, or appears only as an indirect presence as someone else retells the story of the fateful time when she lost her hair. This is a sequel entirely centred on Nanna's frustrated cathexis, her impossible object of desire – Gaudenzio, the novel's "don Giovanni rusticano" – and the *folletto* (little demon) that ruins his life.

"Il folletto": Haunting Tales

As "Il folletto" opens, Gaudenzio is in a bind. Thematically speaking, Gaudenzio's character was built mainly through Nanna's perspective in *In risaia*: he prescribed a specific image of woman, as discussed above, but he was also a winning model of masculinity. Three main elements – his hair, his provocative hip movements, and his powerful control over the instruments of his work, both carriage and horse – eloquently defined his persona. Verticality is, in the case of his hair, the noticeable quality from the very beginning: "Gaudenzio portava la capigliatura divisa sulla tempia sinistra, e rialzata sulla destra in un enorme ciuffo di setole, ritte come tanti pugnali che sfidassero il cielo" (20; Gaudenzio wore his hair parted on his left temple, and combed a giant tuft of bristles high on the right side, as straight as many daggers defying the sky), and his hat is vertically aligned as well: "lo schiacciava là, con un'estremità della tesa sull'orecchio sinistro, e l'altra ritta in su, in linea verticale" (21; he squashed it there, with one extremity of the brim on his left ear and the other standing up, in a vertical line). As *In risaia* draws to a close, Gaudenzio's satisfaction is expressed through an exaggerated verticality of the same hat, as well as by an excessive lateral hip movement: "[L]ui si figurava la sua sposina fra un anno, triplicata almeno, ed era contento, e si dondolava più che mai, e si metteva il cappello tanto sull'orecchio che era un prodigio" (111; [H]e imagined his young bride in a year, three times bigger at least, and he was happy, and he swayed his hips more than ever, and he pushed his hat over his ear [so that the brim was completely vertical on the side of his head] and still miraculously did not fall). Gaudenzio's physicality – in addition to being comical – has a clear sexual undertone.[14]

In the opening lines of "Il folletto," Gaudenzio's changed state is signified by the dismantling of these signs of sexual power: "[O]ra il cappello se l'era tirato sugli occhi, perché non voleva guardare nelle ombre degli angoli" (117; [N]ow he had drawn his hat over his eyes, because he didn't want to look in the shadows of the corners). An even more overt contrast is drawn through his changed relationship with his horse. The almost symbiotic – and economically advantageous – relationship that he had with his animal has become problematic. His instrument for controlling the horse, his *frusta* (whip), no longer works: "[L]a famosa frusta di Gaudenzio, che altre volte schioccava nelle vaste risaie col suono gaio d'una salva di mortaretti e faceva battere il cuore a tutte le fanciulle del circondario, ora gli pendeva lenta dietro le spalle come una biscia morta, mentre lui camminava a fianco del carro adattandosi al passo della mula [*sic*]: era lei che guidava il carrettiere" (112; Gaudenzio's famous whip, which at other times had cracked gaily in the large rice fields like a firecracker and made all the girls' hearts pound, was now hanging passively behind his shoulders, like a dead snake, while he walked at the side of his cart following the stride of the mule [*sic*]: it was she who led the cart driver). The clear sexual reference made by a whip that now looks like a dead snake, devoid of its former vibrancy and vigour, is one of the most obvious symbols of Gaudenzio's defeat. His power over his animal, and over the professional wealth represented by the labour he carried out with mule and carriage, has gone awry.

Moreover, not only does Gaudenzio appear powerless to govern and dominate his work partner; the partner itself has been transformed from the very dignified, disciplined, and male *cavallo* (horse) in the novel into an untamed, completely unreliable, and female *mula* (indeed, the first word used to qualify the mule is "bisbetica," shrew, 112). It is impossible not to recall here the "woman of burden" that Gaudenzio declared to be his ideal woman and draw a connection between *bestia* and *donna*, beast and woman of burden. In the novel, Nanna had already oneirically traced such a connection: while working in the rice fields, she had an anxiety-ridden dream in which she tried unsuccessfully to be the perfect "woman of burden," as described by Gaudenzio. This consisted in simultaneously knitting, carrying a basket of stones, and leading another equine beast, an "asino" (46; donkey), down a steep mountain trail. Overwhelmed by the tasks, however, Nanna was finally dragged across the fields by the animal: "[L]'asino impaurito si dava a fuggire trascinandola dietro pel braccio, e la traeva via traverso campi e prati, ed in quella corsa tormentosa lei udiva da lontano la voce schernitrice di Gaudenzio gridare: – Lo sapevo bene, io. Voi non siete una donna da lavoro" (46; [T]he scared donkey fled, dragging her behind by the arm, and took her farther away through fields and meadows, and during that excruciating race she could hear from far away Gaudenzio's scornful voce that cried: – I knew it. You are not a woman of burden). In a parallel gesture, the ideal *donna da lavoro* Gaudenzio desires in *In risaia* hauntingly reappears here. She is metonymically translated into a beast of burden that leads the carter to his ruin: the obedient partner has eerily turned into a wilful and unruly master.

During their evening gatherings in the stable, the older women turn themselves into narrative authorities by offering specific bits of information and exemplary tales and even by rereading earlier events, such as Nanna's own story as it had been told by her brother (*il folletto* was responsible for her debacle as well, her brother Pietro tells the women at the gathering; 114). The novel's narrator, who had occasionally commented on the peasants' woes from an upper-class perspective, is entirely absent here.[15] Gaudenzio's problem, in the view of the older women, is that his *mula* is possessed by a supernatural and tricky little being: a *folletto*. Santina and her companions know how to get rid of the little demon, and they explain to Gaudenzio the steps he must take. In the final scene of the sequel, Gaudenzio visits his mule in the middle of the night. He follows the folkloric directions to try and free her from the *folletto*, but he ends up being kicked in the head and is sent to the hospital (the same one, of course, where Nanna was sent as a result of the *gallina nera* cure) by the "haunted" mule.

Rereading the Gothic and fantastic tradition of the nineteenth century, Deborah Harter reminds us that the fantastic is, among other things, characterized by "the insistent presence of bodies" as much as by the violence inflicted upon them (8). Her lineage runs from Poe's "Berenice" (1835) to Maupassant's "La chevelure" (1884) and assesses a narrative landscape in which bodies "lend their strangeness to texts that borrow their effect not from the supernatural but from the substance of some utterly familiar domain" (9). In moving from Verga's tale to Marchesa Colombi's folkloric sequel, the presence of (wounded) bodies and their gendered difference is the most evident trace of the novels' divergent ideological paths. It is not just the body of a woman, and the violence inflicted upon it, that is ultimately presented to us in "Il folletto": Marchesa Colombi purposefully resorts to opening a final fantastic space within which the tribulations of a male body can be displayed as well.

The description of the female "beast of burden" in the climax is eerily reminiscent of the characteristics that Verga associates with donna Violante: "la mula ... spaurita, spiritata, si diede a scuotere in furia quella massa fiammeggiante che buttava scintille, a tirar calci, a rotolarsi per terra colle zampe in aria, e mandar certi urli che non parevano di questo mondo" (118; the mule ... frightened, haunted, started to shake that flaming mass that threw out sparks, kicking, rolling on the ground with her feet in the air, and emitting seemingly otherworldly screams). The unruly female body refuses to submit to its master's presence and is associated with an otherworldly dimension. Similarly, Gaudenzio, in the stable with the *mula* trying to save her from the *folletto*, is physically maimed by the encounter. Violently injured by the mule's kick, he is found the following morning "colla tempia aperta e bruciata, che pareva morto del tutto" (118; with his temple opened and burned, so that he seemed altogether dead).

The tale emphasizes the physical mark left on him by the events and also closes with a narrative gesture very similar to that of "Le storie," a reference to the circular, never-ending cycle of storytelling: "E Gaudenzio, che scampò per miracolo, freme ancora adesso, dopo tanti anni, quando racconta nella stalla quella terribile storia del folletto" (118; And Gaudenzio, after that narrow escape, still shakes with fear, after all these years, when he tells the terrible story of the *folletto* in the stable). Just as the castle's ruins bear the ghostly traces of gender violence, his body now bears the traumatic traces of a fantastic revenge – of that moment of uncertainty between the uncanny and the marvellous that can suspend the "natural" order of things.

Gaudenzio's defeat is eloquently signified and displayed as both a professional and a sexual debacle from the very first lines of the sequel. But the generic and formal gestures performed by Marchesa Colombi in this sequel are arguably even more important. In terms of genre, she shapes and organizes this defeat around a specific, and different, narrative form: a marvellous (folkloric) tale. Within this narrative space, storytelling is entirely in the hands of a collective agency, and a gendered one at that. Women's voices organize the story – they provide an (illogical) rationale for Gaudenzio's woes and at the same time preclude him from full access to the knowledge that could remedy his misfortunes. Old Santina, for example, reminds her audience that, while following her directions to free his *mula* from the demon, Gaudenzio should also have recited a specific formula: "[H]a voluto scendere a vedere il folletto, senza dir niente a nessuno. Non sapeva che, nel toccare la bestia stregata, se non gli si vuol dare l'anima al folletto, bisogna dire: Gesù, Giusep e Maria / Follett va via, follett va via!" (118; [H]e wanted to go to see the *folletto*, without telling anybody. He didn't know that, when touching a possessed animal, if one doesn't want to give one's soul to the *folletto*, one must say: Jesus, Joseph and Mary / Folletto go away, Folletto go away!). Had he only said this, he would have avoided disaster. Gaudenzio's defeat is ultimately epistemological as much as it is sexual (bodily) and economic: he is not given unfettered access to knowledge and must instead trust an unreliable (cruel, really) authority with his life.

The deliberateness with which Marchesa Colombi chose to cross the boundaries of her own Christmas tale and walk along the less realistic path of the folkloric tale should thus not be underestimated. As she moves into a different generic territory, she is also free to exert a different authority over her characters (and of course, authorially speaking, she is free to address reviewers' reactions to her novel in the way she finds most appropriate).[16] Folklore, be it in the form of specific medicinal remedies or of narrative paradigms, pertains, in both novel and sequel, to the female universe. In both instances, the recourse to folkloric remedies is catastrophic for the patients. As I outlined in my analysis of Nanna's *gallina nera* moment, folklore is not *always already* a subversive space; Emmanuelle Genevois aptly points out that "on ne trouve donc pas dans *In risaia* de culte romantique du folklore, pas d'attention nostalgique ou sentimentale aux traditions paysannes mais une observation qui, toute riche et minutieuse qu'elle soit, ne commente pas moins sévèrement, quand il le faut, l'obscurantisme de certaines pratiques" (68; we don't find in *In risaia* a Romantic cult of folklore, or a nostalgic or sentimental attention to peasant traditions. We find instead a scrutiny that, no matter how rich and detailed, does not comment less severely, when necessary, on the obscurantism of certain practices).

Within the body of *In risaia*, the realist concern aligns itself with a positivistic view of folklore, one that is uninterested in its possible gender subversion. The sequel, conversely, entrusts the narrative reins to a female folkloric agency. In this sense, I do not subscribe to Genevois's view of the sequel, according to which Marchesa Colombi has let her realist guard down and has been sidetracked by her fascination with peasants' stories: "la curiosité régionaliste a pris le pas alors sur le souci de compréhension globale de l'univers paysan" (68; her regionalist curiosity has taken over her concern to fully understand the peasant universe). Marchesa Colombi's narrative use of folklore in her sequel – her story of the *folletto* as told by a female collective, in contrast to her purely thematic recourse to it in the main novel – represents an ideological stance and a clever way to reinstitute a dissonant agency for a protagonist whose desire has been silently evacuated from the body of the novel. While folklore signals (indeed, causes) the protagonist's aesthetic and economic defeat in the novel, in "Il folletto" it is instrumental in physically punishing the object of her desire and in re-establishing a symmetry of fates between the protagonists of the novel and its sequel. In other words, although Nanna may have been pushed to the background by *In risaia*'s ending, her desire survives and resurfaces in a different narrative dimension in the sequel.

"Il folletto" should be understood, then, as a very literal narrative revenge on the part of the absent desiring subject, one that is thematically built on the punishment of Gaudenzio's economic and sexual appetites by an intentional combination and confusion of productive and reproductive attributes. But it is also a multilayered reflection, both narrative and formal, on the power of narrative, within and outside of a text. In narrative terms, folklore pits the never-ending flow of oral storytelling against the punctual "happy endings" of normative narrative genres. In this respect, the sequel skilfully avoids the discreet conclusion that characterized the novel by reverting to the folkloric continuum of collective life. Gaudenzio is portrayed endlessly retelling his story and shaking from fear ("freme ancora adesso") each time he does so.[17]

From cruel optimism we move on to optimistic cruelty, so to speak. The novel ended under the banner of a conservative happiness: Nanna's acceptance of a belatedly consolatory marriage as the best ending of all signifies her accommodation to "normative form [in order] to get numb with the consensual promise and to misrecognize the promise as an achievement" (Berlant 97). Conversely, the narrative revenge endorsed by this boundary-crossing sequel is emblematic of a gendered reversal of fates, an optimistic cruelty: it *is* possible to rebalance desires and to ensure that happy endings are not always the end of the story. It is possible to place the reins of epistemological and narrative authority back into the hands of marginal subjects – wilful characters and the community that represents them – and also tell the story from their point of view.

As Berlant examines her texts, she finds they are stories in which cruel optimism allows a short-lived hope for social and existential change but that this hope is always dashed by the subjects' lack of control over "the material conditions of their lives": "[T]he vague futurities of normative optimism produce small self-interruptions as the utopias of structural inequality. The texts … stage moments when it could become otherwise, but shifts in affective atmosphere are not equal to changing the world" (116). Whereas Nanna's and donna Violante's stories indeed both end with female (more or less tragic) domestication, Marchesa Colombi's insistence on giving Gaudenzio's life one final fictional instalment bespeaks an ideological commitment to questioning the conservative balance of power and of narrative – or at least to shift the affective burden of cruel optimism onto different shoulders for the length of a coda.

Finally, the revelatory moment in both texts is a complex negotiation of ideological contrasts. Nanna's revelation within the novel serves the very conservative purpose of steering her away from her aspiration to self-sufficiency and towards a sexual compromise. In the case of the baron d'Arvelo, the revelation of the actual presence of his first wife cannot be separated from the violent intervention that this prompts – the revelation of her presence is immediately superseded by the enforcement (the material realization) of her absence. In both instances, the narrative purpose of the revelation aligns with a conservative agenda. However, both revelatory moments, and their subsequent epistemological reversals, leave a trail of unfulfilled desire and of narrative expectations that Verga and Marchesa Colombi significantly decided not to entirely dismiss.

4 Intellectual Experiments: The Philosopher and the Housewife

– Ma perché allora la donna non può fare quello che fa l'uomo?
– Dimmi un po', carina, chi spazza le nostre camere e rifà i letti?
– Quale domanda, mamma! La persona di servizio.
– E chi lava la biancheria? – Il lavandaio.
– E chi taglia i tuoi abiti? – La sarta.
– E chi ci ha fatto i mobili? – Il falegname.
– Perché dunque la sarta non lava i tuoi vestiti, e il falegname non rifà i nostri letti, nè cuce i nostri abiti?
Perchè ognuno deve fare il proprio mestiere.

– But why can a woman not do what a man does?
– Tell me, dear, who sweeps our rooms and makes the beds?
– What a silly question, mom! The maid.
– And who washes your laundry? – The washerman.
– Who sews your clothes? – The seamstress.
– And who made our furniture? – The carpenter.
– Why does the seamstress not wash your clothes, or the carpenter make our beds, or sew our clothes?
Because everyone has to do their job.

(Neera, "Emancipazione," in Neera and Mantegazza, *Dizionario* 143–4)

In chapter 2 I discussed how the very act of placing a female subject at the centre of a novel underscored the dissonance of Neera's protagonists: they are the protagonists of subjective quests and, simultaneously, social objects that are bound to be restrained and contained by traditional gender roles. In chapter 3, I focused on the generic dissonances to be uncovered in Verga's and Marchesa Colombi's projects and examined how different narrative structures can allow different ideological presences (and absences) to resonate with the reader, showing that characters can find an "escape route" within an alternative generic space. The analyses in both of these chapters focused on novels whose basic narrative structures go uncontested, even though there are challenges and power struggles over roles for the characters and over generic choices on the part of the narrator.

In contrast, the texts I examine in this chapter and the next belong to a different ideological space, because the narrative challenges that these texts pose for the novel are more overt and more directly aimed at undoing the structural foundation of novels. Chronologically and contextually, in these chapters we advance well into the twentieth century and towards the crisis of modernity. While the novel is still "the" form through which these stories are told, the gender dissonance at its core deeply influences the narrative pattern – in this chapter, for example, it affects the relationship between character and narrator. It undermines the novelistic promise to offer solutions, to offer a reliable form of reality – of narrative truth – that can solve (echoing Jameson) "unresolvable [*gender*] contradictions" (79).

Just as liberal Italy proved to be extremely contradictory in terms of the ideology of gender in narrative, especially when explored from the standpoint of female writers and characters, the relationship between Italian Fascism and gender roles has also been subjected to a close scrutiny in recent years, one that has increasingly complicated the traditionally univocal critical understanding of notions of femininity and masculinity that were held during the *Ventennio*. From the reminder that early Fascism advocated for institutional revisions of gender prerogatives (such as calling for women's vote) to the description of the "scollamento esistente fra l'immagine femminile ufficiale e la realtà quotidiana" (Mondello 10; existing disconnection between the official female image and day-to-day reality), it is now recognized that Fascist notions of woman were more ambiguous and negotiable than an uncritical reference to Mussolini's demographic campaign would suggest.

As far as the very presence of women artists is concerned, Robin Pickering-Iazzi (along with others) has emphasized that the proliferation of female talent that occurred after the Italian Unification, as exemplified by Neera and Marchesa Colombi, did not significantly decrease during the Fascist years. She has provocatively argued that "women's literary production was repressed not by Fascist cultural management, but by the gaps in visual memory created by the literary establishment after the 'liberation'" (*Politics of the Visible* 5–6). Conversely, scholars such as Lucia Re have also recently illustrated the extent to which Fascist censorship, although not as direct and explicit as one might imagine, "affected women or, rather, *hinged* on the woman question, possibly as much as on the racial questions" ("Women and Censorship" 67).

Writer Paola Masino (1908–89), an "innovative, radical and unorthodox" (Wood 108) author, is a formidable example of both female creativity and the visibility of females during the Fascist regime, and her experiences also exemplify the restrictions and censorship many authors had to endure. Concerning the former, in addition to receiving the Viareggio literary prize in 1931 for her first novel, *Monte Ignoso*, and the Viareggio second prize for her next text, *Periferia* (1933), Masino frequently contributed to literary journals such as *900*, and she was a prolific writer of short stories, novels, and theatre plays during the *Ventennio* – although she received very little critical and editorial attention during the post-war years and is more often than not simply remembered as the (unmarried) companion of Massimo Bontempelli. Concerning the latter, the editorial history of her novel *Nascita e morte della massaia* (and also of her short story "Fame") is replete with conflicted compromises that she had to make in order to have her book published during the last years of the regime.[1]

Masino's third (and last) novel, *Nascita e morte della massaia* (1945), is an especially challenging literary work. By focusing on a female protagonist who is remarkably uninterested in gender conformity – or, rather, interested in it only as an object of philosophical scrutiny – Masino powerfully undermines gendered patterns of knowledge and power. Whereas the *massaia* (who is identified solely through her function, as a bourgeois "housekeeper") remains substantially unchanged throughout the text, the narrator insists at various moments in conforming her story to a conversion, a dynamic model of development through which the protagonist would turn into a perfect incarnation of domestic virtues. The result is a text that, while appealing to traditional expectations of the Bildungsroman as an evolutionary parable, ultimately underscores the failure of the protagonist's supposed conversion to domesticity (or its sole realization, as it were, in the "spectral" epilogue).[2] Masino's novel is not the account of a gendered quest, as are Neera's texts, nor is it the story of wilful characters whose resistance can only be expressed, as the authors in chapter 3 did, via spectral "apparitions" and metonymic displacements from one narrative genre to another. Rather, Masino's novel stages a very sophisticated ideological conflict between a dissonant character and the insistent injunctions that she receives from the narrator, a conflict that, rather than being solved or contained by the end, is paratextually multiplied and propagated.

The Philosopher in the Trunk[3]

Nascita e morte della massaia opens with the refreshingly deathly image of a young woman spending her youth lying in a "baule" (a trunk) "che le fungeva da armadio, letto, credenza, tavola e stanza, pieno di brandelli di coperte, di tozzi di pane, di libri e relitti di funerali" (5; "that served as her wardrobe, bed, dresser, table, and bedroom, a trunk full of blanket rags, bits of bread, books, and funeral remains"; trans. Feltrin-Morris 17).[4] She lives on dust, bread crusts, and nail-biting, reading books and thinking about death. Her mother accuses the *massaia* of leading her to ruin by behaving in such an uncivilized way. The young woman is possessed by nightmares of spiderwebs imprisoning her, and to avoid them, she spends each night reading book after book, resting only when others are awake and can rescue her from her dreams.

What is the reader to make of such a beginning? Lucia Re writes that the young *massaia* behaves as she does "perché intuisce quello che la aspetta se esce e diventa una donna" ("Fascist Theories of 'Woman'" 92; because she intuits what awaits her if she comes out and becomes a woman), while Tristana Rorandelli, in her article about Masino and her cultural environment, reads the protagonist's becoming one with her trunk as becoming an object in the eyes of her family, "una negazione della componente umana della ragazza" ("La questione del corpo materno" 82; a negation of the girl's human component). Both of these remarks are accurate in that they signal, respectively, the protagonist's awareness of her prescribed social destiny and a literalization of the social objectification of women; however, neither Re nor Rorandelli engages directly with the sheer novelty of this female fictional figure, as well as her revisionist references to a Western philosophical tradition founded on the distinction between man as a rational mind and woman as an irrational body and to the tradition's obsession with death.[5]

The young thinker "quotidianamente cataloga[va] pensieri di morte" (5; "day after day ... enumerate[s] her thoughts on death"; trans. Feltrin-Morris 17); she toys with "un'idea di necessità superiore e indiscutibile" ("a notion of necessity as something superior and unquestionable") and aims to "scoprirne le cause e gli effetti" (6; "discover its causes and effects"; trans. Feltrin-Morris 18). She is obsessed and fascinated not by the literal notion of death as the end of an individual's life but by the notion as a philosophical category, a spiritual aspiration: "era attratta verso la morte come a una vetta, un volo" (7; "she was attracted by death as by a summit, a flight"; trans. Feltrin-Morris 18). Death is gradually qualified by the young woman as a detachment from the present, from contingencies and chance, in order to connect with a superior, more permanent order of things; when asked why she brings home all sorts of useless and discarded objects, she replies (with an answer that would have made Descartes quite proud), "Tutto ha una ragione e io devo scoprirla" (11; "Everything has a reason and I must discover it"; trans. Feltrin-Morris 21).

In the rare instances when the girl ventures out of the house, she looks at the material reality of things only in terms of their causal connections with death and with the past, with human history, and with science – in short, with speculative knowledge: "In ogni lumaca schiacciata, in ogni arancio marcito immaginava fasto e declino di grandi dinastie, i tacchi ... pestando i detriti nelle buche della piazza facevano la geologia" (8; "In every crushed slug, in every rotten orange she pictured the splendor and decline of great dynasties; footsteps ... stepping on the rubble stuck in the holes of the piazza, created geology"; trans. Feltrin-Morris 19). Her choice is to isolate herself from the world and to relinquish all care of herself, a decision that reflects the primacy of thought this young philosopher established over mundane concerns: "Su lei cadeva la polvere dei soffitti e le si ammucchiava in capo la forfora sul capo, molliche e residui di carte le entravano sotto le unghie, muschio nasceva tra le fessure del baule" (6; "Dust fell from ceilings and turned into dandruff on her head, while bread crumbs and pieces of paper got stuck under her nails. Moss grew between the cracks of the trunk"; trans. Feltrin-Morris 17).

The fact that such an intellectual role is usually marked as masculine, or rather as a role that refuses sexual specificity and tends towards an ideal neutrality, is made very clear by the contrast played out in these pages between such an ungendered mortality and a bodily (female) "immortality." The young woman realizes that, just like the slaughtered animals she sees at the market, "anche lei nel suo interno doveva avere qualche cosa di cui il mondo aveva bisogno e che gli uomini, se lei non lo offrisse, le strapperanno" (9; "she, too, must have something inside of her that the world needed and that mankind would snatch out of her if she did not offer it willingly"; trans. Feltrin-Morris 20).[6] She is immediately plagued by "la sensazione, per lei terribile, di essere immortale, di non arrivare mai, per quanto faccia, a liberarsi in modo definitivo del corpo che le hanno messo addosso" (9; "the sensation, a terrible sensation for her, of being immortal, of being unable, despite all her efforts, to be rid once and for all of the body they had put on her"; trans. Feltrin-Morris 20). Immortality is here the doomed condition of sexed beings, of all those who cannot do away with the materiality of life. Her nature as a woman is characterized by "something" that men want from her so much that they might end up ripping it away. The immortality – that is, the endless renewal of life signified by the female sex – is rejected by the philosopher as a hindrance and a danger to her speculative enterprise.[7]

In her monograph on Masino, Louise Rozier underscores that, in all of Masino's novels, "la morte è motivo centrale in cui culmina il dramma dei personaggi, che, dopo aver attraversato profonde e crudeli sofferenze, trovano in essa la soluzione ed il senso della loro stessa vita" (52; death is the central motif where the drama of the characters culminates. After going through deep and cruel suffering, they find in it the solution and the direction of their very lives). Indeed, as the title attests, this will also happen to the protagonist of *Birth and Death of the Housewife*: the narrative parable will carry us from her birth to her death. The protagonist's obsession with death and rational thought, nonetheless, needs to be read ideologically, in its philosophical implications: it clearly connects her with the tradition of Western speculative thought, from Plato to Heidegger – with that "being for death" that, according to Hannah Arendt, founds Western philosophy as such. In her book *Nonostante Platone* (*In Spite of Plato*) as well as in her subsequent texts, Adriana Cavarero examines "quella tradizione patriarchale che è da sempre cresciuta sulla centralità della categoria di morte" (8; "the patriarchal tradition that has always thrived on the category of death"; trans. Anderlini-D'Onofrio and O'Healy 7); drawing on Arendt's analysis, she describes the Western philosophical enterprise as characterized by "un desiderio ossessivo di durare che affida agli eterni oggetti del pensiero il compito di 'salvare' gli uomini da quella morte che hanno scelto a luogo del loro senso, decidendo non a caso di chiamarsi *i mortali*" (9; "the obsessive desire to endure, to survive, which leads men to entrust eternal objects of thoughts with the tasks of 'saving' them from the selfsame death they chose as the locus of meaning when they decided, not by chance, to call themselves *mortals* [subject to death, *morte*]"; Anderlini-D'Onofrio and O'Healy 7; the bracketed note is the translators'). Death is the place where (male) individuals find meaning; by rejecting birth as a contingent, limited achievement, and by reducing maternity to reproduction, they deny the possibility of an ontology founded on birth rather than death. Considered as a passive obedience "alla legge di autoconservazione del genere umano" (101; "[to] the law of human self-preservation"; Anderlini-D'Onofrio and O'Healy 100), the physical immortality feared by the *massaia* becomes "una sorta di ciclo cieco misurato appunto sull'angoscia della morte che tutto abbraccia e regge" (101; "a blind, cyclical pattern ... based on a fear of death that embraces and sustains everything"; Anderlini-D'Onofrio and O'Healy 100).

The novel is thus provided with the figure of a philosopher woman who, as primitive, asocial, and a-sexed as she might at first appear, has in fact already very carefully assimilated modes of being that are explicitly connected with masculinity and its narrative of rational universality.[8] She has internalized a frightened consternation about the mysteries of the feminine body and has assumed an approach to the world that wants to explain and eliminate it, rather than ensure its perpetuation. The reason for this attitude in the young girl is provided in the first lines of the text; it is the guilt-ridden relationship between mother and daughter. "[L]a madre s'era dimenticata di educarla" (5; "Her mother had forgotten to raise her"; trans. Feltrin-Morris 17) and now blames her mistake on her daughter, claiming that the girl will soon bring her to her death: "Verrà il giorno in cui m'avrai fatta morire di crepacuore" (5; "A day will come when you'll kill me with all this heartbreak"; trans. Feltrin-Morris 17). The reference to her failed upbringing underscores the reason for the girl's subversive outcome: she has not been properly raised to be a young girl, and she is now being blamed for this.[9]

The *massaia*'s fascination with death in the tightly sketched opening trajectory is thus the result of her internalizing the accusation of being a "figlia assassina" (5; "murderous daughter"; trans. Feltrin-Morris 17), a bearer of death rather than life: it is the result of a thwarted upbringing. In this respect, the formative structure has been completely subverted by an opening that resembles a point of arrival more than a beginning. It presents the figure of the young woman philosopher as a given, as an embodied reality, with her speculative passion juxtaposed to her awareness of the violence ascribed to her, but also to her awareness of the violence that can be inflicted on her gendered body. Her commitment to the model of an asocial, purely speculative life is configured as her only escape from a destiny that infallibly ties her back to her sex and her sex to its social function. Her mother's failure to educate her about society produces a subject who is bound to observe the normal world as an outsider, a philosophical speculator who is eager to learn but also wary of the pitfalls and mystifications of social life and of the unspoken violence within it. In contrast to the dissonant characters that I have analysed in the previous chapters, the *massaia* is not bound to have a revelation as part of her epistemological itinerary; no epiphany awaits this woman who is wise beyond her sex.

The *massaia* is in this sense a subject who, because the chain of prescriptions passed from mother to daughter has been interrupted, explores her "wilfulness" (her awareness of injustice) from a highly intellectual point of view. Indeed, the novel is shaped around her experimental subjectivity, one that refutes preordained models and explores the "normal" of both reality and narrative through an alienated – and alienating – prism. This is a novel in which, as strange as this might sound, the main character at times openly disregards the narrative authority that founds the character's very existence.

Out of the Trunk: The Social Initiation of the *Massaia*

Interestingly enough, the young philosopher decides to leave her trunk because she wants to experience the mystery of birth. As she tries to explain maternity to herself and to her mother, she resorts again to a speculative model: "Nascere è passare attraverso un dolore ostile e altrui che ci conservava, per andare dove il nostro proprio dolore ci attrae, che ci consumerà. Per questo dunque l'amore materno è una forza sempre lacerata" ("To be born is to pass through someone else's hostile pain, a pain that preserved us, so that we may go where our own pain draws us, and where it will consume us. This is why a mother's love is always a torn force"). She tries to understand birth and maternity, and with these the painful destiny of woman, by exercising her intellectual abilities. Her mother reacts with a very pragmatic, socially acceptable version of reality. She exhorts her daughter to be silent – "Taci tu e i tuoi misteri" ("Shut up, you and your mysteries") – and offers her the social *vulgata* about birth: "la nascita non è la madre … La nascita è l'amore, anzi no: il matrimonio" (15; "birth is no mother … Birth is love, or rather, it isn't: it's marriage"; trans. Feltrin-Morris 25).

This encounter fails to bridge the gap between a subjectivity bent on questioning and understanding and one subservient to social dogmas, impermeable to emotional or experiential ties. The novel explicitly contrasts these two positions by explaining that the young woman "da gran tempo pensava agli avvenimenti della materia come ad altrettante attuazioni d'idee e subito si metteva alla ricerca di quelle appena il fenomeno fisico le si palesava. Per la madre invece avevano importanza soltanto i fatti: la domanda della figlia non le apparve dunque che un mal celato desiderio di marito" (15; "For a long time she had regarded every material phenomenon as the realization of a specific idea, and as soon as she noticed a physical occurrence, she would search for that idea. Her mother, on the other hand, only cared about facts: therefore, she interpreted her daughter's question as a poorly disguised desire for a husband"; trans. Feltrin-Morris 25). Radically – indeed, parodically – the mother misunderstands the daughter's yearning for knowledge and initiates her campaign to have her daughter join the human consortium and take a husband.

The young woman ultimately accepts her mother's pleas to conform as another experiment, as an attempt to understand the world: "allora dirò così: poichè io sono più forte di te, cedo. Dimmi soltanto che cosa devo fare per farti piacere" (19; "I'll just say this: because I'm stronger than you, I'll give in. Just tell me what I must do to please you"; trans. Feltrin-Morris 28). Her mother requests that she become beautiful in order to integrate herself into society and find a husband. The aesthetic transformation of the *massaia* takes one week. While she scrubs and polishes off years of dirt, mould, and neglect to emerge as a new, beautifully civilized woman, however, her intellectual approach does not change. She recognizes her body as a text, as matter on which a hermeneutic grid can be superposed: "Questo corpo è abbastanza interessante, ci si può lavorare sopra come il piano regolatore di una città" (21; "Her body was rather interesting; one could work on it as if it were a matter of urban planning"; trans. Feltrin-Morris 30). The awareness that characterizes her apprenticeship exposes this enterprise – the civilizing "lavori di restauro" (21; "renovation work"; trans. Feltrin-Morris 30) on her body – for what it is: a bio-political approach, an intervention through which what was (supposedly) outside of history and power becomes part of, and ruled and described by, that very history and power.

Foucault introduced the concept of biopower in his *History of Sexuality*, describing life as "à la fois à l'extérieur de l'histoire comme son entour biologique et à l'intérieur de l'historicité humaine, pénétrée par ses techniques de savoir et de pouvoir" (189; "at the same time outside history, in its biological environment, and inside human historicity, penetrated by the latter's techniques of knowledge and power"; trans. Hurley 143). Masino's protagonist knowingly uses the similes of urban planning and of renovation work to refer to the topos of a civilizing intervention, one in which the "natural" body of a subject is penetrated, to use Foucault's terminology, by the cultural techniques of knowledge and power and hence transformed into an ideological instrument. However, the *massaia* also exposes the extent to which this narrative – the transformation of her biological attributes into useful social functions and roles – is always already fictional, that is, cultural. For example, during her "make-over" week, she takes long nightly walks to avoid falling prey to her nightmares, and when her family sees her upon her return, they "la credevano composta di una sostanza sottomarina come certo marmo che ha ancora impresso nella pallida carne vene che furono alghe, trasparenze che furono correnti" (22; "thought she was made of some deep-sea substance, like marble that carries on its pale flesh veins like algae and the glow of clear waters"; trans. Feltrin-Morris 30–1). Here, reversing epistemological givens, nature is an achievement, a cultural (fictional) notion, the product of the cultural intervention of knowledge and power. Masino highlights how the *massaia*'s body is conceived and describes it as "natural" only once it has been scrubbed, polished, and worked on, that is, only once it has been moulded by and for history.

The *massaia*-to-be thus accepts her masquerade as a natural woman, although, as she has clearly stated in her "acceptance" speech to her mother, she is also aware that it might not turn out to be a viable role for her: "Sei sicura che esiste, per me, un'altra forma migliore? … Non temi che il ricordo del pensiero che io abbandono mi si insinui poi nella vita e mi sconvolga tutta l'esistenza se io scelgo una vita normale?" (18; "Are you sure that a better form exists for me …? Don't you fear that the memory of the thought I'm about to abandon might creep into my life and overturn my whole existence if I choose a normal course?"; trans. Feltrin-Morris 28). She worries about the consequences of renouncing her subjectivity and her intellectual awareness. This is the dilemma posed by the novel as the young philosopher abandons her old life: Can a thinking individual consciously accept a fate such as the one for which women are destined in Western society and revert, as it were, to nature? What happens to thought, to self-awareness and subjectivity, within the context of a gendered normalization? And, narratively speaking, how will a story handle a character who is as original and self-aware as the *massaia*? What will it *ask* of her?[10]

The Philosopher in the House

The young *massaia* sets out to explore the conventions and customs of twentieth-century Western bourgeoisie and Fascism, trying to analyse her role as a woman in such a society. This is the first epistemological subversion with which the novel confronts us: far from being harmless or clueless, the protagonist is a refined subject who is willing to renounce her monadic status to please her mother and society more generally, but not her intellectual awareness or the analytic ability that goes with it. Such a premise is startling as well as highly innovative: as she applies the skills she has used to decode the world of ideas in order to understand the social status of women, the results cannot but be socially unsettling.[11]

Her bodily metamorphosis complete, the *massaia* is introduced to society. Her mother organizes a ball to which all the city authorities, as well as the city's bachelors, are invited. However, the young woman does not passively comply with the script for her social debut: she remains an actor within – and notwithstanding – her prescribed objectification. As the reception unfolds, the young philosopher does not simply accept being stared at; rather, she consciously turns her own inquisitive gaze towards the spectators of the "crudele mostra di se [*sic*] medesima" (30; "cruel self-exposure"; trans. Feltrin-Morris 36) that she is about to perform. She proposes one condition to her anxious mother when her mother visits her room and begs her to appear among the guests: "Vengo, ma non voglio che mi vedano subito … Se qualcuno mi guarda e mi vede, prima che io voglia, peggio per lui. Dio lo farà diventar cieco" (27; "I'll come, but I don't want them to see me just yet … If anybody looks and sees me before I want them to, so much the worse for them. God shall make them blind"; trans. Feltrin-Morris 34). Evoking a Catholicized Medusa, the young woman reverses the ritual of exposition: she will be the first to lay her gaze upon the others, rather than the other way around. Her mother succeeds – comically enough – in shielding the entrance to the salon with four short-sighted people, so that her daughter can enter and stare at the public without being seen. By the time all the guests turn to look at her, their gazes have lost their usual objective of dominating and hegemonizing and have instead become a tool in her hands, a channel of communication that she uses to convey her subversive message.

Her unsettling performance of the *débutante* topos has distinct consequences for the onlookers:

> A quella festa la sensazione in ognuno, quando apparve la ragazza, fu appunto quella che lei aveva predetto: di non poter guardare, come se dovessero fissare una luce troppo viva e nello stesso tempo il senso che dovevano fissarla a quel modo se non volevano rimanere, loro, come scoperti e nudi dinanzi agli occhi di tutti. (31)

> At the ball, the sensation they all felt when the girl appeared was precisely the one she had predicted: no one could bear to look at her, as if they were staring at a light that was too bright. Yet, at the same time they all felt they had to look at her in that way, lest they might end up uncovered and naked before everyone's eyes. (trans. Feltrin-Morris 37)

Through her performance, she exposes the relationship between social victim and perpetrator and undoes the one-way direction of the gaze: her exposition is not a conciliatory, conservative exercise but rather a performance that affects both spectacle and spectator, an event that promotes a dangerous equating of the one and the many.

Women's traditional introduction to society is a violent gesture of objectification in which their ritualized exposure in fact foreshadows their fate as objects of marital transactions. In this case, however, the young woman performs her cruel display of herself – for the benefit of the audience – with an awareness that her own knowledge of her spectators is far more comprehensive than the knowledge they have of her:

> La figlia fissava diritta davanti a sé, con l'occhio immobile, e non un palpito delle ciglia addolciva per un attimo quella crudele mostra di se medesima. Dritta come una statua davanti a tutti, ormai voleva farsi vedere dopo essere stata, non vista, in quello angolo a osservarli per qualche minuto. Appunto così. *Sapeva chi erano. Sapeva che cosa erano. Non si era mai sbagliata. L'aveva saputo fin da sempre,* fin da sempre li aveva giudicati. (30, emphasis mine)

> The daughter looked straight ahead with a fixed stare. Not a blink from her eyelids alleviated even for a single moment the tension of that cruel self-exposure. Erect like a statue before them all, she now wanted to be

> seen after she had watched them, unseen, for a few minutes. Exactly like that. *She knew who they were. She knew what they were. She had never been wrong. She had always known it*, she had been judging them all along. (trans. Feltrin-Morris 36)

Her social performance confirms, rather than dispels, the hypotheses she had elaborated and the judgments she had made while living in the trunk. The text emphasizes her ontological status as "knower," as a solid, unchanging epistemological authority who faces her new pose with full awareness. At the same time her dissonant behaviour, unsettling as it is, does not change her new social status as a soon-to-be-married commodity. The ambiguity of her power within the debut ritual is expressed, as well, by the ensuing use of a genitive that is both subjective and objective – "il martirio del pubblico durò ancora qualche minuto" (31; "The guests' agony lasted a few minutes longer"; trans. Feltrin-Morris 37) – in which both readings, the public as torturer and the young woman as torturing them, coexist perfectly.

The ball scene draws to a close when the young woman, who hasn't slept well in years, falls asleep out of boredom and is overcome by nightmares: this time, the spiderwebs attacking her in her sleep are dispelled and defeated by a voiceover that tells her not to be afraid because the webs are "tied." This banishing of the nocturnal attacks, however, provokes only sadness for her, as they were her last connection with her previous, purely speculative "trunk" life.[12]

The ball sequence also serves to introduce the character of the "giovane bruno," a young man with "molta ombra sul volto e negli occhi" (32; "a dark look on his face and in his eyes"; trans. Feltrin-Morris 37) who seems to represent the ideal partner for the young philosopher. Among the crowd of potential suitors, he is the only one who recognizes, and admires as such, the *massaia*'s intellectual abilities. The young woman feels she is in love with the dark young man, but the day after the ball he rejects her as a companion because of her uncompromising intelligence: "Perchè non hai esempi e conosci le cose e ti si possono dire le parole vere, mi fai paura e non ti sposo" (41; "Since you have no examples and you know things, and one can tell you true words, you scare me and I won't marry you"; trans. Feltrin-Morris 44). He leaves her with a sort of idealized pact: "Siamo necessari l'uno all'altra e dunque staremo disgiunti per misurare il nostro valore umano" (41; "We need each other, and therefore we'll stay apart so we can measure our human value"; trans. Feltrin-Morris 44). This proposal appears to allude to an eventual romantic connection, that is, to the possibility of a traditional narrative path for the novel, one in which the two Platonic halves might lovingly reconstitute as a perfect unity after many vicissitudes. The reader's anticipation of a resolutive encounter with the dark young man later in the novel will not be completely thwarted, although the outcome of the encounter will be far from romantic or conciliatory.

As her hopes of finding a suitable companion are dashed, the protagonist acquiesces to her mother's choice of an old, rich uncle as her husband (economic considerations having clearly superseded everything else in her mother's ambitions). The *massaia*'s husband brings her to his estate and gives her a tour of his vast house. During this visit, although she is persuaded that from now on her duty will be one "di essere compita e fare piacere a ognuno senza distinzioni e discussioni, a costo di me stessa" (43; "of acting properly and pleasing everyone without distinctions or complaints, at the cost of my own self"; trans. Feltrin-Morris 48), she does not renounce her critical stance towards reality, especially towards the complex display of wealth and social functions about which her husband educates her. When she ironically comments on this display, her groom sharply replies that "La casa è la famiglia: un'istituzione sacra che va rispettata e difesa: più si accresce, più si accresce il bene del paese" (45; "The house is the family: a sacred institution that must be respected and defended. To enhance it is to enhance the good of the country"; trans. Feltrin-Morris 49). He reacts to her disinterest by revealing the underlying anxieties connected with property: just like a country, the house needs to be respected and defended from external threats.[13]

The protagonist also experiences the violent – and violating – nature of the conjugal pact. Immediately after the sequence in which the old uncle displays his domain to his new wife, they consummate the marriage, an event that she suffers in "un'esaltazione di dolore" (46; "painful exaltation"; trans. Feltrin-Morris 49). The young woman wakes up the following morning with her "carne ancora gonfia e battuta" (46; "flesh swollen and battered"; trans. Feltrin-Morris 50) and considers the universal fate with newly opened eyes: she "ha imparato ormai che cosa vuol dire essere squarciati, manomessi, *rivelati*" (47; "had now learned what it meant to be ripped apart, manipulated, *revealed*"; trans. Feltrin-Morris 50, emphasis mine – "manomessi" literally translates as "tampered with"). Her appraisal of the conjugal encounter is a striking example of the intense scrutiny to which she submits the entire institution of marriage, from its economic to its intimate aspects, and of the violent ideology of gender that informs her life. The *massaia* actively reflects on what it means to be "revealed" by the traumatic encounter between the sexes. She concludes that, for both endorser and victim of such violent hermeneutics, "la vita non può essere che contaminazione e decadenza" (47; "Life cannot be but contamination and decay"; trans. Feltrin-Morris 50). The revelatory paradigm does not imply a better understanding of herself. Rather than opening a new epistemological dimension, it merely confirms on her body the direction of the violence of gender, its "ripping," "tampering" nature.

From this point on, the text oscillates regularly between the *massaia*'s attempts to become fully subservient to an economy of non-thought and subjection and her determination to maintain her epistemological awareness. During the first months of married life, for example, her diurnal conduct is blameless: "Ora non leggeva quasi più e ben presto si accorse che quel pensiero entro cui fin qui si era sentita trascinare l'aveva abbandonata del tutto ... Proibì perfino a se stessa di dirsi: – io respiro, io sogno, io maturo – così per provarsi, per mettersi ancora in rapporto con il mondo intimo" (48; "She hardly read anymore and soon became aware that the thought inside of which she had felt dragged along up to that point had abandoned her completely ... She went as far as to forbid herself to say, 'I breathe, I dream, I mature,' which used to be the way she tested herself and tried to relate to her inner world"; trans. Feltrin-Morris 51). At night, though, she wanders through the house harbouring an illusion of non-hierarchical participation in its life: "Io sono libera allora di godere la mia casa, come piace a me, senza responsabilità, senza essere la padrona. Posso se voglio essere anche il cane da caccia o la pentola sul fornellino, posso essere il nascituro o un avo" (50; "That's the time when I'm free to enjoy my house the way I like it, without responsibilities, without being the mistress. If I want, I can be a hound dog or a pot on the stove, I can be an unborn child or an ancestor"; trans. Feltrin-Morris 52).

Her character is soon plagued by this dichotomy, highlighting her inability to simply acquiesce to the social order. The dichotomy, which appears fairly early on in the novel, is arguably the only "dynamic" process we see. Although she alternates between these two modes, she never in fact evolves from one to the other. Such a non-evolutionary, binary conflict is extremely significant in the text because it is gradually juxtaposed to a different desire exhibited by the narrative instance, one that is, in contrast, very much invested in change.[14]

Against Conversion

The passage quoted above, describing the *massaia*'s nocturnal wandering through the house, is followed by the narrator's first explicit intervention in the novel. The novel is narrated in the third person, but the *récit* occasionally gives way to a first-person (singular or plural) narrator whose voice comments (often negatively) on the protagonist's behaviour from a conservative standpoint: "Con queste intenzioni, che noi biasimiamo moltissimo pur trovandole interessanti, si era alzata una prima volta e se ne era andata girovagando per la casa, mettendo alla prova quelle possibilità di libero arbitrio che lei credeva, secondo gli insegnamenti della scolastica, appartenessero indiscutibilmente a ogni uomo. Le fu presto dimostrato che non era così" (50; "It was with such intentions, which we strongly criticize although we find them interesting, that she got up the first time and went wandering about the house, testing that free will which, in line with the teachings of scholasticism, she believed to be mankind's indisputable prerogative. She soon learned that it was not true"; trans. Feltrin-Morris 52–3). The plural "we" of the narrating voice carries with it a conservative criticism of the protagonist's behaviour in a textual move that could be understood as a preventive recognition of the readers' (or censors') anxiety concerning such conduct or, alternatively, as an ironic stance. Lucia Re, arguably the most attentive and subtle critic of Masino's works, considers the narrating voice to be "anonymous and ironic" ("Fame, cibo e antifascismo" 166) and has described "the novel's tone" as "ironic, parodic and mock-heroic" (171).

Irony and parody undoubtedly inhabit more than a few passages of the novel. They are among the elements that complicate the relationships between narrator and protagonist and between a literal and an "other" meaning of the novel. At times, the text appears to be engaged in caricaturing the conservative stance of an omniscient narrator by exaggerating its (his) moralistic posture – for example, when the *massaia* and her equally nameless female alter ego, whose presence in the novel I will discuss later in this chapter, are abruptly qualified as "quelle due bislacche" (166; "those two loonies"; trans. Feltrin-Morris 145) by the text, which then "naively" resumes its narration. However, there also appears to be a different and less formalized strategy of slippage at work within *Nascita e morte della massaia*, a technique for disavowal: the narrator suggests the direction in which the text is heading, only to be conspicuously discredited by the protagonist's actual behaviour.

As she becomes acquainted with her domestic life, for example, the *massaia* pleads to the sky, in a long invective, to rebel against the human order: "Prova ad abbandonare la terra, ti prego, a lasciare questi uomini sociali una volta almeno senza il tuo ausilio" (71; "Try and abandon the earth, I beg you. At least just once try and leave these social men without your assistance"; trans. Feltrin-Morris 67). When she fails to receive an answer, she returns to her room and the narrator takes over, critiquing her arrogance and foreshadowing a change in her life: "Credo che il cielo udì le sue parole e ne rimase offeso. Chi può dirmi di no? Una massaia qualunque che si mette a tu per tu con un magnate dell'universo e dà consigli e fa denunce non può essere ritenuta dal magnate che una presuntuosa da punire ... Non è da maravigliarsi dunque se la massaia quella notte ebbe finalmente sogni, e sogni che la obbligarono a cambiare vita e natura" (72; "I think the sky heard her words and was offended. Who can tell me it is not true? An ordinary housewife who has the nerve to stand up face-to-face with a tycoon of the universe, give advice, and make accusations, cannot but be regarded by that tycoon as a bighead who needs to be punished ... Therefore it is no wonder that, on that night, the housewife finally had dreams, dreams that forced her to change her life and nature"; trans. Feltrin-Morris 68). Subsequently, the *massaia* does indeed have long, dreadful dreams populated by her actual and future domestic personnel, yet, as becomes increasingly clear from the events that follow, she does not change her "life and nature" because of these dreams.

At her husband's suggestion, she throws a large reception for the city notables, a scene that is transcribed in the novel in the form of a theatrical play. As the dinner turns into a stage performance, its individual actors progressively gather into larger groups, or "choruses": a "coro delle signore di una certa età" (92; "chorus of mature women"; trans. Feltrin-Morris 87), a "coro dei mariti" (93; "chorus of husbands"; trans. Feltrin-Morris 88), and a "coro delle donne di piacere" (90; "chorus of women of pleasure"; trans. Feltrin-Morris 95). The *massaia* remains outside of these collective entities, and to the women of pleasure who claim their sexual power over men, she vehemently replies, "E a che cosa serve? Con questo le salvate le mogli e le figlie e le sorelle? ... Le togliete dall'assillo della materialità del vivere quotidiano? dall'attrito delle minime necessità sullo spirito, dal costringere al passo ... l'anima che si divertiva a far capriole?" (95; "And what's it good for? Is that how you save wives, daughters, and sisters? ... Do you free them from the nagging materiality of everyday life? From the friction between bare necessities and spirit? From having to restrain … a soul that enjoyed doing somersaults?"; trans. Feltrin-Morris 90). Her attempt to move beyond clichés powerfully highlights her awareness of her status, an awareness that nonetheless goes unheeded by the rest of the evening's characters.[15]

A very interesting dynamic is thus set up in the novel between passages in which the narrator makes categorical pronouncements concerning the direction of the protagonist's life and the subsequent behavioural disavowal performed by the *massaia* herself. The strategy surfaces more frequently as the novel moves towards its conclusion: the more the narrator insists that the *massaia* is changing her ways, the less this happens. The result is a protagonist who unceasingly challenges the power relationship between herself and the narrative that supposedly contains her, creating an extremely interesting instance of structural dissonance. Her dissonance becomes increasingly apparent as the novel proceeds – as the narrator, that is, attempts to impose a conversion, or formative, paradigm on the story while the protagonist remains almost completely impervious to such a paradigm (or at least more impervious than the story would like her to be).

Several scholars have discussed the extent to which modern subjectivity appears to be shaped by the epistemological model of conversion. For example, Giovanni Carsaniga has emphasized, writing of Monti's, Chateaubriand's, and even Manzoni's famous conversions, that "conversion is an ambivalent phenomenon: on the one hand it is a 'turning upside-down' of one's life; and as such it has almost revolutionary connotations. On the other it is a call to order, a return to tradition, revelation and long-established teaching, the supreme act of obedience to a divine Lord" (428). Carsaniga downplays the extent to which the purportedly dramatic ideological shift of the authors he discusses was really such: "[T]he theme of conversion … lends itself to representing as a radical change what is merely a shift within the boundaries of one's ideology" (428). In his authors' works, conversion is an epistemological model employed to authorize and dramatize change while imparting to it a hegemonic value. This comfortable, well-practiced model of nineteenth-century ideological "shift" became an object of consistent revision and criticism as the new century, with its critique of transcendence and of reassuring models of subjectivity, dawned. Svevo's *La coscienza di Zeno* is a perfect example of the refusal to acquiesce to a conversion narrative as such. John Freccero has convincingly written that this novel presents "a single character who can never change and never evolve, because he does not move" (20); Zeno thus ends up joining the ranks of the successful bourgeois entrepreneurs without ever converting to their ideology.[16]

Masino's protagonist presents a similar kind of resistance to the narrative and ideological paradigm that the novel constantly attempts to enforce upon her, that is, the totalitarian religion of domesticity. She joins the ranks of the domestic angels of her time and is ultimately nominated as a national example in homage to her patriotic efforts during the time of war. But she never changes: the conversion paradigm that is intended to supersede her philosophical approach is denounced for what it is, a social speculation on women's lives and subjectivities. Such a narrative and epistemological model is in fact thematized and caricatured from the beginning of the novel, as we saw in the ironic performance of her social birth (her debut), and denounced as an experience of subjection and objectification that the *massaia* refuses to accept as such (while nonetheless endorsing it by her very existence).[17]

At times, in fact, the *massaia*'s resistance to domestication is much more active than Zeno's resistance to bourgeois sanity. At the end of the reception in her house, she experiences a crisis caused by the claustrophobic universe in which she lives, and she decides to move to the city without her husband; there, she starts working in one of his firms. Her progressive disappointment with independent urban life is recorded in several pages of a diary that, in addition to providing a first-person narration on the part of the protagonist, further exemplifies the contamination of genres and styles that Masino employed to explore and replicate at the stylistic level the multifaceted experience of the *massaia*.

The *Massaia*'s Alter Ego

The *Massaia* (starting from chapter 6, p. 102 her name is capitalized) ultimately renounces her urban experiment, entrusts her belongings to her maid, and sets off to return to her hometown. Her journey soon takes on a metaphysical, oneiric quality that makes time an unreliable measure and space a malleable dimension. Her surrealist wanderings through the countryside with occasional companions – which also include, at one point, the *giovane bruno* – end with her discovery of a babelic conglomeration of buildings, a vast factory on top of which she finds a young, undomesticated woman. She has a "fronte pelosa, i capelli a matasse gommose, e … mani dalle unghie quadrate, molli" (141; "fuzzy forehead covered with rubbery matted hair, … hands with square, soft nails"; trans. Feltrin-Morris 127) and is in love with the dark young man but knows that, ugly as she is, she has no hope. The *Massaia* recognizes in this woman a version of her own "trunk-self," with similar character traits such as "un'esasperazione identica alla mia di allora" (141; "the same exasperation that I used to have back then"; trans. Feltrin-Morris 126–7). The description of the *altra* is contrasted with the appraisal that the *Massaia* has just made of her own body; she can't understand where "[il suo] proprio corpo bianco, trasparente, dalle ossa leggere" (138; "her own white, transparent body, her light bones"; trans. Feltrin-Morris 125) have come from. The protagonist reasserts the cultural vacuity of her appearance: "Donde era uscito [il suo corpo]? Non da sua madre certo, non dal baule e neppure dalla sua volontà. Non era più un corpo il suo, ma rappresentazione" (138–9; "Where did that body come from? Certainly not from her mother, nor from the trunk, and not even from her own will. Hers was no longer a body, but a representation"; trans. Feltrin-Morris 125). Once again, the cultural origin of her bodily identity is stated and critiqued as such, her body the prey of a bio-political intervention that governs it and determines its appearance.

Her alter ego begs the *Massaia* to help her gain the love of the young man, and the *Massaia* decides to bring her back home and initiate her into civilization. This step has an ambiguous corollary: the *Massaia* wants to help her undomesticated double become a more fulfilled individual than she is, yet she remains aware that socializing and civilizing her will mean carrying this woman towards the same objectification that she has never accepted for herself. In addition to being the recipient of social directives, the *Massaia* thus consciously becomes an active enforcer: she "dentro aveva un piacere tempestoso di quanto stava per compiere su quella creatura, ridurla, come lei avevano convinta a ridursi, un'apparenza" (141; "was reveling in the stormy pleasure of what she was about to do to this creature: reduce her, as she had been reduced, to an appearance"; trans. Feltrin-Morris 126). While Neera's protagonist Marta in *L'indomani* had also sealed her narrative parable as a woman transformed from recipient to enforcer of the law that she had set out to understand and possibly contest, Masino's protagonist moves a step further: she shows an awareness of the double yoke that law enforcement is for both subject and object of the ideological equation, but coupled with an awareness of the unexpected pleasure that such enforcement bestows upon the enforcer.

Masino's description of what it means to be a *Massaia* once again goes well beyond a list of rules and chores. She explores the complex relational web and the troubled relationship between victim and perpetrator that characterizes every power relation. As Debarati Sanyal argues in a discussion of the violence inherent in the discourse of modernity, such a narrative engagement "disclose[s] the relations of force that structure a given historical moment from a range of identifications, reminding us that violence is not an immutable condition, or a weapon wielded by readily identified perpetrators, but a dynamic and differential operation" (15). Here Masino comments directly on the violent nature of cultural formations and of social apprenticeships that belong to her era – the bourgeois, Fascist world of 1930s Italy – but also on the violence inscribed in the ideology of gender as an epistemological operation that has characterized the Western world since its philosophical origins.

The protagonist gradually introduces the young woman to food, clothing, and civilized manners; she takes her around to visit her possessions and to acquaint her with other people. When the apprentice *massaia* talks to the servant of an inn by their house and shares the secret of her love for the dark young man, the *Massaia* reacts angrily because she knows that society will exploit this secret to its advantage:

> [N]on ti permetto, a nessun patto ti permetto di metterti nuda in mano di costoro che hanno tramata la mia rovina. Vestita mi hanno voluta, agghindata, adorna dei loro usi, calzata di luoghi comuni per muovere il passo al loro fianco nella vita, coronata di pregiudizi, ammantata d'incomprensione. Ma tu e l'amato no, non dovete gettarvi in questa mola e uscirne triturati, come me, per servire loro, che ci sgranocchino. (173)

> I won't allow you, I absolutely won't allow you to place yourself naked in the hands of those who have plotted my undoing. They demanded that I be dressed, primped, adorned with their traditions, shod in clichés before I moved my first steps in life by their side, crowned with prejudice and wrapped up in misunderstanding. But you and your beloved must not, you must not throw yourself under this grindstone and come out of it crushed like me, for them to munch on. (trans. Feltrin-Morris 150)

Thus emerges the *Massaia*'s lingering hope that the "formation" of her double might produce a civilized woman who is able to pursue her dreams more independently. Her angry reaction is dictated by her realization that her double is about to be caught by the same social traps in which she finds herself, traps whose replication she has enabled by bringing the young woman to civilization. Here the paradigm of formation, that is, the enforced conversion from "cavewoman/philosopher" to sophisticated lady that she has reluctantly decided to promote in her female alter ego (a conversion the novel has been enforcing upon her all along), is openly critiqued for its dangerous ideological significance, like a millstone grinding persons into social servants.

As they return home and pass through the servants' quarters at the *Massaia*'s residence, they discover that the young woman's secret is already publicly scorned: it is written everywhere on the walls. Crushed by the indifference of people, their lack of caring, the young woman disappears into the night. Only towards the end of the *Massaia*'s biographical parable will we come to know what has happened to the young woman and to the *giovane bruno* with her. But before turning to that, I want to highlight a few more instances of the narrator's own insistence on wanting to change the protagonist.

According to the narrator, the young woman's escape from the *Massaia*'s manor provokes yet another change in the *Massaia*: "Da quella mattina fu chiaro che la Massaia era cambiata" (179; "From that morning on, it was clear that the Housewife had changed"; trans. Feltrin-Morris 156). Although the narration subsequently makes clear the extent to which the *Massaia* thoroughly devotes herself to her domestic duties, it also becomes clear, once again, that such a radical change is more the expression of a narrative desire than a textual reality and that the *Massaia* has not changed her attitude towards her life. The change the narrator describes relates to the fact that, right after the girl's departure, the protagonist apparently sets about to truly become a devoted housewife. Yet she does not modify her internal stance, her intellectual gaze upon her own actions: "E ora – pensava allontanandosi in fretta per l'intrico dei corridoi ... che cosa dovrò fare? Come passano le loro giornate senza dubbi la madre, le sorelle, le cognate, le amiche?" (180; "Now, she kept thinking as she hurried down the maze of corridors ... what shall I do? How do mothers, sisters, sisters-in-law, and women friends spend their days so carefreely?"; trans. Feltrin-Morris 156–7).

The narrator's peremptory statement – "fu chiaro che la Massaia era cambiata" – emphatically points towards a narrative trajectory being traced for the protagonist while, in fact, the *Massaia*'s path as a character defies categorizations. There continues a constant slippage between the structural direction that the narrator imparts to the novel and the consequent denials of this direction on the part of the character. The *Massaia* never actually changes: as much as the narrator strives to show progress in her assimilation to society, her intellectual dissatisfaction and her engagement in understanding women's position in society beyond traditional gender roles never fade.

Indeed, the narrator itself at times displays instances of a dissonant sympathy towards its character, for example, when the narrator seems to realize the ridiculousness of the *Massaia*'s situation, caught as she is within the multiple and scattered duties of the bourgeois woman: "Con queste sollecitudini, che noi lodiamo moltissimo pur trovandole avvilenti, l'animo della Massaia si era fatto ansioso d'ogni donnesca attività" (193; "With such diligence, which we highly praise even though we find it degrading, the Housewife's soul had come to crave every female activity"; trans. Feltrin-Morris 167). Although the "conversion" directives occur much more often, Masino is clearly thematizing ideological inconsistency at all levels of her text, including the narrative level.[18]

As a war approaches,[19] the *Massaia* zealously pursues her role of guardian of both home and country, apparently aware that, in order to do this, she must renounce thought and rationality: "La casa, come la patria va difesa contro ogni logica e ogni possibilità" (185; "The house, like the homeland, must be defended in the face of any logic and eventuality"; trans. Feltrin-Morris 160). Her domestic duties go hand in hand with her patriotic activities: she becomes an emblem and example of the perfect female citizen. Her fervent engagement is crowned with her nomination to "Esempio nazionale" (194; "National Example"; trans. Feltrin-Morris 167). Her dedication to the domestic and patriotic causes bring upon her that "provvida ebetudine ... di cui finora la Massaia non aveva fruito" (197; "blessed lethargy ... [that] the Housewife had not had the opportunity to enjoy ... thus far"; trans. Feltrin-Morris 169), a lethargy that momentarily confirms the change the narrator signalled after the young girl's departure. Yet not all is perfect under the totalitarian sun of the *Massaia*'s patriotic dream; the one thing that still sets her apart from the other women – and will do so until the end of the story – is the emptiness of her womb, her sterility. "Forse perchè, nella giornata della Massaia, così perfettamente distribuita, non ci sarebbe stato posto per concepire o partorire?" (197; "Could it be that the Housewife's days were so perfectly planned that there could not possibly be any extra room for conceiving or giving birth?"; trans. Feltrin-Morris 169) wonders the narrator.[20]

A second war begins as soon as the first one ends, and she doubles her efforts while her ascetic aspirations grow even stronger. Once again, the narrator is tempted to assert (and almost celebrate) a transformation, describing her as having adopted the Bible as her reference text and thus renouncing any temptation to think independently: "Fu quello l'ultimo giorno che accadde alla Massaia di riprendere l'antico linguaggio; da allora, ogni volta che avrebbe voluto risolvere un pensiero difficile, si affidava alla Sacra Bibbia, aperta a caso" (209; "That was the last day in which the Housewife happened to pick up her old language again; from then on, every time she wanted to find a key to a difficult thought, she would resort to the Holy Bible. She would open it at random"; trans. Feltrin-Morris 178). This proclamation about the *Massaia*'s sacrifice of her intellect and her conversion to the random wisdom of the Bible turns out to be, once again, completely inaccurate. She is still thinking very lucidly – for example, in comparing her parents' behaviour towards the other members of their family and towards herself (they feel a need to help the others but not their daughter), she realizes that her role as caregiver and its sacrificial nature have turned her into a perfectly autarchic monad in the eyes of her family: "si muore quando non si ha più bisogno della collaborazione umana" (215; "people die when they don't need human cooperation anymore"; trans. Feltrin-Morris 183). Since she has tried to completely suppress her own desires in order to take care of the desires of others, she realizes she has only one desire left: her death. While she awaits this event, she indulges in travelling as a minor form of consolation.

The description of her journeys makes it very clear that the supposed eradication of her rationality through appealing to random biblical wisdom, as well as the novel's repeated claims that such attempts succeeded, was only wishful thinking. She is unable to freely converse with her travel companions because she sees the men "in funzione di mariti, di padri, di fratelli, dunque di aguzzini delle donne" (216; "performing their roles as husbands, fathers, brothers, and therefore as women's tyrants"; trans. Feltrin-Morris 186), and in her thoughts she warns her female companions not to give in to the social call: "Non contemplatevi nell'uomo, abbiate vergogna, resistete alla solitudine: l'unico nostro mestiere sia di tornare indietro e voltare le spalle ad Adamo che ci ha approntato il primo tetto e il primo giaciglio da salvaguardargli" (217; "Don't identify your fulfillment with a man; have some decency, overcome your loneliness: our only goal should be to go back and turn against Adam, he who gave us the first shelter and the first bed to defend for his sake"; trans. Feltrin-Morris 186). Her tracing of the domestic genealogy back to Adam and to the biblical *vulgata* is a direct critique of her stultifying reading.

Nonetheless, her travels also bring her to the realization that she is by now too bound to her domestic duties to relinquish them; she is unable to resist a call for help when an important dinner is organized at home: "capisce che ormai le evasioni le sono impossibili, è più facile rassegnarsi" (220; "she realized that there was no possibility of escape, that it was easier to give up"; trans. Feltrin-Morris 188). Is it easier, indeed, for the *Massaia* to resign herself? As the text draws to its conclusion, she is confronted with an increasingly more appealing alternative to simple resignation: "In realtà il desiderio della morte cresceva in lei a dismisura" (220; "In fact, inside of her the death wish kept growing out of all proportion"; trans. Feltrin-Morris 188). The novel explicitly takes the *Massaia* back to her starting point, to her fascination with death, seen now as the only way out of a social pact that she can no longer bear.

A visit to a fortune teller confirms that her death wish will be fulfilled but also foretells a momentous encounter. This turns out to be an unexpected, temporary reunion with both the "dark young man" and the *Massaia*'s alter ego, the young woman who had escaped from being crafted into a better, more independent version of the *Massaia*. When she encounters them in a cemetery, she first meets an "uomo grasso" (226; "huge man"; trans. Feltrin-Morris 193) surrounded by children. She recognizes him as the disfigured, aged, and fattened *giovane bruno*. The children, the man informs her, should have been theirs – that is, his and the *Massaia*'s – rather than being born to her double, who is called "la madre" from this point on. The mother, reduced to "una catasta di ossa" (227; "a heap of bones"; trans. Feltrin-Morris 194) by her childbearing duty, emerges from behind the fat man. She is nursing two infants, and the couple informs the *Massaia* that all the children bear her (unrevealed) name. The man explicitly articulates the narrative and ideological role that he and the "mother" have served in the novel: they are mere holders of the *Massaia*'s neglected matter: "Sono lembi tuoi, materia che tu hai disprezzato. La tua parte di vita, e non sapevi neppure di avercela data in consegna" (228; "They are patches of you, matter that you scorned. They are your slice of life, and you didn't even know you had deposited it with us"; trans. Feltrin-Morris 194).

The encounter between the protagonist and her two "projections" does not allow any reconciliation between the scattered parts of the social body represented by the Housewife, the Mother, and the Husband.

Lucia Re has written that the *Massaia*'s double is "the obedient half of her personality" ("Fascist Theories of 'Woman'" 95). She is her bodily half, understood as the supposedly biology-driven body. The two women have fulfilled two different womanly imperatives, illustrating that one person could not do both at the same time, while exhibiting the price that is paid, in both cases, for taking on such roles.

Although it is absolutely impossible to do justice to the experimental complexity of Masino's novel, I would argue that in epistemological terms, that is, in terms of the story's investment in the narrative "game" that I have described as characteristic of this text, the most interesting aspect of this second part of the novel, as it works its way towards the biographical ending of the *Massaia*'s story, is the relationship between the *Massaia* and her alter ego. The power to "change" the body and the mind of this young woman, as it is discovered and deployed by the *Massaia*, is a thematic reminder of the main ideological and narrative conflict that shapes the novel, namely the power struggle between the *Massaia* and the narrator. Through the *Massaia*'s decision to intervene in the young woman's life and her attempts to change her, we glimpse the same ideological imperative that pushed the narrator to intervene in the *Massaia*'s own life. In both relations – between narrator and character and between young *massaia* and older *Massaia* – the character that is being "worked on" accepts being subjected to a conservative ideology of gender while refusing the ideological program as such. In both relations the enforcer is somewhat inconsistent – dissonant – in enforcing change upon these wilful characters.

While I do not want to overestimate the connections between the two relationships, there is no doubt that the ideological dissonance that emerges from them undermines the possibility of trusting any textual authority as reliable (be it the narrator or the *Massaia* herself) and, with it, the possibility of understanding the novel as univocally pursuing a specific goal – such as that of "change." "Sadism," Laura Mulvey has famously written in her seminal essay on cinematic narrative, "demands a story": it "depends on making something happen, forcing a change in another person" (43). As Teresa de Lauretis explains, this narrative – and gendered – need for sadism translates into the fact that "women *must either* consent *or* be seduced into consenting to femininity" (*Alice Doesn't* 134). Masino's protagonist initially consents to endorsing the social role of *massaia* as much as she is violently "revealed" in the objectification of her flesh; yet her acceptance is not without conditions. She never forfeits her dissonant subjectivity, nor does she accept the appeasing *vulgata* that a traditional notion of femininity is all that life can offer her. And, as the mother reminds both the *Massaia* and her husband, the price to pay for committing oneself, even intermittently, to such restrictive gender dynamics is, in the end, one's missed existence: "per colpa vostra ho ancora da essere, e voi state a fare le patetiche rappresentazioni ... Dovrò essere io col mio poco corpo a darvi una direzione, sublimi impotenti della vita?" (229–30; "Because of you two, I have yet to be, and still you go on with your pathetic performance ... Do I, with this body, have to be the one to give direction to you, you, sublime and powerless against life?"; trans. Feltrin-Morris 195).

Masino's novel actually points, in its experimental and highly idiosyncratic way, in the direction of a possible demise of the sadism of gender hierarchies as the driving force of narrative. The narrator, far from being a uniquely conservative or seductive force, allows subversion to exist by virtue of its own inconsistencies: it allows the protagonist to explore "the relation of female subjectivity to ideology in the representation of sexual difference and desire" (de Lauretis, *Alice Doesn't* 136) and, in so doing, opens the possibility of a character who, by resisting the hegemonizing structure within which it (she) is inserted, acquires the same degree of (dissonant) authority as the narrative instance.

By the end of the novel, the two gendered rhetorics embodied by the two women – domesticity and motherhood – have been simultaneously endorsed and denounced as alienating. The *Massaia* and the mother constitute themselves as figural symbols, broken allegories of a story that they have – literally – agreed to embody but that has not conquered them. While the mother disappears into the background, for the *Massaia*, at this point, there is only one thing left to do.

Back to the Trunk

When the *Massaia* accompanies the mother and her children to their home (an apartment in a crowded working-class building), she finds that, ironically enough, they are using her trunk, the old philosopher's trunk in which she had spent her childhood, as the children's cradle. With the help of the children, she destroys it and then, in a symmetrical movement, returns home to order architects and carpenters to build her tomb. Her last duty before dying entails finding the attic in which the trunk was supposedly held by her husband after their wedding, before it was stolen by the *giovane bruno* (she discovered all this while visiting the family's apartment). When she finally finds the hidden door to this secret room in the attic, she also detects the last lingering traces of her "first" life: the rectangular mark, still visible, left by the trunk on the floorboards, a clod of dirt and grass – possibly the one she had long kept in a little box as a memory of her life in the trunk and then burned – and one last, surviving spider that could be the final incarnation of her nightly childhood dreams (as well as of an Albertian image of the perfect housekeeper). The *Massaia* is in the process of recuperating her former life, trying to glimpse it from the opposite end of her existence.

When she descends to her living quarters she is "macchiata di polvere, l'erba attorta al braccio, muffe fra i capelli" (243; "covered in dust, grass wrapped around her arm and mold in her hair"; trans. Feltrin-Morris 205). As she abandons her polished, civilized appearance to revert to her trunk-self, she prepares to consummate the fascination with death cultivated by the philosopher in the trunk. Her family is frightened by the sight of her, by "[il] colore verdastro della sua fronte e della fissità degli occhi" (243; "her greenish forehead and the fixity of her gaze"; trans. Feltrin-Morris 205). The *Massaia* dies that same night, attended by her family. The biographic circle is completed with an evocation of her birth: "E sua madre … urlava come quand'ella era nata" (244; "And her mother … screamed like the day her daughter was born"; trans. Feltrin-Morris 206). The inscription on her tomb, long before dictated by the *Massaia*, sanctions the substantial immutability of things: "*quello che è stato è lo stesso che sarà e quello che è stato fatto è lo stesso che si farà; e non vi è nulla di nuovo sotto il sole*" (245; "*That which hath been is that which shall be; and that which hath been done is that which shall be done: and there is no new thing under the sun*"; trans. Feltrin-Morris 207). Her death closes the circle to seal the non-parable of her life and to explicitly repudiate the narrative of conversion.

The Spectre of Domesticity

Her death does not, however, close the novel. There is a very interesting "Epilogo" to the story of this woman philosopher, one that remains enigmatic in its significance yet whose ideological strength demands attention and closer scrutiny. The *Massaia* appears nightly from her tomb to clean and polish the family mausoleum, complaining with the dead neighbours (other *massaie*) about the never-ending job of taking care of their domain. Sometimes she forgets the handkerchief she uses to polish the tomb, leaving it on a bush: "Allora il giorno dopo i maestri portano in fila i bambini delle scuole a vederlo e a rendergli omaggio"

(246; "And so, the next day, schoolteachers line up their pupils and take them to see it and pay homage to it"; trans. Feltrin-Morris 209). The post-mortem traces of her commitment to domestic duties are turned into an *exemplum* for the generations to come. In such an ironic – and iconic – closing image, the only thing that survives is her domestic virtue, her obsession with her womanly duty, the mechanics of the "*Massaia*," as if to suggest that such a non-subjectivity can easily survive a specific death. There is nothing individualistic about these automata cleaning their tombs at night: they are, in the novel's last words, dead who cannot see the living: "i morti non vedono i vivi" (247; "the dead do not see the living"; trans. Feltrin-Morris 209).

What is the reader to make of such an ending? From a thematic point of view, it is clearly a desacralizing image: rather than ascending to heaven, the *Massaia* is consigned to compulsively and ceaselessly repeat her domestic activity for the centuries to come. From a Western philosopher's perspective, that is, by considering the point of departure and the intellectual framework of the *Massaia*'s life, such a finale is shockingly – if parodically – perfect: the *Massaia* endorses death as the only way out of the "material immortality" that was assigned to women and that she wanted to refrain from experiencing as a young woman. Yet she finds herself stuck in precisely that obsessively domestic deathlessness, the "ciclo cieco" (Cavarero, *Nonostante Platone* 101; "blind ... pattern"; Anderlini-D'Onofrio and O'Healy 100) that she had contemplated as the worst possible destiny she could have. Death frees men from the constraints of life, apparently, only when they are "actual" universal subjects – that is, only when they are sexed as men. The *Massaia*'s novelistic afterlife cannot but sarcastically replicate the life she has been brought to lead as a devoted wife and civic icon, the "broken allegory" of domesticity, in a supreme joke about her intellectual aspirations.

In ideological terms, the *Massaia*'s final appearance should also be examined in its "spectral" meaning, that is, as the haunting image that remains of every woman after her disappearance: she turns into a literal spectre of domesticity. Drawing from Derrida's notion of spectre in his essay "The Spectre of Ideology" (although ultimately distancing his interpretation from Derrida's), Slavoj Žižek proposes to identify "the pre-ideological kernel, the formal matrix" of the real, that is, reality before its discursive signification, with "spectral apparitions" (21). In his analysis, "spectral" denotes the "elusive pseudo-materiality that subverts the classic ontological oppositions of reality and illusion" (20), so that it is not, strictly speaking, a synonym for ghosts or for the "return of the dead." Rather, it is a conceptualization of that which remains, un-symbolized and unexplained, as founding reality as such: the spectral apparition "gives body to that which escapes (the symbolically structured) reality" (21). It gives body, in fact, to the "*'primordially repressed,' the irrepresentable X on whose 'repression' reality itself is founded*" (21). The *Massaia*'s literal spectrality can be read through the lens of this ideological trauma. At the end of the story, the reader is allowed to glimpse the spectre of ideology, the repressed image that cannot exist as such. The novel is structured by that which sustains the conservative ideology of gender, an ideology against which the *Massaia* opposes her dissonant behaviour. The intellectually and physically dead, yet devoted, enslaved woman, labouring on the common tomb she shares with her husband, polishing its social appearance ad infinitum, is an image that founds domesticity and the reality that it enables as an ideology.

This is, as the reader surely realizes, not unlike the spectral apparitions in Verga's and Marchesa Colombi's stories that I addressed in chapter 3. The "real" ghost of donna Violante and the *folletto*-plagued beast of burden are also repressed spectres of the real, gendered truths surfacing to remind the readers of their dramatic existence – of the social subjection violently inflicted upon them. "Sadism demands a story," and a story it gets in all of these novels. Yet the enforced annihilation of individuality staged in Masino's last pages is so caricatural as to have a subversive effect. "What emerges via distortions of the accurate representation of reality is the real – that is, the trauma around which social reality is structured" (Žižek 26). "Spectrality" is "that which fills out the unrepresentable abyss of antagonism" (26): the spectre of domesticity is the negative counterpoint to a social discourse within which wilful women are captured and violently domesticated. The trauma of ideology is all that remains of the *Massaia*'s antagonistic subjectivity and of her attempt to move beyond her social fate. It is an extremely pessimistic and highly irreverent ending, sarcastically closing a biographical parable and at the same time denying the very possibility of bringing closure to the *Massaia*'s life.

Of the dissonant projects I have examined so far, Masino's *Nascita e morte della massaia* is the most outrageous and explicit attempt to display in its shocking simplicity the violence on which traditional gender ideology is founded and to ultimately show the kernel of the "real" upon which it hinges. The *Massaia*'s simultaneous compliance with and resistance to sexual and narrative dictates makes her a fully self-aware character whose philosophical attitude shapes the novel itself. Her refusal to change – to give in to the dynamic imperative of the modern novel as the evolution of a self and to the direct interventions of a narrator who appears unable to fully regulate the character – is the most provocative response to a narrative model that closes not with death but with a spectral ("real") parody of life. Her wilful opposition to the imperative of change is an original, innovative strategy of resistance against the ideological power of narrative and against the hierarchy of narrative roles. It proposes a radical experiment in the distribution of power and of knowledge among narrative subjects, and a direct engagement with the narrative and epistemological dynamics of power. It ultimately thematizes the modern impossibility of endorsing one subjective role and one gendered position at once or once and for all.

A Reflection on the Author's Postface

In the novel's final, paratextual twist, it is possible to glimpse this conflictual – and alert – engagement with the dynamics of power "migrating" from the novel to the author. Masino finished the first version of her novel in 1939, and when she submitted it to Fascist censors, they judged it "disfattista e cinico" (251; "defeatist and cynical"; trans. Feltrin-Morris 211). She was asked to remove all references to the Italian context, as well as specific episodes and all quotations from the Bible. She complied. The book was printed soon afterward and was in a Milanese warehouse, waiting to be distributed, when a bomb destroyed the building and the book, down to the very last copy. The publication project was resumed only at the end of the war, and the novel was finally published by Bompiani in 1945. The author relates this story in a "*nota*" postfacing the 1945 edition, a note in which she also informs the reader that, although she has tried, six years after the first printing, to bring the text back to its original version – its unchanged original version, she cannot guarantee the success of this enterprise: "tentai, sulle bozze di stampa che m'erano rimaste, di riportarlo alla prima lezione; ma non potrei giurare che in qualche punto lezione vecchia e lezione nuova non si mescolino" ("I tried, on the basis of the proofs I still had, to restore it to its original concept. But I could not swear that, here and there, the old version and the new version were not getting mixed up"). Then, shifting from her philological discussion of *lectiones* (different textual versions) to the very matter of the text – her protagonist – she simultaneously expresses sympathy for and distance from the *Massaia*. Masino explains that she decided to give up fixing every single change the *Massaia* endured: "se ne è nato qualche assurdo, chi sa non s'intoni fatalmente e saporitamente con le altre originarie assurdità di questo ritratto di donna" ("a few absurdities have cropped up; who knows, they might fatally and delightfully match the other original absurdities of this portrait of a woman"). She closes by saying that such portrait "già a me stessa appare ormai tanto lontano, che appena lo riconosco" (251; "already seems so distant from me that I can barely recognize it"; trans. Feltrin-Morris 211).[21]

This striking authorial note is interesting for the contextual information it offers but also for its hybrid nature as a text that, while defending the author's book and its print history, simultaneously offers a disclaimer – a disavowal – that separates its author from her main character. Beatrice Manetti explains that in 1945 "il libro ottiene buone recensioni, ma sembra ormai appartenere a un altro tempo: e se il 'disfattismo' della protagonista era sembrato ingiurioso ai censori del regime fascista, adesso, nella frenesia della liberazione e della ricostruzione, risulta semplicemente incomprensibile" (52; the book receives good reviews, but it seems now to belong to another era: and if the "resignation to defeat" seemed offensive to the Fascist regime's censors, now, in the frenzy of liberation and of reconstruction, the results are simply unfathomable). Thus, in her postface, Masino is accounting for an epochal and existential change of mood that can, in and of itself, justify the writer's perplexity in the face of her own work. She fashions the vicissitudes of the novel into a very short prehistory that acquires meaning only though a "posthumous" publication that validates the book as it distances it from the author. At the same time, when we connect Masino's ambiguous stance vis-à-vis her novel to the ideological dichotomies that are present *within* her text, we can reasonably draw an analogy between the conflicted compromises that Masino had to make in order to get her book published (in Re's words, "censorship was ... incorporated in the very process of writing"; "Women and Censorship" 72) and the tension that is to be found in the *massaia*'s story, between her decision to conform to social rules and her intellectual and ideological need for autonomy, as well as between a character trying to direct her own narrative parable and the ideological interventions that press on her for "change." The author's note, always included as it is in the subsequent editions of the novel, becomes the appropriate coda to the novel, an illuminating hybrid between an authorial statement and a fictional piece restaging and framing at the paratextual level the ideological complexity that the book has come to embody and represent.[22]

5 A Poetics of Rejection: Elsa Morante and the Gender of the Real

Mi resi conto, difatti, di non sapere, in realtà, esattamente, chi fosse il nemico.

I realized, in fact, that I didn't know, really, exactly, who the enemy was.
(Morante, *Aracoeli* 1234; trans. Weaver 147)

As the fourth novel published by an author whose previous prose text, *La storia*, had sold about 800,000 copies in Italy (in the first year alone) and stirred a vehement debate about its political and literary value, *Aracoeli*, published in 1982, was burdened with the heavy task of proving itself against its antecedent – and what's more, since Elsa Morante died only three years after its publication, it became the author's literary testament. The reviews at the time ranged from surprised to unabashedly mournful, and literary criticism has, ever since, tended to divide itself into two parties: those who think of *Aracoeli* as an "abiura" (an abjuration), as a bleak text that rejects Morante's previously asserted belief in the redeeming powers of literature, and those who find, to the contrary, sufficient elements of continuity with the previous novels, or even sufficient "value" in the novel itself, to endorse a positive (or, at least, a less negative) view of her last text.[1]

Both factions are, in their broader terms, justified: given Morante's thematic coherence and stylistic parable, *Aracoeli*'s origins can be traced to the same narrative obsessions that generated *Menzogna e sortilegio*, *L'isola di Arturo*, and *La storia* at least as much as her tragically parodic and distorted use of these themes in *Aracoeli* can be viewed as a rejection of the previous "affabulations" and as the emergence of a new poetics of rejection that does away with the myths and beliefs that had sustained Morante's previous work. My own view favours this second interpretation, that is, an understanding of *Aracoeli* as a parodic text denying the epistemological possibilities of literature. Such a poetics of rejection, nonetheless, has to be recognized as inevitably built on that which it rejects, in this case the writer's previous reliance on literature as a means to make sense of reality.[2]

In *Aracoeli*, Morante commits herself to an uncompromising critique of traditional paradigms of narration, exposing the impossibility of endorsing such structures any longer. What is particularly interesting here, and what also connects this novel and its protagonist to the texts I analysed in the previous chapters, is the extent to which this critique is built on an indictment of the gender ideology at work in narrative, a critique of the "mythical mechanism" described by de Lauretis and of the cultural logic that structures and defines sexual difference. In *Aracoeli*, though, the critique is built from the standpoint of the male seeker, the subject of knowledge – who is also, here, the narrating instance. Unlike the female problematic characters I have analysed in the previous chapters, this protagonist is problematic not because of his wilfulness – not because of his attempts to become a full seeker – but precisely because he resists the traditional male role as the seeker, the heroic subject of the story. Indeed, this novel dramatically explores what happens when a male character realizes he is performing and framing himself within a narrative and cognitive quest that fully preordains each of his steps and that determines the very outcome of his story. In this respect, Morante's project is extremely ambitious and uncompromising: it unmasks the novel's epistemological endeavour as gendered, and, as a consequence, it goes so far as to reject the very possibility of knowledge of the real.

Journey and Memory

The plot of *Aracoeli* follows the basic traditional thread of a hero setting out to look for the object of his desire. From the greyness of Milan and of a professional and personal life that has long ceased to bring him any happiness or relief, the protagonist and first-person narrator Manuele leaves to search for his mother in her home country, the Spanish region of Andalusia. On 1 November 1975, he boards an Air Iberia flight that takes him, after a layover in Madrid, to the town called Almeria ("mirror" in Arabic). From there, as glimpses of official history inform him of General Franco's death throes, he travels by bus to a smaller town,

Gergal, and then he travels by foot in the hope of finding El Almendral, the village of his mother's origin, and traces of his mother, Aracoeli, who died when he was six years old. When he finally reaches the hamlet, the only human trace he finds is in a bar run by an old Andalusian. The man informs him that every person in the village bears his mother's last name, "Muñoz Muñoz," thus conclusively undermining any possibility of an individualized revelation.

Early on in the novel, however, the very factuality of this journey has been placed under scrutiny by the narrator himself. During his layover in Almeria, he had reflected that "questo viaggio assurdo ... non è forse altro che un fantasma onirico della mia accidia: mentre in realtà il mio corpo dorme, istupidito dagli ipnotici, in qualche mia cameraccia d'affitto a Milano" (1115; "this absurd journey ... is only an oneiric phantom of my acedia, and in reality my body is sleeping, stunned by sleeping pills, in some cheap rented room of mine in Milan"; trans. Weaver 59). The narrator has, in fact, affirmed from the start that he is "incline alle visioni più che alle indagini" (1040; "more inclined to visions than inquiries"; trans. Weaver 4). The "objective" model of the quest is soon juxtaposed to an alternative model of knowledge relying on "ricordi apocrifi" (1050; "apocryphal memories"; trans. Weaver 11) – a model that renounces rationality, objectivity, and universal codes to give way to a personal, completely subjective, epistemological experience.[3]

There are fewer references to the trip to Spain as the text unfolds, and Manuele's memories – "o magari pseudo-memoria?" (1049; "or perhaps pseudomemory?"; trans. Weaver 10) – take up increasingly more space in the narration, their order dictated by free associations and thematic connections rather than chronology. He relates his youth, his mother's encounter with his father in her native Spain, their first clandestine years in Italy before the official wedding, Aracoeli's subsequent introduction into the Italian bourgeoisie, her role as devoted mother and wife, the tragedy of the loss of her second baby and the subsequent onset of a mysterious sickness, her abandonment of the conjugal residence to join a brothel, and her untimely death. The end of Manuele's physical journey (i.e., his arrival in El Almendral) does not coincide with the end of the novel. The final twenty pages are devoted to another portion of Manuele's memories: he recounts his last encounter with his father and his subsequent reaction to the news of his father's death, in the fall of 1946 (seven years after the death of his mother).

The simultaneous presence of two antagonistic narrative models is constitutive of the text, of its goals, and of its shortcomings: although clearly structured around a geographical quest, *Aracoeli* unceasingly underscores the inadequacy of a rational and referential paradigm for single-handedly accounting for Manuele's life experience and fulfilling his hopes of a reunion with his mother. The novel juxtaposes an oneiric, irrational approach to the referential one. In her monograph on Morante's work, Giovanna Rosa has identified *Aracoeli*'s two narrative paradigms as "due tipologie narrative forti: il racconto di viaggio, in una *Bildung* all'inverso, e il *Familienroman* modellato sul paradigma centripeto delle relazioni parentali: a una progressione lineare, poco importa in quale direzione, corrisponde un moto circolare che rinserra il *récit* entro le chiuse pareti del teatrino domestico" (309; two strong narrative typologies: the travel narrative, as a reverse *Bildung*, and the *Familienroman* modelled on the centripetal paradigm of family relations. To the linear progression, no matter in which direction, corresponds a circular motion that encloses the *récit* within the closed walls of the domestic stage). The validity of these two "strong" narrative and epistemological paradigms, though, is undermined by their inability to subsist independently. On the one hand, the travel narrative, or quest, founds the narrative project by contributing a structure and an articulation to it while being denied any epistemological function: "il suo era un richiamo senza nessuna promessa, nè speranza" (1047; "it was a summons with no surprise, no hope"; trans. Weaver 9). On the other, the possibility of using the *Familienroman* ("family romance") to found the narrative, and as such to exist in and of itself, as was the case in Morante's *Menzogna e sortilegio* and *L'isola di Arturo*, is discarded *d'emblée* by the novel. The codependence is initially proposed as a possible solution to the limits of each model, but structurally it undermines the epistemological strength of both.

The geographic model of the quest, together with the theme of the protagonist as seeker, is among the most exploited generic paradigms of Western narrative and the European novel, from the *Odyssey* to *Don Quixote*. Morante clearly refers to this tradition in assigning a wandering role to the narrator: at one point, Manuele describes himself as a "finto Ulisse di Terra, viaggiante fra finti vivi incantati da finte musiche verso colonne d'Ercole anch'esse finte" (1201; "a bogus land-Ulysses, traveling among bogus living people spellbound by bogus music toward Pillars of Hercules also bogus"; trans. Weaver 122), simultaneously endorsing and unmasking the conventionality of his role. He consciously parodies the seeker par excellence, Ulysses, in a quest characterized by the fictionality of all of its elements. At the same time, however, Manuele's *Familienroman*, with its "circular motion" relying on a non-rational paradigm of knowledge, signifies a subjective epistemological project that is motivated not by consciousness but by a "nostalgia dei sensi" (1047; "nostalgia of the senses"; trans. Weaver 9), thus reminding the reader that the entire story might just be apocryphal memories or wishful thinking.[4]

Both of these narrative models (quest and memorial) fail to move past a conservative, dualistic imaginary casting the female object of desire as dichotomous angel/monster. Aracoeli, the title character, is assigned the role of being the passive object of someone else's desire. She remains frozen in a deadly inaccessibility, while the unsettling traces of the "outrage" and violent death she suffered are disseminated throughout the text and projected onto the image of every encountered woman. Eugenio, the father, survives his wife as a puppet animated by social and political forces that transcend him but that cannot grant his individual salvation. Manuele takes on the role of Ulysses (and the requirements of that role) while explicitly refusing to be a seeker, pleading to be shifted back to the passive end of the spectrum. Moreover, each of the two narrative models ultimately fails to know "the other" because the effort remains strictly confined, in both cases, within the "vecchia economia binaria fra il principio attivo del logos maschile e quello passivo della corporeità femminile" (Cavarero and Restaino 135; old binary economy between the active principle of male logos and the passive one of female corporality), while emphasizing, again in both cases, that such a binary economy can no longer be endorsed. In other words, although it is founded on a paradigm that assigns gendered roles to its structures, characters, and themes, *Aracoeli* explicitly undermines the possibility of the epistemological success of such a polarity.

This chapter of *Gender, Narrative, and Dissonance* configures itself as the conceptual terminus to the book's investigation of how the ideological processes regulating the way characters exist and behave within the novel are one and the same with those regulating and defining the epistemological model(s) on which the novel is built; *Aracoeli* provides the most tragic representation in my book of the impossibility of knowing reality (of knowing the truth, of knowing woman) while endorsing the paradigm of the novel. As de Lauretis emphasizes, there is between man and woman "a conceptual opposition that is 'always already' inscribed in what Fredric Jameson would call 'the political unconscious' of dominant culture discourses and their 'master narratives'" (*Figures of Resistance* 1). The sex-gender system is "a sociocultural construct and a semiotic apparatus, a system of representation which assigns meaning" (5) to subjects and shapes narratives. In this sense, an analysis of the three main characters of *Aracoeli* is both necessary and illuminating, since the gender dichotomies structuring the narrative are put directly to work within each of these novelistic signifiers. Each of the dissonant subjects – Aracoeli, Eugenio, and Manuele – can be explored in terms of the gendered "meaning" that is signified and performed.

Aracoeli, or On Femininity

Aracoeli is the centre of both quest and *Familienroman*, the elusive object of Manuele's (double) narrative project. Her story brings together familiar stereotypes of femininity; they are images and roles that thoroughly permeate the patriarchal imaginary and that Manuele unconditionally appropriates to relate his mother's life from his own point of view. The different segments of her biography are offered in a nonchronological order, interspersed within the travel narrative (which I explicate here in linear form for the sake of analysis). Aracoeli is an illiterate, uncivilized girl. The Italian Navy officer Eugenio meets her in her native country in 1931 and, love-struck, asks her to marry him. They immediately become formally engaged, but they have to wait five years for the Royal Navy's permission to marry. In the meantime, the young man brings his fiancée to Italy and entrusts her to Monda, his unmarried sister. Monda finds a house for Aracoeli (and soon-to-be Manuele) on the outskirts of Rome.

The young Aracoeli is the emblem of natural femininity. Years later, her initial ignorance of the most basic forms and manners of civilized life are passed on as amusing jokes: "Sbadigliavi come una tigre. Mangiavi la frutta a morsi. Soffiavi sulla minestra come su una fucina. E ti grattavi la testa con la forchetta ... E una volta, accendesti il fuoco con un'antica stampa francese" (1165; "You yawned like a tiger. You ate fruit in big bites. You blew on your soup as if on a forge. And you scratched your head with your fork ... And once you used an old French engraving to light the fire"; trans. Weaver 95). The narrator explicitly compares her to an animal and describes her as being as uncivilized as a cavewoman. A primitive, superstitious religiosity informs her femininity: she shies away from any manifestation of sexuality, hiding her body and bodily functions from everyone, her son included: "i suoi sensi erano casti come una bambina ignara" (1188; "her senses were as chaste as those of an ignorant child"; trans. Weaver 113). Even after giving birth to her son, writes Manuele, her body "si manteneva quasi virgineo, con certe angolosità fanciullesche, e i movimenti sospettosi e malaccorti dell'animale trapiantato" (1051; "remained almost virginal, with certain girlish angularities and the suspicious, gawky movements of an animal taken from its habitat"; trans. Weaver 12) – she is virginal, childlike, and animal-like. Her religion is a "cattolicesimo elementare" (1089; "elementary Catholicism"; trans. Weaver 40) tainted with polytheism and exotic reminiscences, and her knowledge of the world is limited by her illiteracy and by her instinctive fear of all forms of progress ("un sospetto timorato ... degli automi o meccanismi in genere"; 1281; "a kind of fearful suspicion of ... mechanisms or apparatuses in general"; trans. Weaver 183).

Aracoeli is firmly devoted to the cult of her husband and to taking care of her son. Because her husband is frequently absent because of his work, she spends most of her time with Manuele. During the first few years of Manuele's life, moreover, since she and Manuele are not legally recognized as Eugenio's wife and son, they live sheltered from the rest of the world, in perfect symbiosis: "congiunzione inseparabile per natura e di cui pareva a me naturale anche l'eternità" (1189; "inseparable, natural conjunction, whose eternity seemed to me equally natural"; trans. Weaver 113). This first image of a sacred, childish, and naturally angelic womanhood, sheltered from the weight of sexuality and desire and finding its realization and completion in maternity, founds Manuele's narrative as well as his nostalgia for an unretrievable, originary happiness. This founding myth is then progressively juxtaposed to and contrasted with a very different one. Even before being explicitly familiarized with Aracoeli's existential parable, the reader perceives the inescapable ambiguity that Manuele detects in every representation of femininity he encounters in the novel, especially the ones supposed to be "sacred."

In relating his first, failed, heterosexual encounter during a religious celebration in honour of the Virgin Mary, for example, the narrator writes that "il simulacro della Madonna ... aveva per me qualcosa di cadaverico, al pari di certe bambole antiquate che giacciono morte nelle soffitte" (1119; "the statue of the Madonna ... there was something cadaverous about it, like outmoded dolls that lie dead in attics"; trans. Weaver 62); the image of the Virgin is irremediably corrupted by a destiny of death and a puppet-like status that degrades her saintliness. In another instance, as he enters a small church in Almeria and looks at the image placed at the centre of the altar, Manuele cannot help but read it in a binary manner: "Forse figura un'Assunta, o una Trasfigurazione; ma ai miei occhi essa appare una sorta di sirenide, o altro animale acquatico serpentiforme" (1195; "Perhaps it portrays a Transfiguration, an Assumption; but to my eyes she seems a kind of siren, or some other aquatic animal, serpentine"; trans. Weaver 118). Manuele projects onto reality the dichotomy between his saintly "girl-mother" and her unsaintly negative double, that is, "quell'altra Aracoeli fatta donna" (1066; "that other Aracoeli, transformed into a woman"; trans. Weaver 23) – a siren-like, snake-shaped water creature who is a dangerous and deadly counterpart to the angelic femininity that he knew in his infant years and who appears to take over and irremediably taint every womanly presence in the story.

In a third example, connected with Manuele's second (equally failed) heterosexual encounter, the dichotomy is reversed in its premises but reaffirmed in its binary nature: his attempt at intercourse with a famished old prostitute fails not only because of the woman's monstrosity, that is, because she bares her deadly sex in front of the horrified young man ("un oggetto di strage e di pena orrenda, simile a una bocca di animale macellato"; 1143; "an object of massacre and horrendous suffering, like the mouth of a slaughtered animal"; trans. Weaver 80), but also because of her holy womanliness: "essa era intoccabile dai miei sensi, non tanto ... perchè repulsiva, ma piuttosto perchè sacra" (1144; she could not be touched by my senses, not so much ... because she was repulsive, but because she was sacred).[5] Womanhood is presented from early on in the novel as inextricably woven out of the two "rappresentazioni stereotipiche della madre oblativa [e] della seduttrice impenitente" (Cavarero and Restaino 144; stereotypical representations of the self-sacrificing mother [and] the unrepentant seductress): the virgin and the whore, the angel and the monster. As Adalgisa Giorgio reminds us in her essay on *Aracoeli*, quoting Toril Moi, the patriarchal ideology positions women "as the limit of the symbolic order"; sometimes they represent "darkness and chaos" and sometimes they are seen as "the representatives of a higher and purer nature" (99). The sacred alterity, symbol of life, is eventually revealed as also being (always already) a degraded, deadly one.[6]

Mother and son initiate a process of civilization soon after the official marriage, when they move to the *Quartieri alti*. Manuele begins elementary school and Aracoeli is trained in bourgeois etiquette by Aunt Monda. Their common introduction to the social pact is sanctioned by different, gendered curricula: Manuele studies languages and spends all of his time reading books, while his mother gravitates to magazines and fashion houses. She soon gives up on following her son's education. In Manuele's explanation, Aracoeli's intellect "oramai toccava una frontiera prescritta" (1261; "was now reaching a prescribed frontier"; trans. Weaver 168), a limit beyond which she cannot venture. Her access to civilization is defined and restricted by social prescriptions and limited by physical constraints presented by the narrator as constitutive of female subjectivity. Her intelligence, for example, is explicitly associated with the body and with her own ignorance as to its functioning: "La sua era un'intelligenza diversa dalla nostra: era una sostanza ombrosa, imperscrutabile e segreta, che scorreva in tutto il suo corpo, quale un'infinita memoria carnale" (1261; "Hers was an intelligence different from ours: it was a shadowy substance, inscrutable and secret, which flowed through her whole body, like an infinite carnal memory"; trans. Weaver 168). Her "infinite memory," which originates in and is limited to the body, is the index of a female subjectivity devoid of intellectual awareness and completely grounded in her material body.

Manuele's account of his mother's life fully subscribes to an iconic imagery of womanhood as lacking. By denying the title character a voice of her own, and an intelligence of her own, Morante reproduces within her text the interdiction of self-representation that characterizes women in patriarchal societies; that is, she literalizes the extent to which female subjects are to be known and told only through male eyes (the paradox being, of course, that a female author is writing this story). Aracoeli's life fully exemplifies the extremely limited array of roles available to women in such an ideological system: they can be ignorant mothers and wives, learning their way through the fashion jargon and the bourgeois etiquette, or they can turn out to be, as it happens, uncontrollable sexual predators.

Even more tangibly than Aracoeli's supposed "feminine" essence, *Aracoeli* very deliberately depicts both the narrator's initiation into the social boundaries built around gender – as well as their moral connotations – and the constant self-denial and blame that this provokes in both his mother and himself. For example, the protagonist realizes soon enough that his mother shies away from talking about her childhood and youth, just as his mention of their happy, clandestine years before her official marriage makes Aracoeli blush and prompts Aunt Monda to change the subject. Manuele rapidly understands that there is something socially reproachable about his first years with his mother (1178; trans. Weaver 105), and he internalizes this. He also later perceives just as acutely the changed attitude of the people around Aracoeli as soon as her facade of being respectably bourgeois crumbles under the uncontrollable urges of sexuality (1355; trans. Weaver 237–8).

Aracoeli's parable takes a dramatic turn through the tragedy of a second child, a baby girl, who dies only a month after her birth. Carina's inexplicable death marks the onset of physical and mental disease in Aracoeli. She undergoes surgery, arguably a hysterectomy, but her condition does not improve. Her vital energies, diverted from the vocation of life-bearing, appear to subject her to a dangerous physical drive. Her son witnesses her slow degradation as she turns from a chaste and shy woman into a monstrously sexual being. He describes her transformation thus: "tutte le sue fibre animali ... vibravano nel fervore della sua violenta e strana rifioritura" (1332; "all her animal fiber ... thrummed in the fervor of her violent and strange reburgeoning"; trans. Weaver 221), a description in which the use of animal and vegetable images once again connects Aracoeli to the uncontrollable processes of organic life. She becomes possessed by a burning desire that she initially satisfies with her husband, within the prescribed limits of her conjugal life, but then she begins searching for alternative partners. Her physical appearance changes, her body swells and "doubles": "S'era ingrassata, e sul suo corpo gracile di bambina cresceva un corpo diverso, più colmo e vistoso" (1332; "She had put on weight; and over her frail, little-girl's body a different body was growing, fuller and more showy"; trans. Weaver 221). Here the "monster" superposes itself on the angel.[7]

In tracing Aracoeli's passage from childhood to adolescence and the onset of her desire for "una bambola di carne viva" (1166; "a doll of living flesh"; trans. Weaver 97), that is, the process by which she becomes an icon of natural motherhood, Manuele had already described the gendering process as mechanical and grounded in Aracoeli's body, an urge that she could not but enforce: "la voglia della bambola ... ti fermentava nella carne" (1166; "your yearning for a doll ... fermented in your flesh"; trans. Weaver 96). The young Aracoeli, according to Manuele's "memory," becomes devoted to "l'aspettazione inconsapevole del seme" (1166; "the unconscious expectation of the seed"; trans. Weaver 96), not, as he takes pains to explain, for her sexual satisfaction but for the fulfilment of her function: "tu, come una macchina idiota, eri la serva ignara della tua propria manovra" (1167; "you, an idiot machine, were the ignorant servant of your own intrigue"; trans. Weaver 97). Her latest transformation from chaste mother to restlessly promiscuous woman is ruled by the same "natural" forces running through her body, forces that Aracoeli has no will to oppose in either case. Woman is eloquently mapped out as matter, as a body regulated by extrinsic forces over which the mind has no control – arguably, because there is no such thing as a mind for female individuals.

Aracoeli leaves her family to join a brothel. As is ultimately revealed in the months following her escape, Aracoeli's body is at the mercy of a brain tumour that is ravaging her. Soon she is hospitalized and agonizing, with Eugenio at her bedside, and Manuele, who had been sent to live with his paternal grandparents in Turin after her disappearance, is allowed to see her one final time in her hospital bed. Her last word is "sangre" (1417), which is "blood" in Spanish, another reference to Aracoeli's merely physical awareness of what is happening to her and of the battle taking place in her body. Manuele is sent back to Turin, where Aunt Monda arrives a few days later to inform him of her death.

Aracoeli's behaviour is always already envisaged as conditioned by forces that are beyond her control. Towards the end of the novel Monda offers Manuele a retrospectively "scientific" (and socially appeasing) explanation of his mother's "dichotomy": she argues that Aracoeli's tumour was the inner, organic cause of her degrading behaviour. In Monda's view, Aracoeli's conduct was only "un sintomo ... una conseguenza della sua malattia" (1441; "a symptom ... a consequence of her illness"; trans. Weaver 303), a view that is meant to salvage Aracoeli's subjectivity from the stigma of an essentially duplicitous nature, as it blames her spiritual decay on an organic degeneration. However, Manuele refuses to settle for this explanation; he cannot discard the idea of womanhood as constitutively doomed. Yet the novel combines the two diametrically opposed embodiments of femininity within a single person, forcing the two icons – the innocent woman and the lost one, the angelic woman and the monstrous one – to coexist within a single (absent) body, and the effect is one of estrangement: as in the case of the coupling of epistemological paradigms, these images appear weakened by the juxtaposition. They are the expression of Manuele's apocryphal memories and of his longing for his mother rather than of an actual subjectivity. Moreover, Aracoeli's narrative absence, that is, her existing only through someone else's memory, undermines the very possibility of these signifieds being anything other than imaginary constructs filling the void left by an absent signifier. Aracoeli is no more available as a living body than she is as a reasoning subject, and Manuele's epistemological and narrative enterprise only sanctions the very absence it had set out to remedy.

Thus, an analysis of the restricted imaginary encircling and suffocating femininity in this novel cannot – and does not – exhaust *Aracoeli*'s ideological complexity: this is a text in which contradictory impulses are at work not only in the title character but in all three of the novel's main "actors." It is imperative to analyse the novel more broadly and to consider the intersection of gender and epistemology, an intersection that always already genders the supposedly neutral structures of narrative and knowledge and interpellates both its female *and* its male characters. At the level of the characters, the novel sketches not only traditional femininity, as embodied by Aracoeli, but also – and arguably more so – masculinity, as represented by Aracoeli's husband and counterpart Eugenio and by the narrator Manuele himself, as a social construct regulated by very strict rules and by an imaginary that harshly reprimands, and does not leave room for, "different" males.

Eugenio Oddone Amedeo, or On Masculinity

The novel's representation of stereotypical masculinity similarly draws on familiar topoi. However, the founding of the character of Manuele's father on a dichotomy – he is articulated around two opposite "icons" of masculinity – is similar to Aracoeli's split configuration only structurally. Ideologically, Eugenio's double identity points to a traditional as well as to an alternative masculinity, to the possibility of a nontraditional model of paternity that is longed for yet always harshly punished by the narrative. If the angel-monster configuration of femininity remains well within the boundaries of the patriarchal imagery of womanhood, there appears to be an asymmetric movement in the configuration of the character of Eugenio. On one hand, he is the embodiment of traditional masculinity, the warrant of tradition, of an active, absent virility. On the other, he reveals a weakened, less guarded image of himself, one with which Manuele realizes he could have found an affinity, had the realization not come too late.

Although he receives far less narrative attention than Aracoeli, Eugenio is an important character in the novel for his formative function and arguably precisely because of his minor presence – his fatherly role sketched in absentia. Manuele idolizes his father as Aracoeli's companion but seldom sees him as an actual loving figure or as a possible role model for himself: Eugenio remains "un culto" (1269; "a cult"; trans. Weaver 173). As a father, a navy officer, and a man, he is an absent figure of authority and of mobility, a representative of that "VIRILITÀ adulta" (1270; "adult MANHOOD"; trans. Weaver 175) that makes the young Manuele feel socially out of place.[8]

Manuele's father is presented as Aracoeli's Prince Charming, as the herald of civilization who removes Aracoeli from her wild country. Originally from Piedmont, from a monarchist dynasty that is clearly devoted to a cult of tradition and patriarchy, Eugenio follows the family footprint in choosing a military career. His encounter with the poor Andalusian girl is fortuitous yet fatal: they are the two matching pieces of one (social) body. Describing the way Eugenio gazes at Aracoeli during the celebration of Manuele's fourth birthday, the narrator writes that he "la mirava ... come un'anima che, alla risurrezione dei corpi, ritrova in Paradiso, insieme con la letizia celeste, anche quella carnale" (1206; "would look at her ... like a soul that, at the resurrection of the body, finds once more in Paradise, not only celestial joy but also happiness"; trans. Weaver 126). Such a remark underscores the perfect complementariness of femininity and masculinity in young Manuele's ideological world. The binary opposition between soul and body, nature and culture, and activity and passivity is ideally fused in Aracoeli and Eugenio's legalized romance.[9]

The abstract quality of the male subject, seen by his son as the quintessential representative of authority and virility, is the exact counterpart to Aracoeli's natural, bodily self. They are idealized figures of a traditional masculinity and femininity. Even similar behaviours in the two characters are to be read as having contrasting meanings: just as Aracoeli is embarrassed to show her body to her young son because of her instinctively chaste animality, her husband "neppure in casa non si fa mai vedere se non vestito al completo" (1341; "even at home never was seen unless fully dressed"; trans. Weaver 228), a custom that his sister Monda identifies as the first sign of true education, that is, of civilization. As Elizabeth Grosz remarks, "one and the same message, inscribed on a male or a female body, does not always or even usually mean the same thing or result in the same text" (*Space, Time and Perversion* 156). Whereas female shame is the mark of a body naturally unaware of the dangers of sexuality, of a chastity that precedes civilization, male shame is the expression of a cultural triumph over one's own body, the successful containment of one's urges in order to better fit within the social organization.

Eugenio's reality, as far as Manuele is concerned, lies in his devotion to Aracoeli on the one hand and to the king and his country on the other. The only sign of physical closeness between father and son is that of a "caress" from which Manuele usually withdraws because it seems to him "un simbolo vuoto e poco attendibile" (1270; "an empty and unreliable symbol"; trans. Weaver 174) or an empty gesture. It is nonetheless a physical token of their bond, and it will return as such at the end of the novel, in its lost potentiality. At the same time that Aracoeli's female identity is irreversibly shaken by the denial of motherhood that arises from her daughter's death and the surgery she undergoes shortly thereafter, Eugenio's masculinity is gradually impaired by his decision to sacrifice his career to his sick wife. His "straordinaria offerta sacrificale" (1306; "extraordinary sacrificial offering"; trans. Weaver 201) brings him to renounce active duty and take on a sedentary job at the Ministry, to be closer to her. Manuele experiences Eugenio's decision as the first dent in his father's godlike absence and mobility. His first impression of this new, more present father is that "di non rivedere lui proprio, ma un doppio, proiettato in casa per qualche operazione spiritica. Sbandato ... si muoveva per le stanze come su un veliero bloccato dalla bonaccia" (1307; "I am not actually seeing him, but seeing a double of his, sent into the house through some spiritualistic operation ... [H]e moved around the rooms as if on a becalmed sailing ship, lost"; trans. Weaver 202). The model of masculinity splits into two: a mobile, heroic father and a timorous, immobilized one.

Young Manuele is unable to find an ideological validation for this second model of manhood. The social genealogy of Eugenio's public role is referentially present in the persons of Eugenio's utterly conservative Piedmontese father (a monolithic figure of law and order), above him, the Savoy King of Italy, to whom Eugenio devotes the highest respect (he keeps an effigy of the king in the entrance hall of the house), and then, all the way up, God the Father. There is, in contrast, no such validation for Eugenio's nurturing role, for the suddenly immobilized model of fatherhood and masculinity that he chooses to endorse in the name of his love for Aracoeli.

The theme of an "alternative" paternity, that is, of a more nurturing and private notion of masculinity, is developed very explicitly in at least two other episodes in the novel. The first one (chronologically subsequent but related in the first part of the novel) occurs when Manuele is in boarding school: one night he shelters a new student in his bed, a young boy named Pennati who has chosen Manuele as his surrogate mother. The bliss that Manuele derives from providing the young boy with a refuge from the cold and dark loneliness of the school dormitory is harshly punished the following morning by the boys' caretaker, who separates the two and forces Manuele to offer forty minutes of silent prayer on his knees, supposedly to ask forgiveness by the Male-in-Chief, God himself, while the young Pennati successfully manages to be sent back to his real mother.

The other episode occurs even earlier (but is related later in the novel), during Aracoeli's sickness. Eugenio's attendant, Daniele, is assigned to take care of the young Manuele while the family is busy attending Aracoeli. Manuele remarks that, although he is "abandoned" by his parents, he finds "un'allegria straordinaria" (1314; "an extraordinary happiness"; trans. Weaver 207) in Daniele's company: the young attendant becomes his best friend as well as his own surrogate mother. Daniele cleans the house, cooks, helps Manuele get dressed, and takes him to school: "Era ... un caso inaspettato per me, che un marinaio mi facesse da madre" (1322; "It was ... an unexpected event for me: a sailor acting as my mother"; trans. Weaver 214). This complements, rather than replaces, his virility: "Lui possedeva, invero, della qualità materne: con in più certe rudezze involontarie che mi attestavano la sua grandezza virile" (1322; "He really did possess maternal qualities, plus a certain involuntary roughness that for me testified his manly greatness"; trans. Weaver 214). This blissful period ends when Aracoeli lures the young attendant to her room, thus destroying the rearranged familial configuration. The "monster" that she is becoming eliminates the possibility of an alternative maternity/paternity.

Both the possibilities for Manuele, that of being a nurturing agent and that of being the object of a male mother figure's love, are thus discarded by the text. In the first case, the patriarchal order is reasserted by an appeal to God, understood as the transcendental representative of the male hierarchy. In the second, the text blames "natural" femininity, in its most dangerous connotation, as hampering a possible redistribution of roles.[10]

Domestic masculinity fails in its goals in the case of Eugenio in his weakened condition, as well, in that it does not prevent Aracoeli's ruin or her own tragic mobilization as she abandons the conjugal domicile. Aracoeli's disappearance sanctions the navy officer's definitive "scissione in due se stessi" (1398; "division of himself into two selves"; trans. Weaver 269). This de-doubling is emphasized at various points in the text; it is strikingly conspicuous, for example, as Manuele's grandparents bring their grandson to Turin after Aracoeli's disappearance. As Manuele is leaving Rome, Eugenio first strokes his head and tells his son to be good: "Poi, dopo uno sguardo timorato e quasi peritoso sui genitori, doverosamente aggiun[g]e 'E compòrtati virilmente'" (1397; "And after a timid, almost hesitant glance at his parents, he duly add[s], 'And behave like a man'"; trans. Weaver 269). The loving father who caresses Manuele and invites him to be good is superposed on the patriarchal father who dictates social rules and behaviours to his son.

From this point on, Eugenio maintains a social function only through his profession; in private, he is completely incapable of agency. The failure of his sacrificial act empties one part of his life of any meaning, reducing him to a puppet. After Aracoeli's death, Eugenio asks to be reassigned to active duty in the navy, so as to reintegrate his "public" genealogy, and he remains there until September 1943. The turmoil of Italian history subsequently determines the fate of this navy officer. Fatally disillusioned by the king's (and Prime Minister Badoglio's) secret armistice with the Allies, Eugenio Oddone Amedeo no longer has any reason to live: "Quello, è stato il colpo finale, per lui" (1440; "For him, that was the final blow"; trans. Weaver 301), explains Aunt Monda as she prepares Manuele for his last encounter with his father.

In the very last pages of the novel Manuele recounts his last visit to his father, who still lives in Rome, hidden in a crumbling apartment. The building, which was bombed during the war, is near the cemetery where Aracoeli is buried. After his public disillusionment, Eugenio has withdrawn to a hopeless cult of his lost love, to a drunken domesticity that is the closing, caricatural embodiment of the novel's attempt to negotiate a different virility. When Manuele first sees him, Eugenio is oblivious to his visitor's identity, and he wears "una vestaglia già a me nota, di leggerissima seta indiana" (1445; "a robe, familiar to me, of very light Indian silk"; trans. Weaver 305) – the dressing gown that Aracoeli had worn during the last summer she spent at home. Eugenio hangs on to Aracoeli's memory so closely as to wear her clothes, in a gesture that is both an expression of his never-ending love for his wife and a sign of his defeated virility.

Eugenio is reduced to the motions of a powerless infant, able to articulate only incomprehensible sounds. He is swollen, rather than fattened, from his drinking, and his face is "regredita a una strana immaturità" (1446; "regressed to a strange immaturity"; trans. Weaver 305). He drinks warm beer "come un bambino assetato, reggendo a stento la tazza con tutte e dieci le dita" (1447; "as greedily as a thirsty child, holding the cup with some difficulty, using all ten fingers"; trans. Weaver 307). Yet as soon as he acknowledges the presence of his son, a change occurs in him: he goes to his room to change, and he comes back fully dressed in men's clothes. Manuele thus realizes that his father is still aware of himself and that even in his dissolution he is still ruled by "un pudore atroce" (1448; "a horrible modesty"; trans. Weaver 307), a mark of subjectivity connected to his societal status as a man of order and a naval officer. The son infers that his father must be confusing him with "qualche alto grado della Regia Marina" (1448; "some high-ranking officer of the Royal Navy"; trans. Weaver 307), for he stands up as soon as Manuele does and then walks him to the door and offers his hand for a handshake.

The posthumous realization with which the novel closes is related to this last missed opportunity. Rather than focusing once again on Manuele's mother, as the reader would expect, the novel ends by elaborating on the aftermath of Manuele's encounter with Eugenio. The narrator explains that had this weakened, degraded figure extended a gesture of love to him, one of his awkward caresses, Manuele might finally have come to admit and to accept his love for his father. Thus the novel closes on the lost possibility of establishing a bond of love with something different from the mother – with a present, although diminished, paternity. The importance of the figure of Eugenio within the economy of the novel is surprisingly reasserted in its last lines as the one space in which the possibility of a different gender negotiation is glimpsed, but then even that is discarded by the text. Eugenio's final inability to display his weakness in front of his son, that is, his retirement behind a screen of caricatural, ceremonial conventions as the last bastion of his masculinity, denies Manuele the possibility of identifying with him and prevents Manuele from founding a different genealogy of masculinity.

The significance of this ending, focusing on the paternal rather than on the title character, has been variously understood by critics; many see it as a statement of the historical failure of post–World War II Italy to change and build something new. For example, Rosa considers the novel's circular structure to be indicative of the extent to which this is "il ritratto di una comunità, colta in una fase di trapasso epocale: il fallimento della vecchia borghesia liberale" (340; the portrait of a community, caught in a phase of epochal transition: the failure of the old liberal bourgeoisie), and Di Pascale writes of the final image of the father that "forse è ... simbolo del Potere, forse è questo secolo dominato da una cultura di morte" (302; maybe it is ... a symbol of power, perhaps he represents this century, dominated by a culture of death). These interpretations build on the traditional understanding of the realm of the father as the one tied to public history. Benedetti as well as Fortuna and Gragnolati point out the potential disruption represented by Eugenio, especially in the final encounter with his son. Although Manuele ultimately fails to forge a new bond with Eugenio, Benedetti proposes that the novel closes on this "possibility of breaking the enchanted spell that bound together the woman and her child, perhaps freeing them both" (84), by accepting the weakened model of masculinity of which Eugenio has become exemplary, while Fortuna and Gragnolati say that "Morante's narrative seems to associate Manuele's recovery of the love of his father with the possibility of having words emerge again in their affective corporeality" (17). In the end, if Aracoeli's representation of femininity remains constrained within the boundaries of a dualistic imaginary that portrays her as either the chaste mother or the sexual predator, Eugenio's masculinity appears organized around more dissonant lines. The fact that Manuele cries for love of his weakened, drunken father, and not out of nostalgia for a stronger paternal figure, appears to point in the direction of a necessary renegotiation of gender roles and signals the possibility (or, at least, the narrative desire) of revising traditional notions of femininity and masculinity. It is a revision glimpsed and failed, but which nonetheless has a prominent role in the novel as its closing statement.

Vittorio Emanuele Maria, or The Unwilful Protagonist

Manuele, the narrator, is narratively and ideologically configured as the biological and cultural combination of these two heritages: he is the conflicted product of a double gender identification, a subjectivity attempting to find a place within a traditional gender structure that leaves no room for self-invention. Along with his father's blue eyes, Manuele has his mother's dark complexion and abundant hair, which will later be experienced as degenerating into an excessive, abnormal sign of masculinity. He is christened Vittorio Emanuele Maria. The first two names are in homage to Eugenio's cult, the King of Italy; the third is added by Aracoeli's special request, as an offering to the Virgin. His name marks his double genealogy as much as it anticipates his conflicted gender identification. Everyone, though, follows his mother's example and calls him Manuele or Manuelino, as an explicit homage to Aracoeli's younger brother, Manuel, the young Andalusian man who dies fighting against Franco while Aracoeli is pregnant with her baby girl.[11]

Just like the "first" Eugenio, Manuel is a model of ideal masculinity that Manuele cannot live up to: he recalls Aracoeli describing Manuel as "valente, nel gioco della corrida lui fa sempre l'espada, e da grande farà l'espada, oppure l'esploratore, o il camionista" (1103; "brave; when they play corrida he is always the espada, and when he grows up he'll be a real espada or else an explorer or a truck driver"; trans. Weaver 51). It is arguable that Manuel is the model for the adversary-lover in Manuele's sexual fantasies when he imagines being violently subjugated and killed by "una virilità severa e tragica: data instintivamente all'azione, e anche all'azione estrema" (1131; "a stern and tragic virility, given instinctively to action, and even to extreme action"; trans. Weaver 70), a description that echoes Manuel's sacrifice of his life for the Republican ideal. Unlike Eugenio, however, Manuel never falls from his heroic pedestal: Manuele writes in the first pages of the novel that "il mio EROE fu e rimane, a tutt'oggi sempre uno: mio zio Manuel" (1042; "[m]y HERO was and remains to this day one alone: my uncle Manuel"; trans. Weaver 5). Manuel's premature death, along with the fact that he is part of Aracoeli's Andalusian universe, ensures that he will remain a perfect, godlike idol, an emblem of masculinity adored by his sister well before she met Eugenio. Manuele's one active attempt to emulate Manuel by joining the partisans and fighting for the liberation of Italy during his first escape from boarding school turns into a humiliating farce and ends with his defeated rejection by two fake partisans.

Manuele's first years of life are, as I have already mentioned, related in terms of indescribable bliss. He lives with his mother on the outskirts of Rome, their existence regulated by natural divinities, the "Sempreververgini" (1185; "Evervirgins"; trans. Weaver 110), as much as by the apparition of the ice-cream man. During his infancy with Aracoeli, he writes, "l'io non si distingueva ancora chiaramente dal tu e dall'altro, né i sessi uno dall'altro" (1186; "the form 'I' was not yet clearly distinguished from the 'you' or any other, nor were the sexes distinct"; trans. Weaver 112): he lived in an ahistorical and asocial dimension. His gendering begins in the "Quartieri Alti" ("The Heights") with a haircut: "il taglio dei riccioli ... celebrava non solo la mia promozione virile, ma la fondazione legittima della nostra famiglia, dopo le nozze dei miei genitori" (1204; "the cropping of those curls ... celebrated, in fact, not only my promotion to manhood, but also the legitimate establishment of our family, after the wedding of my parents"; trans. Weaver 125). Legitimization and masculinization are coupled in one gesture.

A year after the wedding, Manuele's cultural initiation is reinforced as he begins primary school, which in turn leads to a new gendering event. During his first winter in school, in 1937, his teachers notice his nearsightedness and suggest that his mother bring him to an optometrist. Aracoeli complies, although very reluctantly. The visit is charged with anxiety for both mother and son: Manuele is seated in front of "un apparecchio astruso" (1257; "a mysterious apparatus"; trans. Weaver 164) that Aracoeli immediately suspects will compromise her son's "materia integra" (1257; intact substance).[12] When the optometrist presents a prescription for glasses to correct Manuele's defective vision, Aracoeli designates the glasses, in Spanish, *i lenti* (1257) – in the masculine. A grammatical gender switch (glasses are referred to in the feminine in Italian) allowed by the use of her native tongue signals Aracoeli's obscure awareness that the glasses are bound to gender her son.

The narrator's experience of putting his glasses on for the first time is traumatic: "gli aspetti del mondo avevano preso, ai miei occhi, una chiarezza e un rilievo inusitati, che me li accusavano come un'unica violenza proteiforme" (1259; "the aspect[s] of the world had taken on an unaccustomed clarity and prominence in my eyes, which beheld them as a sole, protean violence"; trans. Weaver 166). The description of his first walk when he wore his glasses appropriates the stylistic tools of expressionism to signal the deformation of reality when seen through the distorting lenses: "Non m'ero accorto mai, prima, di quanto duri e brutali fossero i segni sulle facce umane ... occhiaie biliose tumefatte, ghiotte narici enormi, gorge tracotanti a macchie paonazze, spaventosi occhioni bistrati e bocche tinte a sangue di macello" (1259; "I had never noticed, before, the harshness and brutality of the marks on human faces ... swollen and bilious eye sockets were followed by enormous and greedy nostrils, aggressive necks with flushed patches, horrifying big, bistered eyes, and mouths painted a slaughterhouse red"; trans. Weaver 166). Manuele is shocked by the "realistic" vision that his glasses offer him, his trauma signifying the extent to which this new, objective perception of reality is an acquired faculty, something in which he has to train ("[i]l mio nuovo esercizio"; 1259; "my new exercise"; trans. Weaver 166–7), rather than an inborn cognitive ability.[13]

The glasses become the signifier of the cultural endorsement of one approach to reality over a different, previous, approach. Manuele gradually gets used to wearing them, but he never discards his originary model of sight; he takes his glasses off whenever referential reality is deemed either uninteresting or unbearable. As he describes his arrival at the airport of Madrid and his refusal to put his glasses on, though, he describes his glassless eyesight in the same expressionistic terms that he used for his "englassed" sight:

> [I]l mondo circonstante, ai miei occhi semiciechi senza gli occhiali, si scioglie, secondo il solito, in un brulicame acquoso, corso da luci stralunate e immagini storpie ... Dal soffitto pende un vasto quadrante tenebroso, fornito di pupille luminescenti e di ciglia verdi movibili; passa una signora obesa con due teste; ... traballano degli individui che al posto della faccia hanno una proboscide. (1064)

> [T]he world around me, to my eyes, half-blind without the glasses, dissolves as usual into a watery swarm streaked with dazed lights and distorted images ... From the ceiling hangs a vast shadowy clock face with luminescent pupils and green, moving eyelids. An obese lady with two heads goes by ... [T]here are some swaying figures who have a proboscis instead of a face. (trans. Weaver 21–2)

Just as he recounts his first encounter with glasses as the enforcement of a flawed objectivity, the narrator also explicitly notes the unreliability of his natural (subjective) vision.

Manuele further informs the reader that a doctor has recently warned him that his sight "è minacciata" (1176; "is threatened"; trans. Weaver 104). His sight is sometimes so impaired, even with the help of lenses, that he wonders "se non dovrei munirmi, già fin d'ora, di un bastone bianco da ciechi" (1105; "Shouldn't I equip myself, now, with a white cane, like the blind?"; trans. Weaver 52). This quasi-blindness signals his radical distancing of himself from the possibility of perceiving reality as it is, with or without the help of a tool such as eyeglasses. By extension, it signals the impossibility of univocally validating any epistemological approach as the provider of an unmediated connection with reality. The text ultimately equates both approaches to vision to arbitrary hermeneutic processes: both paradigms of seeing (and knowing) are always already distorting that which they purport to clarify and understand; they are in both cases subjective interventions over a material subtext that is unreachable and indescribable as such. Reality, with or without glasses, is the product of a mediation between subjects and objects, a mediation in which the subjects read the object through the bias of their own hermeneutic and epistemological categories, projecting onto "reality" that which they want to find (or fear finding) within it.[14]

Thus the initial ungendered bliss that Manuele mourns is contrasted with the process of masculinization and civilization that sanctions his separation from Aracoeli, and with the ensuing consciousness of a divergence between two (gendered) ways to approach reality. His access to civilized knowledge, as signified by the glasses, nonetheless becomes, after the initial trauma, a source of wonder and excitement in the young Manuele. Manuele relates his inescapable fascination with literary representation as soon as he learns to read and write. His initiation into literature captivates him with its "promessa di avventura e smania di esplorazioni e sorprese" (1262; "promise of adventure and the yearning for exploration and surprise"; trans. Weaver 168), that is, with the possibility it offers for approaching reality through representation, and he becomes a voracious reader. While he proceeds through the fields of knowledge, Aracoeli (as I mentioned earlier) renounces their "studi gemelli" (1261; "twin studies"; trans. Weaver 168) because her social training, as a woman, excludes her from intellectual endeavours. Reading and writing are eloquently gendered in the masculine.

The first part of Manuele's life is thus mapped as "*Quando ero un lettore*" (1262; "*When I Was a Reader*"; trans. Weaver 168) and contrasted with the ensuing "*Da quando non sono più lettore*" (1262; "*Since I Am No Longer a Reader*"; trans. Weaver 168), in which he rejects the lures of literature. His abandonment of the "reader" paradigm is accompanied by his endorsement of a visionary one, as exemplified by his experimentation with various kinds of drugs and his addiction to alcohol. Mariuccio, a young "revolutionary" with whom Manuele futilely falls in love in his thirties, introduces him to drugs, which allows him to desert "la fabbrica del tempo ogni volta che i suoi ritmi prescritti mi sbigottivano, nella loro eternità numerata" (1100; "the factory of time whenever its prescribed rhythms dismayed me, in their numbered eternity"; trans. Weaver 48). Drugs provide him with a way to annihilate his relationship with the objectivity of time and to sleep through history; he uses drugs in the vain hope that they might bring him back to Aracoeli, to the fusional bliss he experienced as an infant: "di là dalle croci dei giorni, c'è lei che mi aspetta, coi suoi primi baci" (1100; "beyond the crosses of the days, there she is, waiting for me, with her first kisses"; trans. Weaver 49–50).

However, neither approach to the world can reinstate a unified, ungendered subjectivity. Manuele exposes his "natura scissa, che spesso invalida la mia testimonianza perfino al giudizio mio proprio" (1180; "split nature, which often invalidates my testimony even in my own judgment"; trans. Weaver 106). On one hand, the commencement of his virilization causes him to endorse an analytical paradigm traditionally associated with the masculine: discreetness, analysis, and activity. On the other, his subsequent rejection of this kind of knowledge brings him to endorse a femininization thematized by his renunciation of all social ambitions and by his use of drugs, triggering a form of knowledge associated with passivity, irrationality, and imagination – that is, with the supposedly natural world of femininity.

Manuele's dramatic self-positioning between masculinity and femininity – the narrator's refusal to inhabit a univocal ideological space – is powerfully thematized in his homosexuality. The importance of (homo) sexuality for an understanding of Manuele's ideological "fabric" should not be underestimated. Far from being an exclusively private, subjective event, sexuality is (as Foucault taught us) an extremely dense vehicle of social and ideological conflicts. Through the discussion of his sexual preferences and fantasies, Manuele expresses his awareness of the power struggles he inhabits: he refuses to take an active part in the heterosexual script and falls back, almost by default, into a passive, feminized role.

Early in the novel, Manuele accounts for the failure of his first (and last) two sexual encounters by relating his inability to posit the object of sexual desire as feminine. A drunken girl who approaches him on the beach exudes a natural, animal presence that puts him at ease and enchants him. Manuele tries to arouse himself to pursue the heterosexual script, "disperata imitazione virile" (1122; "in a desperate, manly imitation"; trans. Weaver 64), but he is paralysed by the love he feels for such an animal, innocent femininity that appears to be modelled on his mother's innocence. Actual penetration is prevented by the brutal intervention of a "dark young man" (no connection with the *massaia*'s) who takes over possession of the girl and hastily consummates the act.

This humiliating episode of Manuele's being sexually ambushed by a stronger, arrogant masculinity does not trigger a desire for revenge: to the contrary, it appears to generate, within a few pages, his first homosexual fantasies. The figure of the unknown man is conflated with that of Manuel, the Andalusian uncle, becoming the Other whose object Manuele dreams of being. Manuele enacts a script in which he is passive, fearful, and reduced to self-pity. His identification with the female end of the couple rather than its male end – along with the narrator's insistence on the "stage-like" quality of the role-playing – engenders self-hatred, so that the sexual act is synonymous with murder: "fra noi due non poteva darsi altra intimità che l'assassinio" (1130; "between the two of us there could be no other intimacy except murder"; trans. Weaver 71), a murder in which he is always, necessarily, the victim.

Manuele's refusal to identify with the active end of the (hetero)sexual equation is also explicitly accounted for in the second experience he relates, which occurred when he was eighteen years old. This time, the young Manuele finds himself face-to-face with the opposite end of the spectrum of womanhood: the old, made-up prostitute described earlier, whose face appears to him like a mask of "bianchezza mortuaria" (1142), a deadly whiteness. Whereas Manuele's casual encounter with the young girl had been characterized by her innocent, animal sensuality, in which she adhered to the paradigm of a joyous, life-giving nature whose deadly secret is unveiled only by the man's intervention, this second encounter soon takes on the air of a grotesque dance around the monstrous truth of the female sex: "fra due lembi di povera carne floscia nuda e grigiastra ... mi si lasciò intravvedere appena una sorta di ferita sanguigna" (1143; "I could just glimpse, between two patches of poor flabby flesh, ... a kind of bloody wound"; trans. Weaver 80).

The striking reference to the "ferita sanguigna" revealed during this encounter with the prostitute echoes Niccolò Machiavelli's famous 1509 letter to Guicciardini (as well as Dante's "femina balba" in *Purgatorio*, v. 19).[15] In the letter, Machiavelli recounts his own encounter with an old prostitute. He focuses only on the woman's face – but, as Spackman reminds us, "such reticence is little more than a touch of delicacy ...; by employing such a classic topos, he evokes the entire landscape the topos describes" (*Decadent Genealogies* 165). The topos mentioned here, the "enchantress-turned-hag," is one to which I have already referred in chapter 1, where I discuss it in connection with Manzoni's Gertrude.[16] This is a metaphor for hidden truth as incarnated in the "woman's body, a 'repulsive' common denominator shared by all women" (*Decadent Genealogies* 166). Manuele shies away from such truth. He fails to consummate the act because he is disgusted by such a spectacle, but also because he perceives the old woman as sacred and, even more importantly here, because he refuses to identify with the murderous force that would inflict such wounds on femininity.[17]

Manuele refuses to endorse a strong, active masculinity, but he is also aware of the impossibility of univocally identifying with the feminine. Even within the realm of the homosexual discourse, which supposedly blurs the boundaries between traditional gender roles, he incurs the stigma attached to the failures of his maleness: as his younger (non) lover Mariuccio remarks, Manuele is not a real homosexual; he is rather "un maschio fallito, un rottame di classe fuori servizio" (1096; "a straight who's failed, a class wreck, not in running order"; trans. Weaver 45).[18] He is a subject who is sexed as male yet refuses to endorse the gendered requirements connected to masculinity. He rejects the heterosexual paradigm of the society he lives in as well as the (narrative) definition of masculinity that derives from it: he is not a traditional, active seeker. He has also, nonetheless, internalized the social devaluation accompanying the attributes of femininity.

Manuele's inability to fully identify with either gender role as presented through the figures of his mother, his father, and his uncle is signified by his self-proclaimed homosexuality. More than providing an ethical or political reflection, homosexuality is here a narrative statement, the figure for an epistemological compromise and for the narrator's need to position himself outside of the "compulsory heterosexuality" – as Adrienne Rich puts it – of a conservative narrative structure. Together with the impossibility of reaching the (female) object of knowledge, Manuele's homosexuality in *Aracoeli* serves to literalize the impossibility of a male subject founding a narrative and epistemological project in which his supposed neutrality – his heterosexuality – assures the successful outcome of the enterprise. In this way, the novel exposes the sex/gender system underlying the supposed neutrality of knowledge and thus, like Manuele's glasses, exposes the subjective nature of all epistemological endeavours.

Manuele's problematic status as a novelistic character is thus tied to his "unveiling" (to use a word connected to the epistemology of revelation) the strict gender distribution of roles that rules the narrative and epistemological projects in which he finds himself living: he is a dissonant seeker, a subject who stages his story only to reveal the impossibility of fitting within it. By refusing to endorse the meaning of narrative manhood, he sanctions the defeat of his narrative project and foregrounds himself as parodic. Through the denial of the subject's epistemological possibilities, *Aracoeli* becomes a site of parody, at both the narrative and the epistemological levels. The novel stages a double inaccessibility, a denial of the possibility that literature can make sense of reality, that it can know both subject and object of the epistemological equation. The only opening that the novel appears to allow, as we have seen, is the final structural asymmetry that suddenly displaces Manuele's desire from Aracoeli to Eugenio, simultaneously offering and rejecting the possibility of narrative subversion.

On Narrative, Epistemology, and Poetics: The Gender of the Real

The conclusion of Manuele's journey to El Almendral, which immediately precedes his last encounter with Eugenio, is exemplary in its literalization of the shortcomings of the quest. It is the revelatory ending that the reader expects from the novel, the moment for learning whether Manuele finds his mother. The power and spell of Morante's narrative (and of the structures she relies on) are so strong that, although the narrator has sprinkled disclaimers throughout the text, the reader still hopes that the hero will find his object of desire, Aracoeli (or, at least, will join her by dying). On one hand, the very existence of this first ending is proof of the resilience of the narrative paradigm that it embodies and concludes; on the other, both the parodic structure of this passage and the fact that a second ending follows this one suggest the possibility of a shift in the narrative and epistemological terms that found the novel.

The end of the journey unfolds in two moments: a "false" agnition of the mother is followed by Manuele's actual arrival at his mother's birthplace. As he drunkenly walks towards his final destination, El Almendral, Manuele briefly stops on a scree, a desolate, stony field, to stage an imaginary encounter with Aracoeli: "E non mi resta che inventare il nostro incontro ... In verità, scorgo – o pretendo scorgere – appena un minuscolo sacco d'ombra" (1427; "And I have now only to invent our encounter ... To tell the truth, I can just discern – or pretend to discern – a kind of minuscule sack of shadows"; trans. Weaver 291). The shadow hastily retreats after confirming for him that "non c'è niente da capire" (1428; "there's nothing to be understood"; trans. Weaver 292). The "revelation" of Aracoeli is, indeed, impossible. Manuele's journey can only imagine finding the other: it can only fabricate the other by a suspension of disbelief immediately denounced as such by the protagonist. His subsequent arrival in the hamlet is, then, highly significant in its display of the "actual" result of his quest: as he enters El Almendral and visits the only open house he finds, Manuele realizes that his final point of arrival is only a rudimentary bar, tended by an old Andalusian man. "E che altro potrebbe essere, il mio approdo, se non un'osteria o un bar?" (1429; "And what else could my port be, if not a tavern or a bar?"; trans. Weaver 293), the narrator concedes warily, well aware of the literary model (Ulysses) he himself has evoked for his journey and of the anticlimactic nature of his destination.

On the counter sits an old picture of General Franco, "grosso e panciuto sotto la nota uniforme" ("fat and paunchy under the familiar uniform"); on the wall by Manuele's chair there are several pictures of scantily clad women "che esibiscono le diverse pezzature della propria carne" (1430; "displaying the different areas of their flesh"; trans. Weaver 293). Such is, indeed, the result of his quest. On the one hand, there is a historical icon of manly power, a variation on the Italian king's effigy that Eugenio kept in his entrance hall and the ideal virility that Eugenio himself had embodied up to a certain point in his life. Franco is a living icon that, as the reader has by now repeatedly been informed, is actually (referentially) in his death throes during that same November 1975 in which the novel takes place (Franco died on 20 November) and in the same country, Spain, in which Manuele ends his journey. On the other hand, the magazine clips of semi-naked women are the multiple, interchangeable icons of a femininity reduced to its minimal, bodily terms, to different pieces of flesh. Manuele further remarks that the women carry "l'abituale sorriso stolido di simili esibizioni: col quale sembrano, in fondo, mascherare un'accusa d'oltraggio insanabile" (1430; "the usual inexpressive smile of such displays, with which they seem, privately, to mask an accusation of irreparable outrage"; trans. Weaver 293). These are, it appears, the ultimate fruition of his journey, these discoveries that await him in front of his glass of wine. A quest structured around the model of a male seeker in search of a female object of desire is bound to produce exactly this, an aged photograph of an arrogant virility and a reproduction of objectified femininities that is exactly as reductive and two-dimensional.

What is the outrage, exactly, of which these photographic beauties announce themselves to be victims? It is, to be sure, the same reduction to a bodily essence that sealed Aracoeli's narrative fate from the beginning. The dichotomous model of femininity explored in Aracoeli's story is projected onto every female figure and effigy, from the Virgin Mary to the prostitute; and these figures each reveal, under their lively appearances, their deadly truth. As Aracoeli transforms from the loving mother into the sexual monster, Manuele compares her to a piece of meat besieged by flies ("Aracoeli si accascia intormentita ma senza riposo, come dentro una nube d'insetti assillanti"; 1338; "Aracoeli slumps down, numb but without repose, as if in a cloud of pestering insects"; trans. Weaver 224). In the visions he has of his mother, "le sue nudità scoperte provocano a vederle la stessa vergogna misera e irrimediabile che ci fa torcere lo sguardo dai corpi degli animali scuoiati" (1201; "her bared nakedness, when seen, arouses the same wretched and irreparable shame that makes us turn our gaze away from the bodies of skinned animals"; trans. Weaver 123); even dolls are nothing but "simulacri mortuari" (1295; "mortuary effigies"; trans. Weaver 193). The female life-giving paradigm is always overwhelmed by the unspeakable outrage, the horrifying reality of women's bodies.[19]

Virtually every female incarnation Manuele encounters is coupled with death: his only "visual" encounter with the female sex (the encounter with the old prostitute) results in his describing "an object of massacre and horrendous suffering, like the mouth of a slaughtered animal." Before his encounter with this woman, Manuele had never been to a brothel, shying away from them "come davanti a un lenzuolo che si ha orrore di sollevare, perché copre un cadavere" (1116; "as if before a sheet one is too horrified to raise because it covers a corpse"; trans. Weaver 60). The very last image of womanhood in the novel, as Manuele runs from his father's building, is that of a woman so grotesquely fat that she is stuck lying on her back and looks, as he walks away, like "una morta annegata sull'orlo di una marina in tumulto" (1450; "a drowned woman on the shore of the raging sea"; trans. Weaver 308).

The outrage surfacing through the smiles of the photographed pinup girls is the only trace left of a feminine subjectivity that is reduced to its most elementary, physical given and whose corporality is, in turn, reduced to a merely sexual dimension. This corporality is a body ostracized and demonized, always already condemned to degradation and death – all the while being socially exploited. This "accusation" becomes a denunciation of women's social role as objects of the masculine gaze, a denunciation of their impossible confinement to the passive pole of the knowledge equation, and a denunciation of their being that which is to be known: reality, in its material and deadly consistence. From the epistemological point of view, the "death" of the object of knowledge sanctions the impossibility of knowing it and thus exposes the process as a subjective enterprise.

Manuele's narrative, epistemological, and social defeat signals the schism between reality and representation enacted by this text, the irreversibility of a process by which language and narrative are transformed from being instruments for interpreting and reorganizing the world into devices for recording its scattered manifestations. Worse yet, literature is envisaged here as an ideological machine bent on obliterating what it set out to "faithfully" find and represent. Reality, as the object of knowledge, is compromised because it is confronted by epistemological paradigms that gender it as they represent it and that, by gendering it, actually sanction its inaccessibility. Woman is always her body, and her body is always dead (or deadly).[20] Manuele's renunciation of his status as a strong epistemological subject further indicates that *Aracoeli* subjects the active end of the epistemological equation to the same critique it has carried out for its passive end. Thus, on the one hand, the novel embodies a narrative defeat of both the quest and the family romance, and of both imaginary and analytic cognitive paradigms, because they remain confined to an imaginary that contains "the other" within defined images of femininity. On the other hand, *Aracoeli* also dismantles the monolithic status of the "universal" subject: Manuele's weakening is expressed by his homosexuality and by his refusal to found any knowledge as such. Manuele has fittingly been defined by Anna Maria Di Pascale as "the repulsive, tragic parody of the intellectual" (293). He is the tragic parody of the seeker, its degraded, alcoholic version. *Aracoeli* takes to its extremes the premise of a specific literary paradigm and shows its inherent contradictions and complicities. It literalizes and denounces a model of knowledge founded on the murder of the object of knowledge and on the inaccessibility of the knowing subject. If reality is nothing more than a (female) body, a bloody wound, then the writer's pen – the narrator's journey, the protagonist's memories – cannot bring any life back to (or through) it.

Manuele is painfully conscious of his parodic status, that is, of the impairment befalling the narrator: he has given up trying to find a reliable source of knowledge and considers himself an incongruous, ridiculous "counterfeit." He is, in fact, as unknowable as the object of his quest: Manuele's existence is a "macchia informe" (1213; "shapeless stain"; trans. Weaver 132) against the cosmos, the story of a subject who, rather than leaving his island (like the protagonist of *L'isola di Arturo*), wants to go back and die on it. Moreover, Manuele is aware that his condition is not unique: by the time he writes (and he is historically very precise: the journey begins on 1 November 1975), the weakened status of the epistemological subject needs to be extended and generalized: "e so già che la presente analisi e i suoi pretesi risultati sono immaginari, come immaginaria, del resto, è l'intera mia storia (e tutte le altre storie, o Storie, mortali o immortali)" (1452; "And I already know that my present analysis and its supposed results are imaginary, as, for that matter, my whole story is imaginary (and all other stories, or Histories, mortal or immortal)"; trans. Weaver 310).[21]

Morante's *Aracoeli* is thus a vast parodic gesture, that is, a self-critical replica of one individual's failed attempt to reach the other, and a historicized and contextualized one at that. The conclusion of this parody is not only the failure within the story to find the other – since this failure was contemplated as a possibility from the beginning – but also the more far-reaching conclusion that such a failure is to be ascribed to the very narrative and epistemological structures the subject is relying on. That is, the novel discloses the partiality and relativity of these structures, with the consequent indictment of both epistemological positions (the quest and the *Familienroman*) and of the very possibility of grounding knowledge or literature.

On one hand, the "irreparable outrage" at which Manuele stares as his factual journey ends is the only, and uncanny, trace of a femininity left for dead by a subject unable to move beyond himself. It is the trace of a real that cannot be known as such, yet whose demise is as unbearable as a mother's death. On the other hand, the actual final scene of *Aracoeli* sanctions Manuele's belated realization of the lost possibility of endorsing a different masculinity, that is, of finding in Eugenio's weakened subjectivity an alternative possibility for love. From the narrative point of view, the unexpected shift in desire effected by Manuele comes too late for him to change his enterprise and turn his quest for the mother into a different story; nonetheless, it succeeds in drawing retrospective attention to the figure of the father. By surprising the reader with a closing that does not respect the premise of the novel, that is not organized around the quest for the mother, this ending draws attention to the structural asymmetry of the text. It signals the presence of an unexplored space between the two genders, between seeker and prey, between reader and writer. Manuele's closing "weeping for love" is the surprising "anello che non tiene" (the ring that does not hold) – to use Montale's beautiful expression ("I Limoni," line 27) – an unforeseen deviation of desire, unable to survive its own degradation yet ideologically (phantasmatically) powerful enough to become Morante's very last words.

Conclusion

[T]he world becomes more and more prosaic.

(Lukács 105)

In *Gender, Narrative, and Dissonance*, I have examined specific instances of epistemological, generic, and narrative dissonance in eight Italian novels in order to analyse one of the main ideological concerns of these texts – the variety of ways in which gender informs narrative. I place characters at the centre of my project because a re-examination of the concept of character and its heterogeneous function within each text highlights the interplay of subversion and complicity – the possibility, explored by each story, that one particularly problematic subject might just undo the very structure within which that subject exists.

The solutions to gender negotiations, just as to ideological conflicts in general, are always imaginary, both within and outside of the aesthetic realm (their consequences, of course, are often less so). What changes in the mechanism that rules the functioning of gender is its subversive or complicit charge, its oppositional value in either refusing or acquiescing to the "scene of constraint" within which it operates. The issue of the extent to which novels are gendered arises with the first modern Italian novel, and my opening analysis of the characterization of Geltrude/Gertrude in *Fermo e Lucia* and *I promessi sposi* introduced several fundamental questions about narrative within the space of modernity: Are all (narrated) subjects equal? What is the space that female characters – female protagonists – occupy? How do novels represent gender inequalities, and what do such inequalities signify for the novel itself? In other words, how does gender work in these texts? The evolution of the character of Gertrude is, to a certain extent, coextensive with the introduction of modernity in the discourse of prose narrative. Her ideological objections to an all-knowing novelistic authority are unprecedented and initiate a new, dissonant paradigm for female characters in narrative.

In chapter 2, I focused on the striking importance that Neera assigns to two coexisting cognitive routes in her novels "of the young woman" to outline how the epistemology of gender informs the structure of these texts. The results of the young women's quests for knowledge are determined by a revelatory structure that is not always already "true" but is rather, to put it in Althusserian terms, always a powerful way to mediate the characters' imagination of their relation to the world and the actual conditions of their existence. In chapter 3, which was devoted to Marchesa Colombi and Verga, I focused mainly on how discrepancies in generic choices – that is, in the narrative organization of the texts – can have a momentous impact that produces a different conclusion for the novel, as well as a different reception, and I discussed how a different space can allow for a new, irreverent kind of (gendered) presence. In chapter 4, I emphasized the contradictory relationship that is explicitly established between the protagonist and the narrator in Masino's *Nascita e morte della massaia* – a surprising example of novelistic dissonance that echoes in the relationship between characters and between author and novel itself. Finally, in chapter 5, I examined Morante's novel *Aracoeli* and highlighted the extreme disillusionment it expresses about the very possibility of telling a story, a disillusionment tied to a gender politics that is by then narratively and cognitively unacceptable.

Within each of these texts, the specifics of the modern crisis of representation are seen from the perspective of gendered subjects. The gender of fictional characters becomes a pre-eminent datum not because of its referential import, or at least not uniquely, but because of its structural relevance. Morante's literary calibre and sensitivity do what Manzoni had already done in his novel, but in a most spectacular way. Whereas Manzoni symbolically opened the narrative parable of gender modernity by offering a problematic character gendered as a woman, and one who has an ironic awareness of her own story, Morante closes the circle by turning the cultural logic of patriarchy upon itself. Femininity is predetermined, always already normativized and framed, and now masculinity is undermined in its ability to found knowledge; reality and truth are gendered and as such are unknowable.

This does not mean, of course, that the insistence, indeed reliance, on specific gender roles and models has been compromised once and for all by Morante's last novel. But it does mean that, as I have shown by tracing my own idiosyncratic journey through the modernity of gender, the limits and constraints have been exposed in increasingly stronger terms as Italian novels have evolved across decades and movements. This book calls attention to such ideological twists and to the dissonance of characters who assert the possibilities of narrative – its openness to change – while they also face the novels' almost compulsive predictability, their willingness to go to great lengths to frame subjects within familiar patterns. What is important is to fully understand how productively and effectively, and how often, these dissonances have already been staged and enacted.

Before bringing this book to a close, I want to discuss a haunting image from Morante's *Aracoeli* that clarifies for me both the weight of that which keeps us from changing and the latitude that we have with and within it. To the extent that this final novel reflects on the possibility of literature drawing meaning from the world, its pointed critique of narrative and epistemology brings forth a more generalized reflection on the meaning and function of literature in modern, and postmodern, times. *Aracoeli* contains many textual moments that are useful for appraising the novel as a genre, as well as narrative in general. It could be convincingly argued, of course, that every word of a novel can be read in self-referential terms, that is, as a statement about poetics, as Ross Chambers (among others) has argued: "there is no easier interpretive strategy than to read a text as a commentary on itself as a literary production" (*The Writing of Melancholy* 2). Because the passage I want to discuss is thematically connected to words and literature, it is easy prey for being read in such a way.

The passage is also a telling example of the discrepancies that Chambers believes are characteristic of oppositional narratives, that is, the slippage between textual and narrative function. Chambers's work usefully highlights how the oppositional nature of texts is to be connected with a non-linear relationship between the text's "narrative function" – the "mode of production of the narrative relationship" (*Room for Maneuver* 36), the fact that we are within a narrative context, that a story is being told – and its textual function, its "textual self-representation" (42), the fact that every part of a text can also be understood as saying something about itself. Chambers writes that "it is the *relation* of 'textual function' to 'narrative function' that crucially defines narrative oppositionality, which always depends on the production of difference between the two" (44). In terms of narrative oppositionality, I consider the following passage from *Aracoeli* to be an excellent example of the non-linear relationship between the "literal" (the narrative message) and what the same passage tells the reader about the text as a whole, about its position within an ideological and poetic system of reference.[1]

In the opening pages of *Aracoeli*, while Manuele is reflecting on his mother's name, he writes that since the time that the name seemed to him to be absolutely natural, when he was a boy, it has over the years become an existential "segno di diversità, un *titolo* unico" (1048; "sign of distinction, a unique *title*"; trans. Weaver 10, emphasis mine). The name "Aracoeli" has become so peculiar to him, in fact, that it inspires a comparison with a twisted and massive gilded frame that encloses his mother: "quel nome Aracoeli si è scritto nel mio ricordo quale un segno di diversità, un titolo unico: in cui mia madre rimane separata e rinchiusa, come dentro una cornice tortile e massiccia, dipinta d'oro" (1048; "that name Aracoeli became stamped in my memory as a sign of distinction, a unique title in which my mother remains separate and enclosed, as in a heavy tortile frame painted with gold"; trans. Weaver 10). The name has "written" itself on his memory, ultimately becoming the defining title for his mother. Of course "Aracoeli," the name of his mother, is also "*Aracoeli*," the title of the novel, and the temptation to pursue the implications of a passage equating the novel to a heavy, gilded frame that contains and imprisons a woman is too strong to be ignored, especially given that this "frame," and the mirror it encloses, is one of the founding images of the text.

In the following paragraph, Manuele diverts from his imaginary comparison between a name and a frame to its possible origin: "Forse, questa figura della cornice mi proviene dalla specchiera che esisteva effettivamente nella nostra prima stanza clandestina, da dove poi ci seguì nella nuova casa legittima dei Quartieri Alti" (1048; "Perhaps this image of a frame comes to me from the mirror that did actually exist in our first, clandestine room, whence it then followed us into our new, legitimate house in The Heights"; trans. Weaver 10). The frame becomes the pretext for a memory regress that brings the narrator back to his childhood, to a "grande e vistosa" (1048; "large and conspicuous"; trans. Weaver 10) framed mirror that accompanied the family during their displacements. Manuele then explains that "la primissima visione postuma di me stesso, che fa da sfondo a tutti i miei anni" (1049; "the very first posthumous vision of myself, which serves as background for all of my years"; trans. Weaver 10), is in fact recalled for him through the double mediation of this object. It is the founding myth of his life, and it is a memory that resurfaces "non direttamente ma riflessa dentro quella specchiera, e inquadrata nella nota cornice" (1049; "not directly but reflected in that mirror, and enclosed by the well-known frame"; trans. Weaver 11). His memory is thus doubly mediated, reflected and framed as it is by two highly symbolic objects, the frame and the mirror glass.[2]

The images contained (reflected, framed) by the mirror provide an intricate study of his newborn self, attached to his mother's breast in loving satiation, as well as the first, and extremely detailed, portrait of Aracoeli. This image is *Aracoeli*'s founding myth, a myth in which the mother exists to serve the son and the son does not know that he is a separate individual from the mother. This is Manuele's reason for setting out on his quest, the expression of an unparalleled prehistoric bliss to which Manuele hopes to regress by telling his story. And, in a way, he has just done this: he has recreated the absolute "reality" of his infancy while simultaneously underscoring that it simply might not be as true and immediate as it looks: it is a posthumous vision.

Manuele is quite explicit about the fact that he cannot ascertain the truth of his memory: he entrusts the very possibility of a memorial act to the medium through which reality was supposedly perceived in the first place and to a posthumous, and therefore non-referential, temporality. He also undermines any claim to a univocal connection between the image and reality. It might be a fake memory ("o magari pseudomemoria"; 1049; "or perhaps pseudomemory"; trans. Weaver 10), or then again it might turn out to be truer than truth, but only *later*: "certi ricordi apocrifi *dopo* mi si scoprono più veri del vero" (1050; "some apocryphal memories *later* prove much more true than the truth"; trans. Weaver 11, emphasis mine). The post-mortem nature of these memories is explicit: once Aracoeli is dead, Manuele's "memories" become truer than her disappearance.

The mirror and the frame are the only means through which the knowing subject can access reality. To a certain extent, in fact, the mirror and the frame are the only reality the knowing subject can count on – Manuele prefaces his description with a strikingly assertive note about the "*specchiera*" (i.e., the combination of mirror and frame):[3] "verisimilmente essa ancora esiste, e sopravvive alla famiglia scomparsa" (1048; "In all likelihood, however, it still exists, and survives the family that has vanished"; trans. Weaver 10). He vouches for the survival of the object while contrasting it with the family's disappearance: the object through which Manuele's memory can exist, the mirror, and the frame that "contains" it and as such confers a specific meaning to it have outlived their content. They are, in fact, the very novel that we are reading.

The presentation of the foundational image of blissful union with the (m)other within the heavy frame of a large and conspicuous mirror is thus also a self-referential reflection on the mediating function of literature, on writing as an epistemological tool that both restores and contains that which it sets out to represent. Far from simply being a medium, literature frames words within a discursive structure that determines the way reality is going to be produced. Literature "exists"; reality is long gone, inscrutable and unreachable. While a positive take on such a statement about poetics might hold that literature can successfully preserve that which cannot survive outside of it, the ultimate implication of Morante's model is that the knowing subject (narrator as well as reader) has no way of determining that the image within the mirror antedated the mirror and its frame – there is no way to ascertain the truth of this image.[4]

Although they are unified as a single piece of furniture, Manuele also describes the different characteristics of the two "media." The mirror's glass is "lucida e di fabbrica recente" (1048; "shiny and of recent manufacture"; trans. Weaver 10), while the frame is old and its gilding is slightly faded, because it comes from Eugenio's family, from Manuele's paternal grandparents. As a metaphor for literature, the *specchiera* is dialectically built out of the opposition between the relative novelty of the glass and the majestic baroque-ness – the exuberant antiquity – of the frame: the glass symbolizes the creative process in its discursively productive mode; the frame, conversely, signifies the ideological subtext always already structuring and containing such a process, in this case the patriarchal system of values embodied by Eugenio's parents. This is a partition roughly comparable to Jameson's distinction, within the symbolic act that is literature, between "a prior historical and ideological *subtext*" (always unknowable as such) and the "literary or aesthetic act" (81) itself.

Ross Chambers has written that "literature can designate itself, in its 'textual function,' as a site of discursive oppositionality; that is, … it produces, as the context that makes it meaningful, a context of oppositional relations to power" (*Room for Maneuver* 43). While, at the level of its narrative function, this passage from *Aracoeli* provides narrator and reader with a common understanding of Manuele's starting point, as well as with the foundational myth of the novel, at the level of textual function it undermines the option of believing the epistemological possibilities of literature and of endorsing the founding myth as such. This excerpt portrays literature as a residual form of knowledge whose reality cannot be ascertained by any means and also highlights the oppositional quality of this narrative. It points to the extent to which literary representations are always framed and contained, disarmed and isolated, by an ideological stratum that predetermines the content and conditions the way that content is going to be read. Moreover, the comparison between name and frame, with the accompanying establishment of Aracoeli as the "framed" content, also assigns a gender to such content: reality (or that which is supposed to impersonate it) is a woman.

Sara Fortuna and Manuele Gragnolati have cogently written that "one could affirm that the feeling of unease and irritation produced by the novel (which is so common when the reader approaches *Aracoeli* and which was also our experience, at least when we first confronted it) is the symptom that it achieves its aim at a narrative level by not conforming to the reader's expectations stemming from internalized norms" (17). It is not surprising that *Aracoeli* has emerged in recent years as a text that cannot be overlooked in discussions of Italian (post)modernity or of gender ideology. Aracoeli, Manuele, and Vittorio Amedeo close the critical parable that I began with Geltrude, a parable that aims, via the different stories of the dissonant subjects in the texts of Neera, Verga, Marchesa Colombi, and Masino, to place female characters – or characters whose problem is informed by gender dissonance – at the centre of the ideological analysis. While my book has no ambition of completeness, it proposes a path through the dissonance of gender in novelistic modernity, from the work of its reluctant founding father to the sorrowful, parodic testament of Italy's most famous female author, a journey in which characters – ideological subjects – are that which mediates between what should be and what can be.

The "truth" of literature – its composite status as an antique frame, a sleek, reflective surface, and an image within – echoes throughout these texts as a complex compromise that characters endanger as much as inhabit, by pointing out, in progressively more explicit terms, the narrow limits of literature: its framing restrictions. Within these texts, knowledge is not an open enterprise. The "truth" of gender is attentively "revealed" in its heterogeneous nature, and I have shown these revelations and conversions to be partial at best, because they are each time phantasmatically organized around one specific, relative truth that the novel is engaged in conveying. The violence of gender is expressed in its forceful repression, its tampering interventions on characters, and the haunting reappearances of the "spectres of the real" – these are a few examples of the different techniques through which narratives, even the most complicit ones, always acknowledge the existence of a problem, if only to suppress it.

As I mentioned in the introduction, Mieke Bal compellingly argued that the problem of characters, what often fools us into not taking them seriously, is "this anthropomorphic aspect. The character is not a human being, but it resembles one" (113). However, the opposite is also true. The problem is not that characters are like us – it is not their human "accidentality," their unpredictability, and their genderedness, that should worry us. It is not the bliss of Aracoeli and Manuele's nursing of which we should be wary. It is the extent to which characters always already find themselves informing (and reforming) predictable narrative frames as they move within a universe – the baroque frame, the shiny glass – that is too suspiciously familiar to be taken for granted and too self-explanatory to ever be taken at face value.

Notes

Introduction

1 Unless noted otherwise, translations from the Italian are mine.
2 Indeed, the notorious (and, although short-lived, ever fascinating) experiment with the "death of the character" performed by French nouveau roman authors such as Nathalie Sarraute and Alain Robbe-Grillet is to be considered a confirmation of the centrality of characters to the novelistic enterprise as much as a critique of a specifically realistic and referential notion of character with which the novel can dispense. Far from doing without characters, Alain Robbe-Grillet and Claude Simon, but also Samuel Beckett and Philippe Sollers, simply distance themselves from too simplistic an understanding of the "agents" that inhabit a novel. On this, see also Debenedetti.
3 Aristotle writes, "I use 'plot' to denote the construction of events, 'character' to mean that in virtue of which we ascribe certain qualities to the agents, and 'thought' to cover the parts in which, through speech, they demonstrate something or declare their views. Tragedy as a whole, therefore, must have six components, which give it its qualities – namely, plot, character, diction, thought, spectacle, and lyric poetry … The most important of these things is the structure of events, because tragedy is mimesis not of persons but of action and life; and happiness and unhappiness consist in action, and the goal is a certain kind of action, not a qualitative state" (49–51).
4 Classic analyses of characters by novelists include those of E.M. Forster and François Mauriac; Henry James was among the novelists most committed to proposing a more central notion of character. In his preface to *The Portrait of a Lady* (1881), James spoke of Turgenev's explicit attention

to characters as a characteristic of his own writing, as well, and underscored "the intensity of suggestion that may reside in the stray figure, the unattached character, the *image en disponibilité*" as the starting point of his novels (614). Together with Knights's intervention (1933), influential theories of characters include the structuralist contributions of Vladimir Propp's typology of folktale figures and A.J. Greimas's discussion of characters as actors and of their structural role as actants. In the Anglophone world, a first wave of analytical discussion of characters was initiated by Walcutt and Harvey. Ten years after the latter, Mary Doyle Springer wrote a compelling analysis of characters in Henry James's novels, and Marcia Eaton's coeval essay, under the cover of a linguistic perspective, points in the direction of ideological analysis. Further references that attempt to go beyond too-narrow notions of characters include Seymour Chatman's and James Phelan's works, which I shall discuss further. Another potential source of stimulating research on characters can be found within the dramatic tradition (Fuchs) and in cinematic reflections (Dyer and McDonald).

5 The first trace of this can already be seen in Aristotle's discussion ("plot ... is the first principle, and, as it were, soul of tragedy, while character is secondary," 53). In her book *Stately Bodies: Literature, Philosophy, and the Question of Gender*, Adriana Cavarero offers a description of the Greek political order that is also applicable to the organization of knowledge: it is "both logo- and phallocentric. In its very founding categories, that order clearly excludes a corporeality judged to be mere material support for the human capacity for language and thought, at the same time excluding women, insofar as they are 'naturally' rooted in matters of the body" (16).

6 Among the dictionaries, there are the *Dizionario Bompiani delle opere e dei personaggi: Di tutti i tempi e di tutte le letterature* (1946–50, reprinted in 1983 and 2005), the *Dizionario dei personaggi letterari* (UTET, 2003), and the *Dizionario dei personaggi di romanzo: Da Don Chisciotte all'Innominabile* (Bufalino, 1989).

7 The quote also appears in Caesar (45–46). Caesar's monograph is a substantial contribution to the renewed debate on characters, although mostly from the standpoint of textual mise en abîme, that is, Modernist characters' explicit engagement with their own fictional status *within* the work of art.

8 Although not invested in gender critique, more recent examples of studies on characters can also be found in Italian scholarship. Interestingly enough, a chief example is Franco Marenco's introduction to UTET's *Dizionario dei personaggi letterari*. Marenco surveys different literary epochs and traditions (especially dramatic), from Plautus to Molière and from Hamlet to Kleist, in terms of the "saldo rapporto fra struttura e caratterizzazione"

(xvii; strong relationship between structure and characterization) and between "personaggio e intreccio" (xix; character and plot) that characterize certain archetypal stories and that always already characterize, in fact, every "scrittura di finzione" (xvii; fiction writing). Although Marenco remains tied to the dichotomy "di questa dialettica fra l'interno e l'esterno del personaggio" (xx; of this dialectic between the inside and the outside of the character) and to the theatrical perspective more than the novelistic one, his overview of the modalities of characterization in different literary traditions is very useful. For current approaches to characters see also Bottiroli.

9 Ahmed's contribution appeared in the Spring 2011 issue of *New Literary History*, edited by Rita Felski and devoted to the notion of "character" in all of its meanings.

10 There is also (at least) a third potential meaning of "character": the written sign through which words are constituted. On this point, see Oksenberg Rorty.

11 Greimas proposes a reading of this duplicity in accordance with his discussion of actors and actants: "[A] mask, for example, is an actor having the modality of seeming as its actantial role … We would say that, in this case, the actorial structure is objectivized" (112).

12 Of course, "narrative" includes more than simply literary texts: Pierre Emmanuel Cordoba, for example, extends the problem of the "reality" of characters to that of real-life people, "dés lors qu'[ils sont] object de discours" (34; as soon as they are the subject [literally, the object or topic] of discourse).

13 See, for example, the publisher Feltrinelli's sub-series of feminist works entitled *Gender* in their "Elementi" series. The word for "gender" is currently translated as *genere*, but the original English word is also used.

14 Costa-Zalessow, Zambon, De Nicola and Zannoni, and Cutrufelli, Guacci, and Rusconi have also contributed to this "material" wave of texts. For examples of scholarly analyses of women's works, see Buttafuoco and Zancan's work, as well as those of Frabotta and Kroha.

15 See, for example, Baranski and Vinall and Benedetti, Hairston, and Ross. Zancan also contains a section on women's role in male-authored works. Ryan-Scheutz provides an example of an analysis of the female presence in male narratives specifically in Pasolini's cinema, and Amberson's analysis of Italian Modernism outlines the importance of gender ideology within it. Re ("Passion and Sexual Difference"), Stewart-Steinberg, Ruth Ben-Ghiat, and Spackman (*Fascist Virilities*) provide examples of historically based gender analyses of narrative and ideology, the first two devoted to liberal Italy and the second two devoted to Fascism.

16 On Neera as *trasandata* ("shabby"), see Arslan (*Dame* 97).
17 As Philippe Hamon emphasizes, Lukács's "problematic character," as elaborated in his early work *The Theory of the Novel* (written in 1916–20, but translated into English, French, and Italian only in the 1950s and 1960s), is "inspirée des analyses hégeliennes de la 'conscience malheureuse'" (10n4; inspired by the Hegelian analyses of the "unhappy consciousness"). Hegel's unhappy consciousness, which he detailed in his *Phenomenology of Spirit*, is one of the dialectic phases of experience, a divided state experienced by the individual in which the division is both within the self and between the self and society.
18 One of the limits of Lukács's analysis of characters lies in his "attachment" to characters as individuals, as centres of consciousness whose intellectual physiognomy needs to be fully presented in the novel. In his mature, more rigidly Marxist phase (in *The Historical Novel*, for example), he rejected the modern novels of Dos Passos and Joyce and also of naturalism, in the former case for their disengagement from providing fully executed portrayals of their characters and in the latter case for their inability to elevate characters' portrayals to "typicality," that is, to turn the novel into an epistemological tool.

Chapter One

1 Manzoni (*The Betrothed* 171).
2 The translations of the critical sources and of *Fermo e Lucia* are mine. The translations from Manzoni's *The Betrothed* are Bruce Penman's.
3 In his coeval book, Girardi offers a similar – but not as analytically detailed – apprehension of Gertrude's role in the novel, arguing that Gertrude and her story are "espressioni di un sistema narrativo diverso da quello che governa il romanzo nel suo assieme" (150; expressions of a narrative system that is different from the one governing the novel).
4 See Introduction, p. 18.
5 See Bernstein (165–75) for a discussion of the problematic individual as presented by Lukács.
6 This title appears only in an 1822 letter written by Ermes Visconti to Gaetano Cattaneo. It was never authenticated by Manzoni (Nigro xliii).
7 After completing the first draft on 17 September, Manzoni began to revise it for publication. He made so many corrections working on the galleys of the first eight chapters that he completely rewrote the following parts, reorganizing the entire novel. The first edition of *I promessi sposi* (dated 1826) was published between 1825 and 1827 and distributed in 1827. The second

and final edition of *I promessi sposi*, with revisions that were more linguistic and stylistic than structural, was published in 1840. For a recounting of the writing and editorial history of *I promessi sposi*, see Nigro's excellent "nota critico-filologica" in his edition of Manzoni's novels, Manzoni, *I romanzi*.

8 Nigro's "I Meridiani" edition of the novels – as its title, *I romanzi* (*The Novels*) implies – chooses to explicitly consider them as separate novels, rather than a single creative idea. In his "biography" of the novel, Toschi takes the distinction between the different versions even further. He suggests that Manzoni initially considered *Fermo e Lucia* to be a composition distinct from *I promessi sposi* and that it was only retrospectively that he considered it a "minuta," a first draft of the following versions. This second perspective would amount to a "storicizzazione della propria esperienza ...: l'obiettivo era presentare come un tutt'uno la propria vicenda dal 1821 al 1842, ed anche oltre" (64; historicization of his own experience ...: the goal was to present as a single process his own creative history [*vicenda*] from 1821 to 1842, and even beyond).

9 Alberto Chiari and Fausto Ghisalberti published the full text of *Fermo e Lucia* for the first time in 1954, in Mondadori's seven-volume "Classici Italiani" collection *Tutte le opere di Alessandro Manzoni*. In his essay "Le testimonianze autografe plurime," Dante Isella commented on the "sommarietà" (27; summariness) of this edition and on its corroboration, maintained ever since, of the illusion of *Fermo e Lucia* as "un testo oggettivamente certo" (28; an objectively certain text), something that *Fermo e Lucia* never was. Notwithstanding its philological imprecisions, the Chiari-Ghisalberti edition has the merit of making the text of *Fermo e Lucia* publicly available and of promoting a better critical understanding of Manzoni's writing method. Many studies have been devoted to the *officina* (the "workshop") of the novel. An impressive number of these look at the linguistic revision from *Fermo e Lucia* to *I promessi sposi* (see, for example, Nigro and Paccagnini 1379–80). Another group has investigated the Italian and European sources of the novel and their influence on its three versions (one example being Getto's investigation, which provides an incomparable genealogical analysis of Gertrude's character). A smaller group has looked at the thematic and formal differences between the texts: Isella, for example, applies "critica delle varianti" to the novel and calls for a new critical edition (27–31). Mazza examines the *officina* of the novel in its three versions (1823, 1827, 1840) by juxtaposing passages from the three texts. Varese examines Manzoni's evolution as an author from *Fermo e Lucia* to his last nonfictional writings with respect to the multiplicity

inherent in his ideology and poetics. De Robertis devotes an essay in his book to "Le primizie del romanzo." Raimondi's books contribute to the analyses of both the sources and the laboratory of the novel (including valuable insights about specific characters). In 1985, the proceedings of a national conference entitled *Fermo e Lucia: Il primo romanzo del Manzoni* (Colombo) captured the different critical tendencies. In addition to Getto's and Raimondi's contributions, two recent books by the Italian scholars Girardi and Piero Alberti analyse the novel's characters. Their interests are only tangential to mine: Girardi has an extremely traditional concept of characters, and although Alberti attempts a theoretical excursus on characters in the first four pages of his introduction and subsequently devotes individual paragraphs to at least fourteen characters, he never engages in a study of the character of Gertrude. Jones and McDonald Carolan provide the only two studies that deal explicitly with Manzoni's novel from the standpoint of gender ideology – and, in McDonald Carolan's case, of feminist literary criticism. A gender-focused critical approach is, not surprisingly, not even mentioned in Nigro and Paccagnini's otherwise very useful and detailed "Percorsi bibliografici" integrated in the Meridiani edition of the novels. For a detailed history of scholars' discovery of the first drafts of the novel, see Toschi. For a summary of twentieth-century critiques, with an emphasis on Catholic readings, see Parisi.

10 I quote *Fermo e Lucia* from Manzoni, *I romanzi* (2002), and Manzoni, *I promessi sposi* (1999). In his introductory essay to a new (1985) edition of *Fermo e Lucia*, Sergio Romagnoli describes it as a novel organized by Manzoni in "blocchi … quasi che egli aggiungesse romanzo a romanzo" (xiii; blocks … as if he were adding novel to novel).

11 The narrator of *I promessi sposi* eloquently compares this handling of the characters to an attempt by Manzoni's own son to gather his guinea pigs: "un caro fanciullo … più volte affaccendato sulla sera a mandare al coperto un suo gregge di porcellini d'India … [a]vrebbe voluto fargli andar tutti insieme al covile; ma era fatica buttata: uno si sbandava a destra, … un altro, due, tre ne uscivano a sinistra, da ogni parte. Dimodochè, dopo essersi un po' impazientito, s'adattava al loro genio, spingeva prima dentro quelli ch'eran più vicini all'uscio, poi andava a prender gli altri, a uno, a due, a tre, come gli riusciva. Un gioco simile ci convien fare co' nostri personaggi" (163; "a nice, bright little boy … doing his best, as evening falls, to round up his little herd of guinea pigs … [h]e would like to get them all trotting into the pen together; but that's hopeless. One breaks away to the right, … another one – or two, or three – dash off to the left – or all over the place. After a little impatience he adapts himself to their

methods, and begins by pushing inside those who happen to be nearest to the pen, and then goes to fetch the others, singly, or two or three at a time, as best he can. We have to play much the same game with our characters" trans. Penman 224).

12 I do not analyse here the full extent to which the episodes connected to the *monaca* were reduced between *Fermo e Lucia* and *I promessi sposi.* For a detailed account, see Colombo ("La monaca di Monza") and Varese.

13 Penman's translation is less literal: "the widow replied with some information about the Signora which explained many things that had been puzzling Lucia" (697); "she went to find out what had happened to her previous protectors" (698). I have translated the passages literally to show the repeated use of "thing."

14 For an analysis of the relationship between Manzoni and the Gothic novel, see also Farnetti's "Patologie del romanticismo" (360–2).

15 Introduction, p. 1.

16 In his analysis of the chapters devoted to the nun's story, Getto writes of "quella tendenza, propria dei capitoli del *Fermo* e pienamente superata nei *Promessi Sposi,* al romanzo *terrifiant* o *noir*" (77; that trend, typical of the chapters in *Fermo* and fully overcome in *I promessi sposi,* towards the *terrifiant,* or *noir,* novel). Describing the novel in general, Romagnoli adds that "*Fermo e Lucia* concede più che *I Promessi Sposi* alle tecniche del romanzesco e ne accetta gli ingredienti d'orrore, d'intrigo, di perversione e le astuzie della *suspense*" (Manzoni, *Fermo e Lucia* xvii; *Fermo e Lucia* concedes more than *I promessi sposi* to the techniques of the "romanzesco" [a word that can translate as "novelistic," "romantic," or "fantastic" and here indicates the "spectacular" tendencies of the novel]. It accepts its ingredients of horror, intrigue, perversion, and the ruses of *suspense*).

17 Dombroski analyses this same passage in "Reforming the Monster" (250).

18 The English passages are Jones's quotations of Wellek and Warren. Jones also quotes Northrop Frye's analysis of the "dark heroine": "as a rule passionate, haughty, plain, foreign or Jewish" (94).

19 See also Pozzi's analysis of the beauty canon.

20 Commenting on this same image, Dombroski wrote, "In *Fermo e Lucia,* Geltrude seems to have emerged from the mysterious and satanic atmosphere of the gothic novel" ("Reforming the Monster" 249).

21 See also Spackman's *Decadent Genealogies,* esp. 160–8.

22 As found, for example, in Freidson.

23 And vice versa: myths degenerate into fictions, and these fictions hold such organizational power that they are conceived as true, as *the* truth. The assumption of de Lauretis's study, in both Lotman's premises and the

conclusions de Lauretis draws, might succumb to the same mythologizing temptation she denounces, that of a tendency to universalize that does not do justice to the heterogeneity of narrative cultures and procedures. To borrow Natalie Zemon Davis's formulation, written in the context of women's history, "we would do better to use these polarities only when our [historical] *narrative* evidence supports them, and not assume that they always represent the fundamental meanings that society sees in the sexes" (91).

24 For a discussion of women as commodities, see Irigaray.

25 Manzoni's irony is analysed, for example, by Spinazzola. However, Spinazzola's conception of irony is so broad that it encompasses humour, satire, caricature, and the grotesque – practically every narrative play with the literality of the text.

26 To my knowledge, this occurrence of the term "ironico" has not been commented upon by any critic (including Dombroski, who called the first article he devoted to Gertrude's role within the novel "The Irony of Self-Discovery"). Getto noted that this line represents a "sostituzione attenuata della frase più cruda che si legge nella prima stesura" (90n95; "a substitution that tones down the harshest sentence we read in the first draft") but did not elaborate specifically on the unique appearance of "ironico."

27 McDonald Carolan analyses Gertrude's role in the novel in the light of the "repudiation of the imagination" (81) that, in her view, characterizes her story. She argues that an analysis of *I promessi sposi* in this context "confirm[s] the standard presentation of female desire squashed by male power, the annihilation of female self-determination at the hands of a male writer" (79). While I agree that annihilation is at work in Gertrude's case, I consider this process to be only one side of the dialectics defining Gertrude's character, one that cannot be said to completely succeed. Indeed, McDonald Carolan's own conclusions entrust the character of Gertrude with a highly active – if "merely" symbolic – role rather than a passive one. McDonald Carolan establishes an analogy between Gertrude's "repudiation of the imagination" and that of the later Manzoni, as the author of *Del romanzo storico*: she believes both "condemn … imaginative powers," so that her story as such can be viewed as a momentous "critique of the nexus of fact and fiction, history and romance" (81).

28 For a discussion of the ascetic practices of seventeenth-century nuns, see Matthews Grieco.

29 There is, to be sure, a difference between Foucault's understanding of the body as a surface to be written upon – he presupposes an "essence" preceding the inscriptions – and Grosz's "fictionalized" body (*Volatile Bodies* 118), where the body does not exist prior to the social practices that shape it.

30 Getto was one of several critics who pointed out that Manzoni's representation of Gertrude "sorvola sulla conversione e sulla penitenza che la realtà storica pur non mancava di proporgli" (95; glosses on the conversion and the penance that historical reality nevertheless offered him). Guglielminetti writes of Manzoni's "rifiuto di fare della Monaca di Monza un'eroina sacra" (153; refusal to turn the *Monaca* into a holy heroine). Conversely, in a brief religious reading of this character, Freidson finds an elaborately allegorical explanation of the ending, because otherwise, she says, in its utter lack of transcendental meaning, it would come across as a "weak and inconclusive bit of patchwork" (32).

31 Penman's translation – "without endangering her life" – is milder than the literal translation, "without taking her life."

Chapter Two

1 An earlier version of this chapter was published in *The Italianist* in 2008, under the name "Gendered Quests: Analysis, Revelation, and the Epistemology of Gender in Neera's *Teresa*, *Lydia*, and *L'indomani*."

2 Anna Zuccari was born in Milan in 1846 and spent her childhood in Lombardy (Casalmaggiore and Caravaggio). She married Adolfo Radius in 1871. In 1875, under the Horatian pseudonym Neera, she began writing short stories and articles for various magazines and soon thereafter full-length novels. Her peak period of production was the decade from 1880 to 1890, during which she published the three novels *Teresa* (1886), *Lydia* (1887), and *L'indomani* (1889), conceived as a cycle of naturalistic (à la Zola) inspiration. She also co-authored the *Dizionario d'igiene per le famiglie* with physiologist Paolo Mantegazza (1881) and published several collections of essays, including *Le idee di una donna*, which was popular for its anti-feminist stances, in 1903. Neera was quite famous during her lifetime and was reviewed and befriended by Luigi Capuana, Matilde Serao, the feminist Ersilia Majno, and Benedetto Croce, among others. She died in 1918. Her poems and the autobiography she wrote in the last year of her life, *Una giovinezza del secolo XIX*, were published posthumously in 1919. In 1943, Croce edited a copious anthology of her works, entitled *Neera*, for Garzanti.

3 Catherine Ramsey-Portolano reports that, according to Arslan, Neera herself referred to these novels "in several unpublished letters as a 'ciclo della fanciulla'" (359; cycle of the young woman).

4 "[T]he fundamental form-determining intention of the novel is objectivized as the psychology of the novel's heroes: they are seekers" (Lukács 60).

Heroes – conjugated in the masculine in Lukács's text – embody and confirm the structural restlessness of the novel and its quest for meaning; the novel is, in Lukács's words, "the art-form of virile maturity" (71).

5 See Bassanese for a similar reading of Sibilla Aleramo's fictional memoir *Una donna*.

6 Two other interesting contributions to the literature about the female Bildungsroman can be found in Fraiman and in Summerfield and Downward.

7 Two of the scholars who are more invested in reassessing the importance of Neera's work are Arslan and Folli. Arslan edited the most recent editions of *Teresa* (1995 and 2009) together with Gian Luca Baio, and she published an edition of Neera's short stories and her private correspondence with Benedetto Croce, among other works, together with Folli (Arslan and Folli). For other analyses of Neera's works, see Finucci, Folli ("Le arpe Eolie" and *Penne leggère*), Kroha (esp. 67–98), Wood (esp. 26–39), and Boylan. The most recently published volume on Neera is the collection *Rethinking Neera* (2010), edited by Mitchell and Ramsey-Portolano.

8 On this point, also see Kroha, Pierobon ("La diversità del femminile"), and Finucci. Mettifogo devoted a thoughtful chapter of her dissertation to Neera's *trittico* and an appraisal of her anti-feminist essays in light of her more progressive stance in these novels. The translations of critical sources (with the exception of Foucault and Cavarero) and of *Lydia* and *L'indomani* are mine. The translation of *Teresa* is Martha King's.

9 All references in Italian are to the 1995 Periplo edition. The English text is from Martha King's translation. Because the passage quoted here is omitted in Martha King's translation, the translation is mine.

10 The unborn baby is marked by default as male (a *fratellino*) during the pregnancy.

11 Ceserani and De Federicis write that "il modello *letterario* dell'amore romantico si diffonde largamente e rapidamente … [esso] diviene *modello di comportamento*" (the *literary* model of romantic love spreads widely and quickly … [it] becomes a *pattern of behavior*). They also explain that such a model "si diffonde, gradatamente, in tutti gli strati sociali. Gli strati sociali più bassi palpitano, accanto a quelli più alti … per il dramma paterno e la seduzione di Gilda, casta e pura, nel *Rigoletto*" (754–5; spreads, gradually, through all social strata. The lower social strata palpitate, next to the highest … for the paternal drama and the seduction of chaste and pure Gilda in *Rigoletto*).

12 For a discussion of the theme of femininity throughout Freud's works, see Brennan.

13 On the theme of hysteria and narrative, see also Beizer.

14 For example, Boylan, reading the novel in light of Kroha's thoughtful analysis, argues that "even in the unconventional step she takes of going to the now broken Orlandi, she sacrifices herself for the sake of a man and places herself once again in the role of caretaker" (458). Morandini says of the finale, "Teresa arriva a lasciare l'ambiente, a sfidarne l'opinione, ma questo finale quasi si dissocia dal suo modo di essere tanto da sembrare improbabile" (16; Teresa gets to leave her environment, defying the opinion of others, but this ending almost dissociates itself from her way of being, so much so that it appears improbable), an opinion that Baldacci discusses in similar terms in his foreword to the Einaudi edition of the novel ("Nota Introduttiva," xi). For Folli, Egidio's last letter "apre una storia apparentemente antitetica all'altra, all'insegna di un ordine di cui la nuova Teresa è portatrice" ("Le arpe Eolie" 112; opens a story seemingly antithetical to the other, in the name of an order that is carried forward by the new Teresa), while Finucci argues that "Neera is not granting Teresa a wish-fulfilling, consolatory fantasy after a soporific life, but some mature parity with a man" (236).

15 De Giorgio confirms that women's strong presence in the teaching profession by the beginning of the twentieth century, "present from the north to the south of the country, all the way to the most remote villages," began precisely with the generation personified by Teresa's sister: "[i]n 1901 Italian female teachers are 62,643 … they are born in little more than a generation" (464). For more about the character of Ida in the novel, see Finucci and Boylan (453 and 458–9).

16 As Finucci has observed, *Teresa*'s ending "is in literary kinship" (236) with *Jane Eyre*'s, that is, with Jane's return to her master and lover, Rochester, now blind and invalid, in Charlotte Brontë's 1847 novel. *Teresa*'s ending similarly portrays a weakening of the masculine position in order to allow a more egalitarian relationship between the sexes. Just as "Jane … appears to grow strong, because those around her diminish or die" (Chase 78), Teresa becomes a mobile, active subject as a consequence of her parents' death, her brother's weakened social position (he impregnates and subsequently marries an innkeeper's daughter), and Egidio's immobilization.

17 Famously, the founding epistemological grid of Western philosophy was formulated by Aristotle. As Lydia Lange explains, "Since Aristotle ranked animals according to amount of vital heat, the female was identified at the start as a notch below the male in the graduated differentiation of animals" (9–10). The grid in *Lydia* inverts the poles of this standard, associating Calmi's rational masculinity with coldness. Such an alternative

grid is influenced by a Romantic vision in which passion – that is, warmth – is highly valued in both genders, at least as far as matters of love are concerned.

18 For a discussion of the association between hermaphrodites and fin-de-siècle active women, see Re's excellent analysis of post-Unification gendering practices in "Passion and Sexual Difference" (esp. 180).

19 The plot of this heiress's story, and of the treachery prepared by her best friend, recalls the central part of Isabel Archer's story in Henry James's *The Portrait of a Lady* (published in 1881, five years earlier than *Teresa* and six years earlier then *Lydia*. I mention *Teresa*'s and *Lydia*'s thematic connections with Anglophone novels not only to point to the possible direct influence of the latter, showing where female authors such as Neera, in Italy, could find inspirational narrative models to draw upon, but also more generally, to recall that the literary discussion of women's social roles and the possibilities for self-determination was increasingly relevant in many Western countries, from *Madame Bovary* (1856–7) in France to *Anna Karenina* (1878) in Russia. In this sense, Neera's fiction fits neatly within a European panorama increasingly interested in women as social and literary subjects.

20 The presence of a doctor is fundamental, for example, in Igino Ugo Tarchetti's novel *Fosca* (1869). He acts as a Cupid-like figure for the protagonists, and he entangles the discourse of science with that of love. As the male protagonist explains, for example, "più che il racconto di una passione d'amore, io faccio forse qui la diagnosi di una malattia" (Tarchetti 22; "more than the story of a passionate affair, what I offer is perhaps the diagnosis of an illness"; trans. Venuti 8). In Aleramo's *Una donna*, the doctor has a role similar to the one in *Teresa*, during and following the birth of the protagonist's son: he is a male individual who, aside from his professional role, reveals a spiritual proximity with the protagonist (Aleramo 67 and 72). For the relationship between Neera and positivism (and between Neera and Capuana) see Ramsey-Portolano as well as Arslan's discussion of Neera's historical and ideological context (*Dame* 87–98, esp. 92–5). Both scholars discuss Neera's interest in positivistic and naturalistic ideological trends, on the one hand, and idealistic and symbolist influences, on the other, the former interests being more apparent in her writings up until the early 1890s and the latter becoming prevalent in her later work.

21 Lydia witnesses a scene of intimacy between the baroness and Keptsky earlier in the novel (148–9), but she chooses to forget rather than to try to understand. The imagery of veiling is eloquent in immediately signalling the non-revelatory nature of this scene: "le pupille le si velarono,

le si piegarono le gambe e così, senza sapere il perché, ... si lasciò sdrucciolare lungo lo stipite dell'uscio" (149; her pupils veiled themselves, her legs bent and so, without knowing why, ... she let herself slip along the doorpost). The second time around, Calmi's presence leaves her unable to disavow what she hears.

22 De Giorgio writes that "dal 1871 al 1951 circa il 20% delle donne che abitano nelle grandi città e che hanno raggiunto la fine del loro periodo produttivo sono nubili" (348; from 1871 to 1951, about 20% of women who live in big cities and who have reached the end of their productive life are unmarried).

23 "Bazza a chi tocca" today has a uniquely negative connotation (as a synonym of "peggio per lui" [all the worse for him]) but it is attested by the Tommaseo and Bellini *Dizionario della lingua italiana* to have had the meanings "earning," "luck," "success," and "abundance of choice" at the turn of the century, which might better correspond to the notion of randomness evoked in this passage.

24 In several of her essays, Neera endorsed a much more triumphant portrayal of maternity. Her 1881 entry on *maternità* for the *Dizionario d'igiene per le famiglie*, co-written with Paolo Mantegazza, is centred on an emphatic message to new mothers: "Siete persuase che compite in questo momento la missione primissima della donna, che toccate l'apogeo della vostra grandezza, che mai in nessuna circostanza sarete così, come ora, collocate nella prima gerarchia degli esseri viventi?" (221; Are you convinced that you are at this moment accomplishing the very first mission of woman, that you are touching the pinnacle of greatness, and that never again, under any circumstances, will you be placed, as you are now, first in the hierarchy of the living?). The message is that maternity is women's first and most important function, yet Neera's rhetorical question, paradoxically, also invites an oppositional reading: that woman's social value is uniquely connected to her physiological functions, and once her reproductive duty is depleted, she will be declassed back to a second-class status. For an account of the relationship between Neera and Mantegazza, see Arslan and Ganazzoli.

25 In her chapter on Neera, Mettifogo considers this revelation to be authentically veil-ripping and concludes that "[m]aternity offers the only possible consolation in this dismal reality" (193). However, maternity itself should also be understood as ideologically manipulated by the social (and narrative) system in which Marta finds herself.

26 Neera's preface to the 1909 edition of the novel is unpaginated; this quotation comes from the second page of the preface.

27 As Neera relates in her preface to the 1909 edition of the novel, George Hérelle insisted they close the novel with the penultimate chapter (with Marta falling into her mother's arms), and she answered by withdrawing permission for the translation. In several unpublished letters, she replied to Hérelle's criticisms of the last chapter, quoted above, by emphasizing its absolute structural necessity vis-à-vis idealism and morality and writing that the novel, if stripped of its last chapter, would be "un poème de monstres" (a poem of monsters; in French in the original; letter by Neera to Hérelle, 15 November 1899, quoted in Folli, "Le arpe Eolie" 104). For a recounting of the attempt at a translation, see Folli's "Le arpe Eolie" and Arslan's *Dame, galline e regine* (117–35); however, their interpretation of the episode differs substantially from mine.

28 Freud discusses the primal scene theme in "From the History of an Infantile Neurosis ('Wolf Man')," among other texts. In her preface to *Lydia,* Azzolini assesses these recurrent scenes in the trilogy as topical, fundamental to the novel's development. She considers the final revelation in Lydia to be not only a "topical scene" (12) but also a previous revelation: during a visit to her friend Eva, Lydia spots red marks on her friend's arms, possibly traces of Eva's interrupted love encounter with her husband. Folli highlights the importance of Teresa's revelations as a "movement from false knowledge (illusions, readings, social conventions, family prohibitions) to the true one" (*Penne leggère* 108).

Chapter Three

1 Most of the translations of the primary and secondary sources in this chapter were provided by my research assistant, Danila Coppola, whose assistance was invaluable.

2 "[T]here occurs an event which cannot be explained by the laws of this same familiar world. The person who experiences the event must opt for one of two possible solutions: either he is the victim of an illusion of the senses, of a product of the imagination – and laws of the world then remain what they are; or else the event has indeed taken place, it is an integral part of reality – but then this reality is controlled by laws unknown to us. Either the devil is an illusion, an imaginary being; or else he really exists, precisely like other living beings – with this reservation, that we encounter him infrequently. *The fantastic occupies the duration of this uncertainty*. Once we choose one answer or the other, we leave the fantastic for a neighboring genre, the uncanny or the marvelous" (Todorov, *The Fantastic* 25; emphasis mine).

3 I quote from the 1980 Garzanti edition of Verga's *Le novelle*, a collection that gathers all of Verga's stories.

4 "Addentellato" is a fascinating architectural term. It indicates, literally, "quella serie di risalti che si lasciano in alcun lato del muramento per potervi collegare nuovo muro" (Tommaseo and Bellini; the series of ridges that are left in any side of a wall to be able to connect a new wall to it).

5 For an analysis of sadism in narrative, see Mulvey as well as de Lauretis's chapter on "Desire in Narrative" in *Alice Doesn't*.

6 My analysis of the housewife's "spectral" return at the end of the next chapter, pp. 141–2, provides a lengthier reflection on the spectrality of ideology.

7 At the end of the sixth chapter, as Luciano ends his account of the first part of the baroness's legend, following Matilde's exclamation "E' una storia spaventosa!" (It's a frightening story!), he takes pains to distance present from the legend: "'Una storia la quale non sarebbe più possibile oggi che i mariti ricorrono ai tribunali, o alla peggio si battono'; rispose Luciano ridendo" (110; "A story that could not be possible now that the husbands turn to the courts, or in the worst case duel"; Luciano laughingly answered).

8 Farnetti also suggests that with this "estrema, isolata postilla … l'autore ottiene, per esclusiva virtù di struttura, l'effetto di una inquietante e ideale continuità, inducendo nel lettore già emotivamente placato dalla conclusione della vicenda una reazione estrema e inattesa, approdante a uno stato di irrisolto turbamento" (*Il giuoco del maligno* 150; "extreme, isolated note … the author achieves, exclusively by virtue of the structure, the effect of a disturbing and ideal continuity. This causes the reader, who was already emotionally soothed by the end of the story, to have an extreme and unexpected reaction, arriving at a state of unresolved disturbance).

9 The novel, dated 1878, was printed and distributed before Christmas 1877 (De Gubernatis 1879, quoted in Benatti 141). Quotations from the novel are from the 2001 Interlinea edition, edited by Benatti and Bermani.

10 It should be noted, at the same time, that endings are often problematic for female writers of this generation. Arslan, for example, remarks in a study of Neera's work that "in diverse novelle la parte più debole [è] proprio la conclusione" (*Dame* 110; in several short stories the weakest part [is] really the conclusion. This is hardly surprising, given the generic and ideological constraints under which female writers operated. In most instances, they found it impossible to bring to their logical conclusions the very premises that they had laid out for their female characters.

11 On the relationship between Marchesa Colombi and Verga, and with Nedda in particular, see Genevois, esp. 64–8.

12 In an analysis influenced by Zambon, Barbarulli and Brandi also write that in the conclusion, Nanna "[accetta] la sua situazione operando una scelta consapevole" (42; [accepts] her situation and makes a conscious choice). Genevois reads it in terms of a coherent "évolution psychologique personnelle" (71; personal psychological evolution).

13 Other traits of the ideal woman, as envisaged by Gaudenzio, are described with the words "[I]l bello ideale era arabo o sanscrito per lui. Ammirava le spalle tarchiate, i fianchi sporgenti, le gambe grosse come colonne, i petti turgidi da squarciare il corsetto" ([T]he ideal beauty was Greek or Sanskrit for him. He admired square shoulders, protruding flanks, legs as thick as columns, a bosom so turgid as to rip the corset) and "contadinotte massicce che scoppiano di salute" (21; massive countrywomen bursting with health).

14 Part of the appeal of this story, it must be said, lies in the ironic distance that Marchesa Colombi is able to create between Nanna's perception of Gaudenzio and that of the reader, who is made well aware of Gaudenzio's vanity and pretentiousness very early on.

15 See Bermani's analysis (esp. 132–4) of the changes from the first to the fourth edition for examples of the massive presence of an upper-class narrator addressing her upper-class readers in the first edition, and also for examples of the same class difference between narrator and characters in the final edition – parenthetic interventions such as "la Nanna, co' suoi pregiudizi da Contadina, ebbe un istante di repulsione" (quoted in Bermani 134; *In risaia* 110; Nanna, with her countrywoman bias, momentarily felt revulsion).

16 I thank Francesca Parmeggiani for pointing out that the author's decision to append a sequel to *In risaia* might have originated precisely from the opinion that De Gubernatis and other book reviewers shared about the unrealistic ending. From this perspective, Marchesa Colombi's choice of continuing the story along a folkloric line might be read as her very personal response to the accusations of a fairy-tale ending – an ironic response to be sure, as befits as ironic an author as she.

17 As Benatti also reminds us in her overview of the critical reactions to the novel, Gaudenzio (as portrayed in *In risaia*) was by far the most popular character, the one most praised by (male) critics – e.g., as "uno dei personaggi più vivi e più veri che da un pezzo abbiamo trovato nei romanzi italiani" (anonymous reviewer from *Gazzetta letteraria*, Benatti 138; one of the most lively and real characters that we have found in the Italian novel in a long time). It is striking to see this narrative parable close with Gaudenzio shaking from fear every time his story is told.

Chapter Four

1 Paola Masino published her first collection of stories, *Decadenza della morte*, in 1931, with a preface by Massimo Bontempelli. Along with her first two novels, she wrote short stories, later collected in *Racconto grosso e altri* (1941). In September 1938, the publication of her story "Fame" ("Hunger") in the first issue of the magazine *Le grandi firme* was responsible for the magazine's discontinued publication (enforced by Mussolini himself). As Manetti explains in the biography she wrote for the volume *Paola Masino*, "I rapporti col regime cominciano a deteriorarsi" (48; The relationship with the regime [began] to deteriorate). Although conceived between 1938 and 1939 (and published in fifteen episodes in the periodical *Tempo* between 16 October 1941 and 22 January 1942), her third novel *Nascita e morte della massaia* was only published in 1945 (this is further discussed in the last section of this chapter, "A Reflection on the Author's Postface," 204). After the war, Masino published a collection of poetry, *Poesie*, at which point, apart from a libretto she wrote for a lyrical drama in 1956, "[her] creative life virtually ended" (Gieri 199). From then on, she was the devoted curator of Bontempelli's work and, after his death in 1960, of his literary legacy and archive. In 1995, Rusconi published a posthumous anthology of her work, *Io, Massimo e gli altri: Autobiografia di una figlia del secolo*.

2 Virtually ignored when it was published in 1945, the *Massaia* was reprinted by Bompiani in 1970, with a preface by Garboli, and then again in 1982, in a new edition by the feminist publisher La Tartaruga, with an introduction by Giacomoni. The most recent edition is from 2009. Vittori edited a posthumous collection of her short stories from the 1930s and 1940s (*Colloquio di notte*) in 1994. The literature on Masino's last novel (as well as on the rest of her work) is not extensive: in 2001 the Fondazione Mondadori, which holds many of Masino's papers, published a volume devoted to the writer. Ben-Ghiat discusses *Nascita e morte della massaia* in the fifth chapter of her book *Fascist Modernities*. In her 2002 entry about Masino for the *Dictionary of Literary Biography: Italian Prose Writers, 1900–1945*, Gieri lists only four articles about Masino – of these, Re's "Fascist Theories of 'Woman' and the Construction of Gender" is the central reference. However, there has since been a steady increase in the scholarly output about Masino. To mention just a few texts (D'Ortenzi offers many other useful bibliographic references), Rozier published the first comprehensive monograph about Masino's works (*Il mito e l'allegoria*) in 2004, and Re has written two more articles. Several dissertations are

devoted to her work, including dissertations by Boero and Rorandelli. Rorandelli also published a thoughtful essay on the theme of maternity in Masino's work. In 2009, Feltrin-Morris translated *Nascita e morte della massaia* into English (*Birth and Death of the Housewife*). For an analysis of women's discourses during the Fascist regime, see Pickering-Iazzi's collection *Mothers of Invention* (which also contains Re's first essay) and her preface to *Unspeakable Women*, an anthology of texts by women from the interwar years (1–22).

The translations of secondary sources in this chapter were prepared by my wonderful research assistant, Danila Coppola.

3 Masino began writing *Nascita e morte della massaia* in 1938. As Ben-Ghiat synthesizes, 1938 was "[a] year marked by Hitler's takeover of Austria, the Munich crisis, the Kristallnacht pogrom, and the onset of the Italian anti-Jewish laws" (158). The increasingly oppressive regime imposed sanctions against Masino's work, along with the work of Bontempelli, whose Europeanist beliefs came to be regarded as starkly opposed to Fascist orthodoxy. When Bontempelli was sent to confinement, Masino left for Venice with him. Their new domicile in a Patrician palace on the Canal Grande provoked housekeeping anxieties for Masino. She was in charge of the residence's upkeep, and in a letter to her sister Valeria she wrote, "[Q]ui c'è la casa da mettere su che vuol dire questo: piedi gonfi e duri, capelli spettinati e color di cenere per la polvere" (*Io, Massimo e gli altri* 80; [H]ere there is the house to set up which means this: swollen and stiff feet, hair in disarray and grey with dust). She seems to have decided to write about it as a therapeutic exercise to banish her domestic obsessions. Yet, sure enough, *Nascita e morte della massaia* is much more than an exorcism of housekeeping phantasms; it is, again in Ben-Ghiat's words, "one of the most incisive critiques of fascist attempts to (re)socialize, militarize, and discipline Italians" (163–4), as well as a very lucid attempt to analyse the restrictions of women's social role in Western society.

4 All quotations and page references are from the 1945 Bompiani edition.

5 Also see Namer for a reading of the trunk as a "figura estrema dell'*emboitement*" (extreme figure of *emboitement*) and as a prelude to "le pattumiere dei genitori beckettiani" (182; the garbage of Beckettian parents).

6 The original "uomini," translated by Feltrin-Morris as "mankind," has a specific gendered meaning here, as "men."

7 On the theme of men "snatching out," see also Rorandelli ("*Nascita e morte della massaia* di Paola Masino" 88).

8 Later in the novel the protagonist uses the word "philosopher" to ironically congratulate herself: "Omaggi alla filosofa" (81; My respects to the

philosopher; translation mine, as Feltrin-Morris translates "filosofa" as "philosophy," 75).

9 Even as the novel continues, references to her "trunk" wisdom alternately qualify it as "saggezza istintiva" (44; "instinctive wisdom"; trans. Feltrin-Morris 48), i.e., as originary, and as acquired – "recitare la parte che d'ora in poi mi è stata assegnata è facile. Difficile era quanto avevo conquistato finora, a costo della mia vita, a costo della mia morte" (30; "playing the part I have been assigned from now on is easy. The difficult phase had been conquering what I had conquered, risking my life and my death"; trans. Feltrin-Morris 36) – and also as "quelle possibilità di libero arbitrio che lei credeva, secondo gli insegnamenti della scolastica, appartenessero indiscutibilmente a ogni uomo" (50; "that free will which, in line with the teachings of scholasticism, she believed to be mankind's indisputable prerogative"; trans. Feltrin-Morris 53).

10 The theme of the "masquerade" in the novel also surfaces in a passage during the reception at the *massaia*'s house, when she affirms, "è come se fossi in maschera" (91; "it's as if I were wearing a mask"; trans. Feltrin-Morris 86).

11 A more recent example that exploits this archetype of the thinking woman can be found in Dacia Maraini's *La lunga vita di Marianna Ucria*. Although it is superposed and inextricably intertwined with the pressing theme of childhood (gendered) trauma, Maraini develops the theme of a strong, monadic individuality through the character of Marianna, who is deaf and dumb, and hence isolated from the world, but much more alert and intellectually developed than anyone would suspect.

12 A subsequent reference to a woman who has had to renounce mathematics, with its "aracnei rapporti di giranti piani" (112; "spidery ratios of rotating planes"; trans. Feltrin-Morris 106), could be a clue suggesting that spiderwebs are used to represent knowledge, although the *massaia*'s unpleasant encounter on a train with a lustful ticket inspector who wants a lock of her hair is probably more pertinent. As he draws closer to her, "[p]areva a lei che un ragno con la sua bava trascinante le corresse lungo il filo della schiena, … e rivedeva le notturne tele della sua infanzia" (144; "[s]he felt as if a spider, with its streaming drool, were running along her spine. She … saw again the nightly spider webs of her childhood"; trans. Feltrin-Morris 129). Connected to this second mention of a spider, her nightmares would be the index of a direct, uncensored sexuality, an impulse that is reigned in and domesticated as she enters society. The use of the theme of spiderwebs in connection with the life of the *massaia* may possibly be an intertextual reference to Leon Battista Alberti's *Della famiglia*, in the third book

of which Giannozzo contrasts the traditional association between good (male) housekeepers and ants with the more graphic one portraying male "*massai*" – as they are called – as spiders. Read in this light, the disappearance of the spiderweb imagery at this point in the text would symbolically allude to the *massaia*'s actual imprisonment in a model of domestic management. I am grateful to Albert R. Ascoli, Amyrose Gill, and Sara Russell for pointing out this possible intertextual reference.

13 Lucia Re, who has examined the political references in the home-touring excerpt, points out that "the regime of the home, even in its very physical being, its furniture and layout, turn[s] out to be a reflection of the hierarchy and bureaucracy of the Fascist state" ("Fascist Theories of 'Woman'" 93). See also Ben-Ghiat (165–6). In general, rather than emphasizing the necessity to guard and enhance one's property, the *massaia* points to the internal economy of crime to which both masters and servants end up being subservient: "Se son ladri, io sono in carcere con loro. Criminali e carcerieri vivono nella stessa prigione" (62; "If they're thieves, I'm a prisoner with them. Criminals and their guard live in the same prison"; trans. Feltrin-Morris 60).

14 The most explicit reference scholars have made to the possibly non-evolutionary nature of Masino's text is found in Re's "Fame, cibo e anti-fascismo": "the meaning of the novel goes beyond the typical individual dimension of the bourgeois *Bildungsroman* that recounts the formation and maturation of a single individual and protagonist. The protagonist's hunger is indeed her real and sole 'art,' and means first and foremost the refusal to become the type of individual and above all the type of woman that fascism – and the bourgeois and patriarchal ideology – wanted" (180). Rorandelli insightfully refers to the novel as constituted by a basic dichotomy in which "il corpo e la vita quotidiana della Massaia sono oggetto di una tensione fra una spinta "sovversiva" iniziale ed una "repressiva" successiva ad essa, la quale finisce per avere il predominio" ("*Nascita e morte della massaia* di Paola Masino" 86; the *Massaia*'s body and daily life are the subject of a tension between an initial "subversive" push and a subsequent "repressive" one, which ends up being predominant).

15 This formal shift from novel to drama is only one example of the constant challenge to traditional forms and styles to be found in Masino's text, and it is highly indicative of this writer's idiosyncratic style, of her ability to mix genres and tones.

16 Of course, Zeno is also "the" example of the modern antihero and *inetto*, and his relationship to traditional models of masculinity poses a different, if complementary, set of questions than Masino's *massaia*. Concerning

Zeno (and Pirandello's novelistic *inetti*, or Montale's Arsenio) as antihero, see Biasin (esp. ch. 3). For a historical overview of the *inetto* in both literature and cinema, see Reich (esp. ch. 1).

17 Kenneth Burke approaches conversion in *The Rhetoric of Religion* by pairing it with the contrasting "form of 'turning'" (101) developed by Augustine in his *Confessions*: "perversion." In the *massaia*'s case, what the narrator presents as a conversion is experienced by the protagonist as a perversion, as a negative turning away from her true vocation – thought and speculation – to the mundaneness of household and nationalistic chores.

18 Another example of the narrator's sympathetic side can be found at the beginning of chapter 6, as the *Massaia* multiplies her efforts to become a prominent public figure of womanly virtue: "Da qui cominciano le sofferenze della Massaia vera e propria. Raccontarle? Non raccontiamole. Vogliamo aver pietà di quel trascorrente e pervicace esercito donnesco che in tali torture s'accampa e procede; non gli metteremo ancora sotto gli occhi quanto ha, forse, appena finito di soffrire e già si avvia a sopportare di nuovo" (191; "From this point, the sorrows of the real Housewife began. Shall we recount them? No, we shall not. We want to have mercy on that ephemeral and stubborn army of women who establish and perpetuate these tortures. We will not confront them with what they have just suffered and are about to suffer again"; trans. Feltrin-Morris 165).

19 Re writes, of the references to two wars in the novel, that they are veiled references to, respectively, "la Guerra d'Africa e la Guerra di Spagna" ("Fame, cibo e antifascismo" 169).

20 On the refusal of maternity and its political significance see Rorandelli's cogent analysis ("*Nascita e morte della massaia* di Paola Masino"), explicitly focused on the theme of the "maternal body" in the novel, as well as Rozier's "Motherhood and Femininity."

21 On this point, see also Re's "Women and Censorship in Fascist Italy." For a gripping account of the destruction of Bompiani's typography in the same bombings, see Valentino Bompiani's preface to the *Dizionario Bompiani delle opere e dei personaggi*. A different, yet equally fascinating, case involving material destruction is that of Anna Banti's novel *Artemisia* (1947), whose original manuscript was destroyed in the 1944 bombings of Florence. Banti rewrote the novel thematizing such trauma within the very fabric of the text. The "Nota" ("Author's Note") is unnumbered in the original text. I assigned the page numbers relative to the last page (247) of the novel itself.

22 I am grateful to Rhiannon N. Welch for calling my attention to the parallelism between postface and novel. In *Tempo*, the novel occupies an almost

oxymoronic position as a subversive text within the magazine's otherwise conservative content. The contrast between the magazine's visual advertisements, for example, and Masino's text are at times so strident as to become comical: the *massaia*'s monologue to the sky, in which she states "io credo che il desiderio della morte e del nulla siano un attributo che mi spetta davvero fin dalla nascita" (71; "I believe that the desire for death and nothingness has truly been an attribute of mine ever since I was born"; trans. Feltrin-Morris 68), is printed in *Tempo* next to an advertisement for Bayer's headache drug Gardan. The ad proclaims in big letters that the housewife is "Sempre simpatica" (always likeable), and an insert in the lower part of the image explains in smaller font, "Essa propaga a tutti, ovunque si trovi, la sua gioia di vivere … Il **GARDAN** giova a eliminare i piccoli dolori e i disturbi quotidiani e ripristina subito il solito buon umore" (*Tempo* 159, 13 November 1941, p. 40; She conveys to everybody, everywhere she is, her joy of living … **GARDAN** helps to eliminate little aches and day-to-day nuisances and immediately restores a good mood).

Chapter Five

1 Among the first reviews of the novel, Garboli read *Aracoeli* as undoing the dyad mother/son exalted in *L'isola di Arturo* and *La storia*: "il vecchio schema glorioso (madre/figlio; Nunziata/Arturo; Ida/Useppe) viene lapidato e dato in pasto ai cani perchè ne facciano strazio. La parodia è un autodafé; un'esibizione oscena; il gesto con cui si straccia ciò che abbiamo amato di più" ("Aracoeli" 199; the old glorious pattern (mother/son; Nunziata/Arturo; Ida/Useppe) is stoned and thrown to the dogs so that they can tear it apart. The parody is an *auto-da-fe*, an obscene exhibition, the gesture with which one tears to pieces what one loved most). Together with Garboli's essay, Fortini's review set the ground for a negative – in the sense of nihilistic – assessment of the novel: "*Aracoeli* è un libro definitivo. Non se ne torna indietro … [L]a Morante vuol farci varcare le frontiere oltre le quali nessuna abitazione c'è più; oppure non c'è più quel mondo di libertà e anche di equivoco che viene detto letteratura" (240; *Aracoeli* is a definitive book. There is no way back … Morante wants us to cross borders beyond which there is no home; or there is no more that world of freedom and even of misunderstanding that is called literature). For Fusillo, the main theme in *Aracoeli* is the tragic dismantling of the archaic truth of *barbarie* (barbarism), in terms close to the anthropological catastrophe that Pasolini had denounced years before (111). Although concentrating on the linguistic and stylistic features of Morante's novels, Mengaldo

eventually ventures to say that "forse il tremendo romanzo terminale nega tutto ciò che precede" (12; perhaps this terrible, terminal novel negates all that precedes it). Capozzi ("Sheherazade") emphasizes the continuities between *Aracoeli* and Morante's previous novels but also identifies it as a novel that ultimately denies any possibility of healing life's wounds through literature. Among the recent interventions, the imposing and subtle analysis proposed by Giovanna Rosa in *Cattedrali di carta* confirms a view of the last novel as "la riscrittura 'postuma' e definitiva dell'intera opera morantiana, di cui scopre in figura negativa il significato più autentico" (295; the posthumous and definitive rewriting of the entirety of Morante's works. Of these, it discovers in negative terms its most authentic meaning). Several critics have proposed a more positive interpretation, one that maintains the possibility of a relationship between reality and representation and that proposes an understanding of the novel as not solely devoted to dismantling literary and existential myths. In his preface to the volume *Vent'anni dopo La storia*, De Michelis considers the novel to be coherent with the previous ones in that its message, "tanto inquietante quanto perentorio" (as unsettling as it is peremptory), prescribes that "con tutte le forze bisogna resistere all'orrore del mondo" (8; with all our strengths we need to resist the horror of the world). He quotes Morante directly: "la mia vera speranza era di smuovere – straziandomi – con le mie stesse mani – l'indifferenza totale della terra" (8; my true hope was to shake – tearing myself apart – with my own hands – the complete indifference of the earth). For D'Angeli and Venturi, the pessimism *Aracoeli* expresses about literature is ultimately denied by the novel's very existence and excellence: "E tuttavia il cerchio non si è chiuso ancora, se l'esito di un percorso che dichiara la più assoluta sfiducia nella parola poetica è la grandezza di questo romanzo estremo" (D'Angeli 74; And yet the circle is not yet closed, if the result of a process that declares the most absolute lack of confidence in the poetic word is the greatness of this extreme novel);"la scrittura negata, afferma la sua esistenza proprio nel momento che viene rifiutata" (Venturi 127; the writing that is denied affirms its existence precisely in the moment in which it is rejected). For Marrone and Filippelli, *Aracoeli* is still born out of the unified vision of art and life that Morante had expressed in "Nove domande sul romanzo" ("Nine Questions on the Novel") and in "Pro o contro la bomba atomica" ("For or Against the Atomic Bomb"). Agamben argues for a similar poetic coherence of all of Morante's novels on the basis of her parodic approach to literature. In her 2009 essay on Manuele's distorted vision, West eloquently sums up the debate: "It remains an open question whether the book is fundamentally an expression of defeat of long-held beliefs in the vitalistic, integrative essence of art, no matter how tragic or fractured the content, or a sort of last challenge to the downward, disintegrating pull of age, disillusionment, and the silence of death" (25–6). All translations from secondary sources (and from Morante's works other than her novels) are mine.

2 Although essays on *Aracoeli* commonly begin by lamenting the limited amount of critical literature devoted to the novel, the lament is far from true (unless, of course, one takes *La storia* as the standard for comparison). Among the many contributions devoted to this novel, several essays analyse *Aracoeli* from the point of view of its gender ideology. The most stimulating of these are essays written by Volpi, Poeti, and Giorgio and, although it is not uniquely devoted to the analysis of gender (nor is it invested in a gender reading), Rosa's book-length analysis of Morante's works. See also the edited collection on *Aracoeli, The Power of Disturbance,* especially the editors Fortuna and Gragnolati's own "Between Affection and Discipline." Several analyses of Morante's gender ideology were also written prior to the publication of *Aracoeli* and devoted to her earlier works; of these, the essays by Nozzoli and Pickering-Iazzi ("Designing Mothers") are especially interesting.

3 All quotations are from the Meridiani edition of Morante's works, *Opere,* in two volumes, edited by Garboli and Cecchi. *Aracoeli* is part of the second volume. The translation of *Aracoeli* is by William Weaver.

4 On the theme of seekers in novels, see my discussions of Lukács's theory in the introduction (23–4) and chapter 1 (29, 30, 43, and 52). It should also be noted the novel hints at (at least) another archetypal quest in addition to Ulysses's: Orpheus's descent to the Realm of the Dead to bring Eurydice back.

5 My translation. Weaver's translation, "she could not touch my senses" (81), is inaccurate.

6 My analysis of Aracoeli's character rehearses in part Giorgio's exploration of the novel from the standpoint of its representation of femininity. In her essay, Giorgio emphasizes that, "although the title indicates that Aracoeli is the focus of attention, she exists only in Manuele's discourse: her silence reflects the silenced condition of all mothers in patriarchy" (111). On the one hand, Giorgio sees her initial, natural incarnation as a happy mother as "the reconstruction of a maternal pre-culture or of an alternative maternal culture marginal to patriarchal culture, seen as a site of power and sexual pleasure for both mother and child" (107). On the other, Giorgio reads her subsequent introduction to civilization, as well as the way in which her family silenced her maternal (and sisterly) mourning, as "mutilations

of her femininity" (114) and denials of her subjectivity. Ultimately, Giorgio reads Aracoeli's escape from the house as "an unconscious attempt to rebel against a thwarting way of life and to express her sexuality" (115). Fascinating as such a hypothesis of rebelliousness is, Giorgio recognizes that Aracoeli's gesture is, and remains, "ambiguous" (115). Further in this chapter I explore other textual (and figural) spaces that are arguably more incisively disruptive of patriarchy than the tragedy of femininity embodied by Aracoeli.

7 It has been remarked before that her name, Aracoeli, appears to evoke both the church of Santa Maria in Aracoeli (Ara Coeli) in Rome and the Roman prison of Regina Coeli (see, for example, Capozzi's "Sheherazade" 62). Thus, her very name carries an allusive ambiguity, divided between the angelic and the criminal. On this point also see Di Pascale: "le altezze vertiginose, il Paradiso, e l'abisso infernale sono ugualmente contenuti nel mistero di questa parola: Aracoeli" (287; the dizzy heights, Heaven, and the abyss of Hell are equally contained in the mystery of this word: Aracoeli).

8 The traditional, patriarchal dichotomy between a present mother and an absent father has been analysed by many feminist critics. Coppélia Kahn summarizes Dinnerstein's, Rich's, and Chodorow's research, for example, as engaged in describing "the father-absent, mother-involved nuclear family as creating the gender identities which perpetuate patriarchy and the denigration of women … they present, in effect, a collective vision of how maternal power in the nursery defines gender so as to foster patriarchal power in the public world" (33).

9 In her essay on *Aracoeli*, Serkowska deploys the Platonic myth of androgyny to read Manuele's homosexuality. The reference to the "two halves" myth is in my view more fitting here, in that, in the case of Eugenio and Aracoeli, it is a myth literally endorsed by the text. As I will discuss later, Manuele's homosexuality can be more productively read figurally, i.e., in connection to the narrator's epistemological status.

10 Giorgio touches upon the fact that the novel "challenges Manuele's idea of maternity as an instinct generated by the biological-genetic make-up of being female" (100). She subsequently considers this alternative maternity as naturalized in "humble people from Southern cultures" and "specific to an ethnic group" (101). This naturalization is true in the case of Daniele but not the case of Manuele himself or his father.

11 The custom of adding "Maria" to a male name is not foreign to Italian onomastics. It is nonetheless particularly relevant in this story, in that it institutionalizes and foretells Manuele's gender confusion. As is by now

apparent, the characters' names, as well as the appellations of places, are extremely significant in the novel and very carefully chosen by the author. "Aracoeli" evokes both sanctity and sin (see note 7); "Eugenio Oddone Amedeo" perfectly describes the benign, yet profoundly conservative and patriarchal nature of the narrator's father; and "Emanuele" and its Spanish version "Manuele," in addition to being an homage to the Italian monarchy (see also Paduano 314), are among the traditional signifiers for Jesus Christ. An original contribution on names in *Aracoeli* is Deuber-Mankosky's "Baubo." In terms of toponymy, the narrator's arrival in the municipality of "Almerìa" – which contains within its administrative boundaries both El Almendral and Gergal – confirms the regressive nature of Manuele's journey: the "almeria," that is, the "mirror" he spatially reaches, is clearly connected with the image of originary bliss contained within the "framed mirror" described by Manuele shortly before his arrival in the city (for a discussion of the image of the mirror, see this book's conclusion, pp. 177–82). Finally, the name of El Almendral clearly has an anticlimactic (and parodic) value: as has been remarked, instead of a "field of almond trees" Manuele only finds a bruised, desert landscape (see, for example, Di Pascale 299).

12 My translation. Weaver's "integral substance" does not fully convey the reference to the loss of innocence, of wholesomeness, that the passage evokes.

13 On this novel's use of expressionism as one of the traits that distinguish it from Morante's previous novels, see Rosa (317–21) and Mengaldo. Pischedda and Siddell have correctly pointed out the echoes of Anna Maria Ortese's opening short story in *Il mare non bagna Napoli*, "Un paio di occhiali" ("A Pair of Glasses"), in this episode. Beyond the attempts to prove a direct affiliation, the thematic connection is important by virtue of the shared theme of objective versus subjective vision that is developed with similar intensity in both texts. It might also be worth noting the thematic closeness with Ingeborg Bachmann's short story "Occhi felici" ("Happy Eyes") from her collection *Tre sentieri per il lago*, written in 1972 but only translated into Italian in 1994 (Morante and Bachmann knew each other in the 1960s and 1970s, when Bachmann lived in Rome).

14 Marrone writes that "l'uso strutturale degli occhiali suppone un livello di realtà come miraggio coscientemente messo in scena" (272; the structural use of glasses posits a level of reality as a consciously staged illusion). D'Angeli explains Manuele's putting on and taking off his glasses in hermeneutic terms: taking off the glasses would correspond to passing from *irrealtà* to *realtà* (66), that is, following Morante's own understanding of

these two terms, from "non-authenticity" to "fullness and completeness of life, and the fundamental justification of art" (49). The subjective, glassless approach is, however, described in the novel as no fuller or more complete than the other approach. West cogently focuses on the theme of Manuele's distorted vision by connecting it to the tradition of the European novel, from Don Quixote to Pirandello's Mattia Pascal.

15 In *Purgatorio*, canto 19, Dante's "femina balba" (v. 7) is an old, stuttering woman who parades as a "sweet siren" (v. 19) for Dante and whose spell is broken by the arrival of a lady saint who prods Virgil to intervene. He bares her body, showing Dante her "ventre" (v. 32; belly), and the stench awakens Dante from her spell.

16 See pp. 41–2.

17 Rosa emphasizes that Manuele's description of the female sex in his encounter with the old prostitute is "the first and last in all of Morante's works" (333). On the theme of the fascination with the female sex and on its (ir)representability in novels, see Peter Brooks.

18 The expression "rottame di classe fuori servizio" is ambiguous in the original, and not easily translated. "Classe" can be translated as "social class" or "class/type," or – in "di classe" – as "classy." "Fuori servizio" can refer to a "wreck" (that is William Weaver's choice in the English translation of the novel) or to "class" itself – a "class not in running order" (thus the phrase is translatable as "a wreck belonging to a class not in running order").

19 For the theme of women's bodies as slaughterhouse material, see also one of the passages from Paola Masino's novel that I discussed in chapter 4: the young girl sees "i ventri concavi dei buoi appesi con uncini di ferro alle travi delle macellerie" ("the concave stomachs of oxen hanging from iron hooks on the ceiling beams of the butcher shops") and infers that "anche lei nel suo interno doveva avere qualche cosa di cui il mondo aveva bisogno e che gli uomini, se lei non lo offrisse, le strapperanno" (*Nascita e morte della massaia* 9; "she, too, must have something inside of her that the world needed and that mankind would snatch out of her if she did not offer it willingly"; trans. Feltrin-Morris 20).

20 In *Over Her Dead Body*, Bronfen has argued that "both death and femininity are necessarily constructed by culture and as such always in some sense tropic," that is, they always "serve as ciphers for other values, as privileged tropes" (xi). As her analysis shows, "to represent *over her dead body* signals that the represented feminine body also stands in for concepts other than death, femininity and body – most notably the masculine artist and the community of the survivors" (xi). Her chapters on works

by women writers cogently argue that "these narratives by women writers self-consciously install the cultural paradigm that links femininity with death in the same gesture that they critique it. They simultaneously perform the terms of the production of both woman and death as text so as to duplicitously comply with this convention even as they also resist an identification with this Janus-faced image" (432–3). This is an insight that applies to Morante's work as well as to the works that Bronfen discusses.

21 Pier Paolo Pasolini died during the night of that same 1 November 1975. Several critics have gone so far as to state that Manuele *is* Pasolini. While I think that such a juxtaposition remains rather reductive, in that it does not do justice either to Pasolini or to this novel and does not contribute to a deeper understanding of *Aracoeli,* it is clearly impossible to consider it a simple coincidence. See, for example, Fortini's review of the novel and Siti's essay "Elsa Morante and Pier Paolo Pasolini."

Conclusion

1 Chambers exemplifies this non-linearity of narrative and textual function in the first chapter of *The Writing of Melancholy*, "On Being *Nouveau*," with an analysis of the opening scene of *Madame Bovary*: the entrance of the young Charles Bovary into the classroom as "un *nouveau* habillé en bourgeois" (5) is, at the narrative level, "easily classifiable in the well-known genre of 'schoolday memories'" (6). "But," Chambers continues, "is that all there is to the text? Suppose that, alerted by the parallel between his 'entrance' into the text and the new boy's entrance into the class, ... it should occur to some reader that the text may be figuring itself in this way?" Chambers's analysis brings him to find that through its textual function, the text "raises the question of *nouveauté* or 'newness' – including that of the text itself – in a universe so rigidly structured that everything is always already *classé*, that is, identified *by class*" (7). See also my reference to Chambers in chapter 1, p. 51.

2 The theme of the mirror as the medium for a first identification of and, at the same time, alienation from one's self is reminiscent of Lacan's theory of the "mirror stage," summarized in "Le stade du miroir comme formateur de la fonction du Je": "We have only to understand the mirror stage as an identification, in the full sense that analysis gives to the term; namely, the transformation that takes place in the subject when he assumes an image – whose predestination to this phase-effect is sufficiently indicated by the use, in analytic theory, of the ancient term imago. Here, the first identification is not with the father, but with the false mirror image. This

jubilant assumption of his specular image by the child at the infant stage, still sunk in his motor incapacity and nursling dependence, would seem to exhibit in an exemplary situation the symbolic matrix in which the I is precipitated in a primordial form, before it is objectified in the dialectic of identification with the other, and before language restores to it, in the universal, its function as subject" (2). In Lacan's formulation, the infant gazes at itself in the mirror and finds in the mirror its own reflection, a full, coherent picture of itself that coalesces its previous scattered perceptions and visual experiences into an ideal, unified subjectivity. This experience founds consciousness and subjectivity, but also potentially disrupts it, in that it is founded not on identity but on difference: the child's sense of self is predicated on the distance between the child's firsthand perceptions of itself and the "ideal" image that the mirror sends back to the child. From this standpoint, Manuele's troubles arise from his inability to relinquish his mirror-stage self, that is, to vacate the symbiotic mother-child icon and recognize himself as a separate person from his mother.

3 "*Specchiera*" translates as "mirror," but it refers specifically to a mirror as a piece of furniture, inserted within a frame, or as part of a vanity.

4 For a discussion of the importance of the mirror in literature, and for an analysis of its unsettling power in Luigi Pirandello, see Ascoli: "The mirror, classical figure of resemblance and self-discovery, becomes now [in Pirandello] its opposite, a trope of alienation and otherness, of self-division (as it already was in Ovid's myth of Narcissus)" (36).

Works Cited

Abel, Elizabeth, Marianne Hirsch, and Elizabeth Langland, eds. *The Voyage In: Fictions of Female Development*. Hanover: University Press of New England, 1983.

Agamben, Giorgio. "Parodia: Un concetto per la letteratura italiana da Dante all'Isola di Arturo." *Il Caffè Illustrato* 18 (2004): 74–9.

Ahmed, Sarah. *The Cultural Politics of Emotion*. New York: Routledge, 2004.

– "Willful Parts: Problem Characters or the Problem of Character." *New Literary History* 42.2 (2011): 231–53. http://dx.doi.org/10.1353/nlh.2011.0019

Airoldi Namer, Fulvia. "La terra e la discesa: L'immaginario di Paola Masino." *Otto/Novecento* 3 (2001): 161–86.

Alberti, Leon Battista. *Opere volgari: I Libri della Famiglia: Cena Familiaris: Villa*. Ed. Cecil Grayson. Bari: Laterza, 1960.

Alberti, Piero. *I porcellini d'India e il pastorello: Personaggi dei Promessi Sposi di Manzoni: Fine di un messaggio cattolico*. Rome: Armando, 2001.

Aleramo, Sibilla. *Una donna*. 1906. Milan: Feltrinelli, 2000.

Alighieri, Dante. *Purgatorio: La commedia secondo l'antica vulgata*. Ed. Giorgio Petrocchi. Milan: Mondadori, 1967.

Althusser, Louis. "Ideology and Ideological State Apparatuses (Notes Toward an Investigation)." Trans. Ben Brewster. In *Lenin and Philosophy and Other Essays*, 121–73. London: New Left, 1971.

Amberson, Deborah. *Giraffes in the Garden of Italian Literature: Modernist Embodiment in Italo Svevo, Federigo Tozzi and Carlo Emilio Gadda*. Oxford: Legenda, 2012.

Arendt, Hannah. *The Human Condition*. Chicago: University of Chicago Press, 1958.

Aristotle. *Poetics*. Trans. and ed. Stephen Halliwell. Cambridge: Cambridge University Press, 1995.

Arslan, Antonia. *Dame, galline e regine: La scrittura femminile italiana fra '800 e '900*. Milan: Guerini, 1998.

– "Introduction." In *Teresa*, by Neera, 5–13. 1887. Lecco: Periplo, 1995.

Arslan, Antonia, and Anna Folli. *Il concetto che ne informa: Benedetto Croce e Neera: Corrispondenza (1903–1917)*. Naples: Edizioni Scientifiche Italiane, 1989.

Arslan, Antonia, and Margherita Ganazzoli. "Neera e Paolo Mantegazza: Storia di una collaborazione (con 32 lettere inedite)." *Rassegna della letteratura italiana* 87.1–2 (1983): 102–24.

Ascoli, Albert R. "Mirror and Veil: *Così è (se vi pare)* and the Drama of Interpretation." *Stanford Italian Review VII* 1–2 (1987): 29–46.

Azzolini, Paola. "Preface." In *Lydia*, by Neera, 5–16. 1886. Lecco: Periplo Edizioni, 1997.

Bachmann, Ingeborg. *Tre sentieri per il lago*. Trans. Amina Pandolfi. Milan: Adelphi, 1994.

Bal, Mieke. *Narratology: Introduction to the Theory of Narrative*. 3rd ed. Toronto: University of Toronto Press, 2009.

Baldacci, Luigi. "Nota Introduttiva." In *Teresa* by Neera, v–xiv. Turin: Einaudi, 1976.

– "Nota." In *Le idee di una donna e Confessioni letterarie*, by Neera, xvii–xix. Florence: Vallecchi, 1977.

Banti, Anna. "Manzoni e noi." *Paragone* 78 (1956): 24–36.

Baranski, Zygmunt, and Shirley W. Vinall, eds. *Women and Italy: Essays on Gender, Culture and History*. London: Macmillan, 1991.

Barbarulli, Clotilde, and Luciana Brandi. *L'arma di cristallo: Sui "discorsi trionfanti," l'ironia della Marchesa Colombi*. Ferrara: Tufani, 1998.

Barbi, Michele. "I 'Promessi sposi' e la critica." In *Annali manzoniani*, vol. 3, 31–231. Milan: Casa del Manzoni, 1942.

Bassanese, Fiora. "Una Donna: Autobiography as Exemplary Text." In *Donna: Women in Italian Culture*, ed. Ada Testaferri, 131–52. Ottawa: Dovehouse, 1989.

Battaglia, Salvatore. *Mitografia del personaggio*. Milan: Rizzoli, 1968.

Beccaria Manzoni, Giulia. *Lettere di Giulia Beccaria Manzoni conservate nella Biblioteca Nazionale Braidense*. Ed. Maria Grazia Griffini. Milan: Il Polifilo, 1974.

Beizer, Janet. *Ventriloquized Bodies: Narratives of Hysteria in Nineteenth-Century France*. Ithaca: Cornell University Press, 1994.

Benatti, Silvia. "La fortuna critica di *In risaia* dai veristi a Croce." In *In risaia*, by Marchesa Colombi, ed. Silvia Benatti and Cesare Bermani, 135–42. 1878. Novara: Interlinea, 2001.

Benatti, Silvia, and Roberto Cicala, eds. *La Marchesa Colombi: Una scrittrice e il suo tempo: Atti del convegno internazionale: Novara 26 maggio 2000*. Novara: Interlinea, 2001.

Benedetti, Laura. *The Tigress in the Snow*. Toronto: University of Toronto Press, 2007.

Benedetti, Laura, Julia L. Hairston, and Silvia M. Ross, eds. *Gendered Contexts: New Perspectives in Italian Cultural Studies*. New York: Peter Lang, 1996.

Ben-Ghiat, Ruth. *Fascist Modernities: Italy 1922–1945*. Berkeley: University of California Press, 2001.

Berlant, Lauren. *Cruel Optimism*. Durham, NC: Duke University Press, 2011. http://dx.doi.org/10.1215/9780822394716

Bermani, Cesare. "Dalla prima alla quarta edizione: Evoluzione linguistica e sociale." In *In risaia*, by Marchesa Colombi, ed. Silvia Benatti and Cesare Bermani, 130–4. 1878. Novara: Interlinea, 2001.

Bernstein, Jay M. *The Philosophy of the Novel: Lukács, Marxism, and the Dialectics of Form*. Minneapolis: Minnesota University Press, 1984.

Biasin, Gian Paolo. *Montale, Debussy, and Modernism*. Princeton: Princeton University Press, 1989.

Billiani, Francesca, and Gigliola Sulis, eds. *The Italian Gothic and Fantastic: Encounters and Rewritings of Literary Traditions*. Madison, NJ: Fairleigh Dickinson University Press, 2007.

Boero, Silvia. "Vite parallele di Paola Drigo e Paola Masino: Voci femminili di dissenso nella letteratura del periodo fascista." Diss., University of North Carolina at Chapel Hill, 2005.

Bompiani, Valentino. "Nascita e vita d'un dizionario: Un'arca di Noé della cultura." In *Dizionario Bompiani delle opere e dei personaggi di tutti i tempi e di tutte le letterature*, ix–x. Milan: Bompiani, 1946.

Bottiroli, Giovanni, ed. *Problemi del personaggio*. Bergamo: Bergamo University Press, 2001.

Boylan, Amy. "Teresa by Neera." In *World Literature: Italian Literature and Its Times*, ed. David Gaden and Joyce Moss, 451–61. Detroit: Thomson Gale, 2005.

Brennan, Teresa. *The Interpretation of the Flesh: Freud and Femininity*. New York: Routledge, 1992.

Brewer, David A. *The Afterlife of Character, 1726–1825*. Philadelphia: University of Pennsylvania Press, 2005.

Bronfen, Elizabeth. *Over Her Dead Body: Death, Femininity and the Aesthetic*. Manchester: Manchester University Press, 1992.

Brooks, Peter. "Storied Bodies, or Nana at Last Unveil'd." *Critical Inquiry* 16.1 (1989): 1–32. http://dx.doi.org/10.1086/448524

Bufalino, Gesualdo. *Dizionario dei personaggi di romanzo: Da Don Chisciotte all'Innominabile*. Milan: Bompiani, 1989.

Burke, Kenneth. *The Rhetoric of Religion: Studies in Logology*. Berkeley: University of California Press, 1961.

Butler, Judith. *Bodies That Matter: On the Discursive Limits of "Sex."* New York: Routledge, 1993.
– *Gender Trouble: Feminism and the Subversion of Identity*. 1990. New York: Routledge, 1999.
– *Undoing Gender*. New York: Routledge, 2004.
Buttafuoco, Annarita, and Marina Zancan, eds. *Svelamento: Sibilla Aleramo: Una biografia intellettuale*. Milan: Feltrinelli, 1988.
Caesar, Ann H. *Characters and Authors in Luigi Pirandello*. Oxford: Clarendon, 1998. http://dx.doi.org/10.1093/acprof:oso/9780198151760.001.0001
Cannon, JoAnn. "Women Writers and the Canon in Contemporary Italy." In *Italian Women Writers from the Renaissance to the Present*, ed. Maria Ornella Marotti, 13–23. University Park: Pennsylvania State University Press, 1996.
Capozzi, Rocco. "Elsa Morante's *Aracoeli*: The End of a Journey." In *Donna: Women in Italian Culture*, ed. Ada Testaferri, 47–58. Toronto: Dovehouse, 1989.
– "'Sheherazade' and Other 'Alibis': Elsa Morante's Victims of Love." *Rivista di studi italiani* 4.1 (1988): 51–71.
Capuana, Luigi. *Giacinta*. 1879. Milan: Mursia, 1980.
Carcereri, Luciano, and Francesco Fiorentino, eds. *Il personaggio romanzesco: Teoria e storia di una categoria letteraria*. Rome: Bulzoni, 1998.
Carsaniga, Giovanni. "The Age of Romanticism (1800–1870)." In *The Cambridge History of Italian Literature*, ed. Peter Brand and Lino Pertile, 397–456. Cambridge: Cambridge University Press, 1999.
Cavarero, Adriana. *In Spite of Plato: A Feminist Rewriting of Ancient Philosophy*. Trans. Serena Anderlini-D'Onofrio and Áine O'Healy. New York: Routledge, 1995.
– *Nonostante Platone: Figure femminili nella filosofia antica*. Rome: Editori Riuniti, 1990.
– *Relating Narratives: Storytelling and Self-Hood*. Trans. Paul A. Kottman. New York: Routledge, 2000.
– *Stately Bodies: Literature, Philosophy, and the Question of Gender*. Trans. Robert de Lucca and Deanna Shemek. Minneapolis: University of Michigan Press, 2002.
– *Tu che mi guardi, tu che mi racconti: Filosofia della narrazione*. Milan: Feltrinelli, 1997.
Cavarero, Adriana, and Franco Restaino. *Le filosofie femministe*. Turin: Paravia, 1999.
Ceserani, Remo, and Lidia De Federicis. *Il materiale e l'immaginario: Laboratorio di analisi dei testi e di lavoro critico*. Milan: Loescher, 1981.
Ceserani, Remo, and Pierluigi Pellini. "The Belated Development of a Theory of the Novel in Italian Literary Culture." In *The Cambridge Companion*

to the Italian Novel, ed. Peter Bondanella and Andrea Ciccarelli, 1–19. Cambridge: Cambridge University Press, 2003. http://dx.doi.org/10.1017/CCOL0521660181.001

Chambers, Ross. *Room for Maneuver: Reading (the) Oppositional (in) Narrative.* Chicago: University of Chicago Press, 1991.

– *The Writing of Melancholy: Modes of Opposition in Early French Modernism.* Trans. Mary Seidman Trouille. Chicago: University of Chicago Press, 1993.

Chase, Karen. *Eros and Psyche: The Representation of Personality in the Works of Charlotte Brontë, Charles Dickens, and George Eliot.* New York: Methuen, 1984.

Chatman, Seymour. *Story and Discourse: Narrative Structure in Fiction and Film.* Ithaca: Cornell University Press, 1978.

Chiari, Pietro, and Fausto Ghisalberti. *Fermo e Lucia: Prima composizione del 1821–1823: Tutte le opere di Alessandro Manzoni.* Vol. 2. Milan: Arnoldo Mondadori, 1964.

Chodorow, Nancy. *The Reproduction of Mothering: Psychoanalysis and the Sociology of Gender.* Berkeley: University of California Press, 1979.

Colombo, Umberto. "La monaca di Monza del *Fermo e Lucia.*" In *Fermo e Lucia: Il primo romanzo del Manzoni: Atti XIII Congresso Nazionale Studi Manzoniani,* ed. Umberto Colombo, 183–214. Lecco: Centro Nazionale Studi Manzoniani, 1986.

– *Vita e processo di suor Virginia Maria de Leyva monaca di Monza.* Milan: Garzanti, 1985.

Cordoba, Pierre Emmanuel. "Prénom Gloria: Pour une pragmatique du personnage." In *Le personnage en question: Actes du IVe colloque du S.E.L.,* by Jean Alsina et al., 32–42. Toulouse: Presses universitaires de Toulouse Le Mirail, 1984.

Costa-Zalessow, Natalia. *Scrittrici italiane dal 13° al 20° secolo: Testi e critica.* Ravenna: Longo, 1982.

Croce, Benedetto, ed. *Neera.* Milan: Garzanti, 1943.

Culler, Jonathan. "Issues in Contemporary American Criticism." In *American Criticism in the Poststructuralist Age,* ed. Ira Konisberg, 1–18. Ann Arbor: University of Michigan Press, 1981.

Cutrufelli, Maria Rosa, Rosaria Guacci, and Marisa Rusconi, eds. *Il Pozzo segreto: Cinquanta scrittrici italiane.* Florence: Giunti, 1993.

D'Angeli, Concetta. *Leggere Elsa Morante: Aracoeli, La Storia e Il mondo salvato dai ragazzini.* Rome: Carocci, 2003.

D'Angeli, Concetta, and Giacomo Magrini, eds. *Studi novecenteschi.* Special Issue: "Vent'anni dopo La storia: Omaggio a Elsa Morante" 21.47–8 (1995).

Davis, Natalie Zemon. "Women's History in Transition: The European Case." *Feminist Studies* 3.3/4 (1976): 83–103. http://dx.doi.org/10.2307/3177729

Debenedetti, Giacomo. "Commemorazione provvisoria del personaggio-uomo." In *Saggi*, 1283–322. Ed. Alfonso Berardinelli. Milan: Mondadori, 1999.

De Giorgio, Michela. *Le italiane dall'Unità a oggi: Modelli culturali e comportamenti sociali*. Bari: Laterza, 1992.

De Gubernatis, Angelo. *Dizionario biografico degli scrittori contemporanei ornato di oltre 300 ritratti diretto da Angelo De Gubernatis*. Florence, 1879.

de Lauretis, Teresa. *Alice Doesn't: Feminism, Semiotics, Cinema*. Bloomington: Indiana University Press, 1984.

– *Figures of Resistance: Essays in Feminist Theory*. Ed. Patricia White. Urbana: University of Illinois Press, 2007.

– *Soggetti eccentrici*. Milan: Feltrinelli, 1999.

– *Technologies of Gender: Essays on Theory, Film, and Fiction*. Bloomington: Indiana University Press, 1987.

De Michelis, Cesare. "Preface." In D'Angeli and Magrini, *Vent'anni dopo La storia*, 7–9.

De Nicola, Francesco, and Pier Antonio Zannoni. *La fama e il silenzio: Scrittrici dimenticate del primo Novecento*. Venice: Marsilio, 2002.

De Robertis, Domenico. *Carte d'identità*. Milan: Il Saggiatore, 1974.

Deuber-Mankosky, Astrid. "Baubo – Another and Additional Name of Aracoeli: Morante's Queer Feminism." In Fortuna and Gragnolati, *The Power of Disturbance*, 73–83.

Dinnerstein, Dorothy. *The Mermaid and the Minotaur: Sexual Arrangements and Human Malaise*. New York: Harper and Row, 1976.

Di Pascale, Anna Maria. "Senza i conforti di alcuna religione." In D'Angeli and Magrini, *Vent'anni dopo La storia*, 287–302.

Dizionario Bompiani delle opere e dei personaggi di tutti i tempi e di tutte le letterature. Milan: Bompiani, 1946.

Dizionario dei personaggi letterari. Turin: UTET, 2003.

Dombroski, Robert. "Alessandro Manzoni: The Cultural Transformation of Narrative." In *Properties of Writing: Ideological Discourse in Modern Italian Fiction*, 1–22. Baltimore: Johns Hopkins University Press, 1994.

– "Gertrude's Story: The Irony of Self-Discovery." *Forum Italicum* 19.2 (1985): 247–58. http://dx.doi.org/10.1177/001458588501900203

– *L'apologia del vero: Lettura ed interpretazione dei Promessi Sposi*. Padua: Liviana, 1984.

– "Reforming the Monster: Manzoni and the Grotesque." In *Monsters in the Italian Literary Imagination*, ed. Keala Jewell, 247–62. Detroit: Wayne State University Press, 2001.

D'Ortenzi, Silvia. "*Nascita e morte della massaia*: Paola Masino." *Quaderni del Novecento* 5 (2005): 39–52.

Dyer, Richard, and Paul McDonald. *Stars*. London: British Film Institute, 1998.

Eaton, Marcia M. "On Being a Character." *British Journal of Aesthetics* 16.1 (1976): 24–31. http://dx.doi.org/10.1093/bjaesthetics/16.1.24

Farnetti, Monica. *Il giuoco del maligno: Il racconto fantastico nella letteratura italiana tra Otto e Novecento*. Florence: Vallecchi, 1988.

– "Patologie del romanticismo: Il gotico e il fantastico tra Italia e Europa." In *Dal barocco all'Ottocento: Mappe della letteratura europea e mediterranea*, ed. Gian Mario Anselmi, 340–66. Vol. 2. Milan: Paravia Bruno Mondadori, 2000.

Felski, Rita, ed. *New Literary History*. Special Issue: "Character" 42.2 (Spring 2011).

Fido, Franco. "Per una descrizione dei *Promessi sposi*: Il sistema dei personaggi." In *Le metamorfosi del centauro: Studi e letture da Boccaccio a Pirandello*, 255–63. Rome: Bulzoni, 1977.

Filippelli, Fiammetta. "L'ultima Morante e la storia come memoria: *Aracoeli* (1982)." *Annali Istituto Universitario Orientale* 31 (1989): 397–415.

Finucci, Valeria. "Between Acquiescence and Madness: Neera's *Teresa*." *Stanford Italian Review* 7 (1987): 217–39.

Fleming, Ray. "Happy Endings? Resisting Women and the Economy of Love in Day Five of Boccaccio's *Decameron*." *Italica* 70.1 (1993): 30–45. http://dx.doi.org/10.2307/479987

Folli, Anna. "Le arpe Eolie: Lettura di Neera." *La Rassegna della Letteratura Italiana* 91 (1987): 98–120.

– *Penne leggère: Neera, Ada Negri, Sibilla Aleramo, scritture femminili italiane fra Otto e Novecento*. Milan: Guerini, 2000.

Forster, E.M. *Aspects of the Novel*. New York: Harcourt, 1927.

Fortini, Franco. "Aracoeli." In *Nuovi Saggi Italiani*, 240–7. Milan: Garzanti, 1982.

Fortuna, Sara, and Manuele Gragnolati, eds. *The Power of Disturbance: Elsa Morante's Aracoeli*. Oxford: Legenda, 2009.

Foucault, Michel. *Histoire de la sexualité I: La volonté de savoir*. Paris: Gallimard, 1976.

– *History of Sexuality: An Introduction*. Trans. Robert Hurley. New York: Vintage, 1988.

– "Nietzsche, Genealogy, History." In *The Foucault Reader*, 76–100. Ed. Paul Rabinow. New York: Pantheon, 1984.

Frabotta, Biancamaria. *Letteratura al femminile*. Bari: De Donato, 1980.

Fraiman, Susan. *Unbecoming Women: British Writers and the Novel of Development*. New York: Columbia University Press, 1993.

Freccero, John. "Zeno's Last Cigarette." *MLN* 77.1 (1962): 3–23. http://dx.doi.org/10.2307/3042679

Freidson, Marion Facinger. "The Meaning of Gertrude in *I promessi sposi.*" *Italica* 28.1 (1951): 27–32. http://dx.doi.org/10.2307/475949

Freud, Sigmund. "From the History of an Infantile Neurosis ('Wolf Man')." In *The Freud Reader*, 400–26. Ed. Peter Gay. London: Vintage, 1995.

Fuchs, Elinor. *The Death of Character: Perspectives on Theater after Modernism.* Bloomington: Indiana University Press, 1996.

Fusillo, Massimo. "'Credo nelle chiacchiere dei barbari': Il tema della barbarie in Elsa Morante e in Pier Paolo Pasolini." In D'Angeli and Magrini, *Vent'anni dopo La storia*, 97–129.

Garboli, Cesare. "Aracoeli." In *Il gioco segreto: Nove immagini di Elsa Morante*, 193–200. Milan: Adelphi, 1995.

– "Cronologia." In *Opere*, by Elsa Morante, vol. 1, xix–xc. Milan: Arnoldo Mondadori, 1988.

– "Preface." In *Nascita e morte della massaia*, by Paola Masino, 5–10. Milan: Bompiani, 1970.

Genette, Gérard. *Narrative Discourse.* Trans. Jane Lewin. Ithaca: Cornell University Press, 1980.

Genevois, Emmanuelle. "Entre naturalisme et feminisme: *In risaia* de la Marchesa Colombi (1840–1920)." In *Les femmes écrivains en Italie au XIX et XX siècles*, ed. Emmanuelle Genevois, 63–76. Aix-en-Provence: University of Provence Press, 1993.

Getto, Giovanni. *Manzoni europeo.* Milan: Mursia, 1971.

Giacomoni, Silvia. "Introduction." In *Nascita e morte della massaia*, by Paola Masino, 5–10. Milan: La Tartaruga, 1982.

Gieri, Manuela. "Paola Masino." In *Dictionary of Literary Biography*, vol. 264, *Italian Prose Writers, 1900–1945*, ed. Luca Somigli and Rocco Capozzi, 193–9. Detroit: Gale, 2002.

Giordani, Pietro. *Lettere inedite a Lazzaro Papi.* Lucca: Tipografia Baccelli, 1851.

Girardi, Enzo Noé. *Struttura e personaggi dei Promessi Sposi.* Milan: Jaca, 1994.

Giorgio, Adalgisa. "Nature vs Culture: Repression, Rebellion and Madness in Elsa Morante's *Aracoeli.*" *MLN* 109.1 (1994): 93–116. http://dx.doi.org/10.2307/2904930

Greimas, Algirdas Julien. *On Meaning: Selected Writings in Semiotic Theory.* Trans. Paul J. Perron and Frank H. Collins. Minneapolis: University of Minnesota Press, 1976.

Griffini, Maria Grazia, ed. *Lettere di Giulia Beccaria Manzoni conservate nella Biblioteca Nazionale Braidense.* Milan: Il polifilo, 1974.

Grosz, Elizabeth. *Space, Time and Perversion*. New York: Routledge, 1995.
– *Volatile Bodies: Toward a Corporeal Feminism*. Bloomington: Indiana University Press, 1994.
Guglielminetti, Marziano. "Le Gertrudi impossibili." *Revue des Etudes Italiennes* 32–33 (1986–87): 148–54.
Hadlock, Heather. "The Career of Cherubino." In *Siren Songs: Gender and Representation in Opera*, ed. Mary Ann Smart, 67–92. Princeton: Princeton University Press, 2000.
Hamon, Philippe. *Le personnel du roman: Le système des personnages dans les Rougon-Macquart d'Emile Zola*. Paris: Droz, 1983.
Harter, Deborah H. *Bodies in Pieces: Fantastic Narrative and the Poetics of the Fragment*. Stanford: Stanford University Press, 1996.
Hartsock, Nancy. "Foucault on Power: A Theory for Women?" In *Feminism/Postmodernism*, ed. Linda J. Nicholson, 157–75. New York: Routledge, 1990.
Harvey, W.J. *Character and the Novel*. London: Chatto & Windus, 1965.
Irigaray, Luce. *This Sex Which Is Not One*. Trans. Catherine Porter and Carolyn Burke. Ithaca: Cornell University Press, 1985.
Isella, Dante. "Le testimonianze autografe plurime." In *Le carte mescolate: Esperienze di filologia d'autore*, 21–31. Padua: Liviana, 1987.
James, Henry. "Author's Preface." In *The Portrait of a Lady*, 611–27. 1881. Oxford: Oxford University Press, 2009.
Jameson, Frederic. *The Political Unconscious: Narrative as a Socially Symbolic Act*. Ithaca: Cornell University Press, 1981.
Jones, Verina R. *Le Dark Ladies manzoniane e altri saggi sui* Promessi sposi. Rome: Salerno, 1998.
Kahn, Coppélia. "Excavating 'Those Dim Minoan Regions': Maternal Subtexts in Patriarchal Literature." *Diacritics* 12.2 (1982): 32–41. http://dx.doi.org/10.2307/464677
Keen, Suzanne. *Empathy and the Novel*. New York: Oxford University Press, 2007. http://dx.doi.org/10.1093/acprof:oso/9780195175769.001.0001
Kermode, Frank. *The Sense of an Ending: Studies in the Theory of Fiction with a New Epilogue*. 1966. Oxford: Oxford University Press, 2000.
Knights, Lionel Charles. *How Many Children Had Lady Macbeth? An Essay in the Theory and Practice of Shakespeare Criticism*. Cambridge: Minority, 1933.
Kroha, Lucienne. *The Woman Writer in Late Nineteenth Century Italy: Gender and the Formation of Literary Identity*. New York: Edwin Mellen, 1992.
Lacan, Jacques. *Écrits: A Selection*. Trans. Alan Sheridan. New York: Norton, 1977.
Lange, Lydia. "Woman Is Not a Rational Animal: On Aristotle's Biology of Reproduction." In *Discovering Reality: Feminist Perspectives on Epistemology, Metaphysics, Methodology, and Philosophy of Science*, ed. Sandra Harding and

Merrill B. Hintikka, 1–15. 2nd ed. Boston: Kluwer Academic, 2003. http://dx.doi.org/10.1007/978-94-010-0101-4_1

Lotman, Jurij M. "The Origin of Plot in the Light of Typology." Trans. Julian Graffy. *Poetics Today* 1.1/2 (1979): 161–84. http://dx.doi.org/10.2307/1772046

Lucamante, Stefania. *A Multitude of Women*. Toronto: Toronto University Press, 2008.

Lucamante, Stefania, and Sharon Wood, eds. *Under Arturo's Star: The Cultural Legacies of Elsa Morante*. West Lafayette, IN: Purdue University Press, 2006.

Lukács, Georg. *The Theory of the Novel: A Historico-Philosophical Essay on the Forms of Great Epic Literature*. Trans. Anna Bostock. Cambridge, MA: MIT Press, 1971.

Machiavelli, Niccolò. "Spectabili viro L. Guicciardini in Mantova tanquam fratri carissimo." In *Lettere*, 26–7. Ed. Giuseppe Lesca. Florence: Rinascimento del Libro, 1929.

Manetti, Beatrice. "Biografia." In *Paola Masino*, ed. Francesca Bernardini Napoletano and Marinella Mascia Galateria, 38–63. Milan: Fondazione Arnoldo e Alberto Mondadori, 2001.

Manzoni, Alessandro. *Fermo e Lucia*. Ed. Sergio Romagnoli and Luca Toschi. Florence: Sansoni, 1985.

– *I promessi sposi*. Ed. Vittorio Spinazzola. 1966. Milan: Garzanti, 1999.

– *I romanzi*. Ed. Salvatore Silvano Nigro. 3 vols. Milan: Arnoldo Mondadori Editore, 2002.

– *The Betrothed*. Trans. Bruce Penman. London: Penguin, 1972.

Maraini, Dacia. *La lunga vita di Marianna Ucria*. Milan: Rizzoli, 1990.

Marchesa Colombi [Maria Antonietta Torriani]. *In risaia*. Ed. Silvia Benatti and Cesare Bermani. 1878. Novara: Interlinea, 2001.

Marenco, Franco. "Avventure del personaggio." In *Dizionario dei personaggi letterari*, vol. 1, ix–xxv. Turin: UTET, 2003.

– "Il personaggio e l'intreccio come funzioni testuali: Programma di ricerca." Università degli studi di Torino. 30 August 2012.

Marrone, Gaetana. "La fantasia della voce maternale in *Aracoeli* di Elsa Morante." In *Maria Vergine nella letteratura italiana*, ed. Florinda M. Iannace, 267–82. Stony Brook, NY: Forum Italicum, 2000.

Masino, Paola. *Birth and Death of the Housewife*. Trans. Marella Feltrin-Morris. Albany: SUNY Press, 2009.

– *Colloquio di notte*. Preface by Maria Rosa Cutrufelli. Ed. Maria Vittoria Vittori. Palermo: La Luna, 1994.

– *Decadenza della morte*. Rome: Alberto Stock, 1931.

– *Io, Massimo e gli altri: Autobiografia di una figlia del secolo*. Milan: Rusconi, 1995.

– *Monte Ignoso*. Milan: Bompiani, 1931.

– *Nascita e morte della massaia. Tempo: Settimanale di politica, informazione, letteratura e arte.* Publication of the novel in installments from 16 October 1941 (n.125) to 22 January 1942 (n.139).
– *Nascita e morte della massaia.* Milan: Bompiani, 1945.
– *Periferia.* Milan: Bompiani, 1933.
– *Poesie.* Milan: Bompiani, 1947.
– *Racconto grosso e altri.* Milan: Bompiani, 1941.

Matthews Grieco, Sara F. "Modelli di santità femminile nell'Italia del Rinascimento e della Controriforma." In Scaraffia and Zarri, *Donne e fede,* 303–25.

Mauriac, François. *Le romancier et ses personnages.* Paris: Correa, 1933.

Mazza, Antonia. *Studi sulle redazioni de I promessi Sposi.* Milan: Paoline, 1968.

Mazzoni, Cristina. "Parturition, Parting and Paradox in Turn-of-the-Century Italian Literature." *Forum Italicum* 31.2 (1997): 343–66. http://dx.doi.org/10.1177/001458589703100202

McDonald Carolan, Mary Ann. "La Monaca di Monza: Manzoni's Bad Girl and the Repudiation of the Imagination." *Rivista di studi italiani* 19.2 (2001): 65–85.

Mengaldo, Pier Vincenzo. "Spunti per un'analisi linguistica dei romanzi di Elsa Morante." In D'Angeli and Magrini, *Vent'anni dopo La storia,* 11–36.

Mettifogo, Mariarosa. "Feminism between Theory and Practice: Mary Wollstonecraft, George Sand, and Neera." Diss., University of California, Davis, 2005.

Mitchell, Katharine, and Catherine Ramsey-Portolano, eds. *Rethinking Neera.* Supplement to *The Italianist* 30.3 (2010).

Mondello, Elisabetta. *La nuova italiana: La donna nella stampa e nella cultura del Ventennio.* Rome: Editori Riuniti, 1987.

Montale, Eugenio. *Ossi di seppia.* Turin: Piero Gobetti, 1925.

Morandini, Giuliana. *La voce che è in lei: Antologia della narrativa femminile italiana tra '800 e '900.* Milan: Bompiani, 1980.

Morante, Elsa. *Aracoeli.* Turin: Einaudi, 1982.
– *Aracoeli.* Trans. William Weaver. New York: Random House, 1984.
– *L'isola di Arturo.* Turin: Einaudi, 1968.
– *La storia.* Turin: Einaudi, 1974.
– *Menzogna e sortilegio.* Turin: Einaudi, 1948.
– "Nove domande sul romanzo." *Nuovi argomenti* 38–9 (1959): 17–38.
– *Opere.* Ed. Cesare Garboli and Carlo Cecchi. 2 vols. Milan: Arnoldo Mondadori, 1988–90.
– "Pro o contro la bomba atomica." *Europa letteraria* 6.34 (1965): 31–42.
– *Pro o contro la bomba atomica e altri scritti.* Ed. Cesare Garboli. Milan: Adelphi, 1987.

Moretti, Franco. *Il romanzo*. 5 vols. Turin: Einaudi, 2001–3.
Mulvey, Laura. "Visual Pleasure and Narrative Cinema." In *Feminism and Film*, ed. E. Ann Kaplan, 34–47. Oxford: Oxford University Press, 2000.
Neera [Anna Radius Zuccari]. *Addio!* 1877. Milan: Baldini & Castoldi, 1919.
– "Il libro di mio figlio." In *Neera*, 701–49. Ed. Benedetto Croce. 1891. Milan: Garzanti, 1943.
– *Le idee di una donna e Confessioni letterarie*. Ed. Francesca Sanvitale. Florence: Vallecchi, 1977.
– *L'indomani*. 1889. Milan: Fratelli Treves, 1909.
– *Lydia*. 1886. Lecco: Periplo Edizioni, 1997.
– *Monastero e altri racconti*. Ed. Antonia Arslan and Anna Folli. Milan: Scheiwiller, 1987.
– *Neera*. Ed. Benedetto Croce. Milan: Garzanti, 1943.
– *Teresa*. 1887. Ed. Antonia Arslan and Gian Luca Baio. Lecco: Periplo Edizioni, 1995.
– *Teresa*. 1887. Ed. Luigi Baldacci. Turin: Einaudi, 1976.
– *Teresa*. Trans. Martha King. Evanston, IL: Northwestern University Press, 1998.
– *Una giovinezza del secolo XIX*. Milan: Cogliati, 1919.
Neera and Paolo Mantegazza. *Dizionario d'igiene per le famiglie*. 1881. Milan: Scheiwiller, 1985.
Nigro, Salvatore Silvano. "Nota critico-filologica: I tre romanzi." In Manzoni, *I romanzi*, vol. 1, xli–lix.
Nigro, Salvatore Silvano, and Ermanno Paccagnini. "Percorsi bibliografici." In Manzoni, *I romanzi*, vol. 1, 1373–1402.
Nozzoli, Anna. *Tabù e coscienza: La condizione femminile nella letteratura italiana del novecento*. Florence: Nuova Italia, 1978.
Oksenberg Rorty, Amélie. "Characters, Personas, Selves, Individuals." In *Mind in Action: Essays in the Philosophy of Mind*, 78–98. Boston: Beacon, 1988.
Ortese, Anna Maria. *Il mare non bagna Napoli*. Turin: Einaudi, 1953.
Paduano, Guido. "La svolta nella produzione di Elsa Morante: Domande e ipotesi di lavoro (e una verifica su *Aracoeli*)." In D'Angeli and Magrini, *Vent'anni dopo La storia*, 303–19.
Parati, Graziella. *Public History, Private Stories: Italian Women's Autobiography*. Minneapolis: University of Minnesota Press, 1996.
Parisi, Luciano. *Come abbiamo letto Manzoni: Interpreti novecenteschi*. Alessandria: Edizioni dell'Orso, 2008.
Phelan, James. *Reading People, Reading Plots: Character Progression, and the Interpretation of Narrative*. Chicago: University of Chicago Press, 1989.
Pickering-Iazzi, Robin. "Designing Mothers: Images of Motherhood in Novels by Aleramo, Morante, Maraini and Fallaci." *Annali d'italianistica* 7 (1989): 325–40.

– ed. *Mothers of Invention: Women, Italian Fascism, and Culture*. Minneapolis: University of Minnesota Press, 1995.
– *Politics of the Visible: Writing Women, Culture, and Fascism*. Minneapolis: University of Minnesota Press, 1997.
– ed. *Unspeakable Women: Selected Short Stories Written by Italian Women during Fascism*. New York: Feminist, 1993.
Pierobon, Ermenegilda. "La diversità del femminile: Neera femminista ed antifemminista." *Studi d'italianistica nell'Africa australe / Italian Studies in Southern Africa* 9 (1996): 30–44.
– "Per la conquista della bellezza." In Benatti and Cicala, *La Marchesa Colombi*, 101–11.
Piperno, Alessandro. "Questo sesso non mi eccita." *L'espresso*. 31 March 2010: 112–15.
Pirandello, Luigi. *Eleven Short Stories*. Trans. Stanley Appelbaum. Mineola, NY: Dover, 1994.
– *Novelle per un anno*. Vol. 1. Milan: Mondadori, 1956.
Pischedda, Bruno. "L'apocalisse del cristianesimo." *Belfagor* 55 (2000): 397–412.
Poeti, Alida. "Riflessi speculari e identità femminile nell'opera di Elsa Morante." *Studi d'italianistica nell'Africa australe / Italian Studies in Southern Africa* 7 (1994): 21–36.
Pozzi, Giovanni. "Temi, topoi, stereotipi." In *Letteratura italiana*, ed. Alberto Asor Rosa, 391–436. Vol. 3. Turin: Einaudi, 1982.
Propp, Vladimir. *Morphology of the Folktale*. Trans. Laurence Scott. Austin: University of Texas Press, 1968.
Prosperi, A. "Lettere spirituali." In *Donne e fede: Santità e vita religiosa in Italia*, ed. Lucetta Scaraffia and Gabriella Zarri, 227–51. Rome and Bari: Laterza, 1994.
Raimondi, Ezio. *Il romanzo senza idillio: Saggio sui Promessi sposi*. 1974. Turin: Einaudi, 2000.
– *La dissimulazione romanzesca: Antropologia manzoniana*. Bologna: Il Mulino, 1990.
Ramsey-Portolano, Catherine. "Neera the *Verist* Woman Writer." *Italica* 81.3 (2004): 351–66. http://dx.doi.org/10.2307/27668927
Re, Lucia. "Fame, cibo e antifascismo nella Massaia di Paola Masino." In *Il cibo e le donne nella cultura e nella storia: Prospettive interdisciplinari*, ed. Lucia Re and Maria Giuseppina Muzzarelli, 165–81. Bologna: CLUEB, 2005.
– "Fascist Theories of 'Woman' and the Construction of Gender." In Pickering-Iazzi, *Mothers of Invention*, 76–99.
– "Passion and Sexual Difference: The Risorgimento and the Gendering of Writing in Nineteenth-Century Italian Culture." In *Making and Remaking Italy: The Cultivation of National Identity Around the Risorgimento*, ed. Albert Russell Ascoli and Krystyna Von Henneberg, 155–200. Oxford: Berg, 2001.

– "Women and Censorship in Fascist Italy: From Mura to Paola Masino." In *Culture, Censorship and the State in Twentieth-Century Italy*, ed. Guido Bonsaver and Robert S.C. Gordon, 64–75. London: Legenda, 2005.

Reich, Jacqueline. *Beyond the Latin Lover: Marcello Mastroianni, Masculinity, and Italian Cinema*. Bloomington: Indiana University Press, 2004.

Rich, Adrienne. "Compulsory Heterosexuality and the Lesbian Experience." In *Blood, Bread, and Poetry: Selected Prose 1979–1985*, 23–75. New York: Norton, 1986.

– *Of Woman Born: Motherhood as Experience and Institution*. New York: Norton, 1976.

Ripamonti, Giuseppe. *Historiae Patriae Libri*. Milan, 1641.

Romagnoli, Sergio. "Il primo romanzo." In Manzoni, *Fermo e Lucia*, vii–xxi.

Rorandelli, Tristana. "Female Identity and the Female Body in Italian Women's Writings: 1900–1955 (Sibilla Aleramo, Enif Robert, Paola Masino and Alba de Cespedes)." Diss., New York University, 2007.

– "*Nascita e morte della massaia* di Paola Masino e la questione del corpo materno nel fascismo." *Forum Italicum* 37.1 (2003): 70–102. http://dx.doi.org/10.1177/001458580303700105

Rosa, Giovanna. *Cattedrali di carta: Elsa Morante romanziere*. Milan: Il Saggiatore, 1995.

Rozier, Louise. *Il mito e l'allegoria nella narrativa di Paola Masino*. Lewiston, NY: Edwin Mellen, 2004.

– "Motherhood and Femininity in Paola Masino's Novels *Monte ignoso* and *Nascita e morte della massaia*." *Italica* 88.2 (2011): 245–61.

Ryan-Scheutz, Colleen. *Sex, the Self and the Sacred: Women in the Cinema of Pier Paolo Pasolini*. Toronto: University of Toronto Press, 2007.

Sanyal, Debarati. *The Violence of Modernity: Baudelaire, Irony, and the Politics of Form*. Baltimore: Johns Hopkins University Press, 2006.

Savoca, Giuseppe. *Strutture e personaggi: Da Verga a Bonaviri*. Rome: Bonacci, 1989.

Scaraffia, Lucetta, and Gabriella Zarri, eds. *Donne e fede: Santità e vita religiosa in Italia*. Rome and Bari: Laterza, 1994.

Scholes, Robert, James Phelan, and Robert Kellogg. *The Nature of Narrative: Fortieth Anniversary Edition*. Oxford: Oxford University Press, 2006.

Serkowska, Hanna. "Percorsi androgini: *Aracoeli*: Il romanzo definitivo di Elsa Morante." *Il lettore di provincia* 115 (2002): 3–27.

Shemek, Deanna. "Introduction." In Cavarero, *Stately Bodies*, 1–11.

Showalter, Elaine. "Towards a Feminist Poetics." In *Women Writing and Writing About Women*, ed. Mary Jacobus, 25–33. London: Croom Helm, 1979.

Siddell, Felix. "*Aracoeli*: A Journey through Map Space in Quest of the Garden." *Spunti e ricerche* 9 (1993): 69–96.

Siti, Walter. "Elsa Morante and Pier Paolo Pasolini." In Lucamante and Wood, *Under Arturo's Star*, 268–89.
– "La Morante nell'opera di Pier Paolo Pasolini." In D'Angeli and Magrini, *Vent'anni dopo La storia*, 131–48.
Spackman, Barbara. *Decadent Genealogies: The Rhetoric of Sickness from Baudelaire to D'Annunzio*. Ithaca: Cornell University Press, 1989.
– *Fascist Virilities: Rhetoric, Ideology, and Social Fantasy in Italy*. Minneapolis: University of Minnesota Press, 1996.
– "Monstrous Knowledge." In *Monsters in the Italian Literary Imagination*, ed. Keala J. Jewell, 297–310. Detroit: Wayne State University Press, 2001.
Spinazzola, Vittorio. "La costruzione ironica dei personaggi nei *promessi sposi*." In *Miscellanea di studi in onore di Vittore Branca*, vol. 4, tome 2, *Tra illuminismo e romanticismo*, 615–33. Florence: Olschki, 1983.
Springer, Mary Doyle. *A Rhetoric of Literary Character: Some Women of Henry James*. Chicago: University of Chicago Press, 1978.
Stewart-Steinberg, Suzanne. *The Pinocchio Effect: On Making Italians, 1860–1920*. Chicago: University of Chicago Press, 2008.
Summerfield, Giovanna, and Lisa Downward. *New Perspectives on the European Bildungsroman*. New York: Continuum, 2010.
Svevo, Italo. *La coscienza di Zeno*. Trieste: Licinio Cappelli, 1923.
Tarchetti, Igino Ugo. *Fosca*. 1869. Milan: Mondadori, 1981.
– *Passion*. Trans. Lawrence Venuti. San Francisco: Mercury, 1994.
Todorov, Tzvetan. *The Fantastic: A Structural Approach to a Literary Genre*. Trans. Richard Howard. Cleveland: Case Western Reserve University Press, 1973.
– "Les hommes-récits." In *Poétique de la prose*, 78–91. Paris: Seuil, 1971.
Tommaseo, Niccolò, and Bernardo Bellini. *Dizionario della lingua italiana: 1861–1879*. 30 August 2012. http://www.dizionario.org/
Toschi, Luca. *La sala rossa: Biografia dei Promessi sposi*. Turin: Bollati Boringhieri, 1989.
Valisa, Silvia. "Gendered Quests: Analysis, Revelation and the Epistemology of Gender in Neera's *Teresa Lydia* and *L'indomani*." *Italianist* 28.1 (2008): 92–112. http://dx.doi.org/10.1179/ita.2008.28.1.92
Varese, Claudio. *Fermo e Lucia: Un'esperienza manzoniana interrotta*. Florence: Nuova Italia, 1964.
Venturi, Gianni. "La menzogna della bellezza: *Aracoeli*." *Narrativa* 17 (2000): 123–36.
Verga, Giovanni. *Eros*. Milan, 1875.
– "Nedda." 1874. In *Le novelle*, 1–31.
– *Le novelle*. Ed. Nicola Merola. 2 vols. Milan: Garzanti, 1980.
– *Primavera e altri racconti*. 1876. In *Le novelle*, 33–130.
– *Vita dei campi*. 1880. In *Le novelle*, 131–237.

Vermeule, Blakey. *Why Do We Care about Literary Characters?* Baltimore: Johns Hopkins University Press, 2010.

Vigorelli, Giancarlo. "La monaca di Monza: Dal 'romanzo' al 'documento.'" In *Fermo e Lucia: Il primo romanzo del Manzoni: Atti XIII Congresso Nazionale Studi Manzoniani*, ed. Umberto Colombo, 91–101. Lecco: Centro Nazionale Studi Manzoniani, 1986.

– "Presentazione." In Colombo, *Vita e processo*, vii–xix.

Volpi, Marisa. "I miei Sahara futuri." In D'Angeli and Magrini, *Vent'anni dopo La storia*, 91–6.

Walcutt, Charles Child. *Man's Changing Mask: Modes and Methods of Characterization in Fiction*. Minneapolis: University of Minnesota Press, 1966.

Wellek, René, and Austin Warren. *Theory of Literature*. New York: Harcourt, 1977.

West, Rebecca. "Seeing and Telling: Anamorphosis, Relational Identity, and Other Perspectival Perplexities in *Aracoeli*." In Fortuna and Gragnolati, *The Power of Disturbance*, 20–9.

Woloch, Alex. *The One vs. the Many: Minor Characters and the Space of the Protagonist in the Novel*. Princeton: Princeton University Press, 2003.

Wood, Sharon. *Italian Women's Writing 1860–1994*. London: Athlone, 1995.

Zaccaria, Giuseppe. "L'alternarsi dei punti di vista nell'opera della Marchesa Colombi." In Benatti and Cicala, *La Marchesa Colombi*, 91–100.

Zambon, Patrizia, ed. *Novelle d'autrice tra Ottocento e Novecento*. 1987. Roma: Bulzoni, 1998.

– "Un genere di occasione: I 'racconti di Natale' della Marchesa Colombi." In Benatti and Cicala, *La Marchesa Colombi*, 121–38.

Zancan, Marina. *Il doppio itinerario della scrittura: La donna nella tradizione italiana*. Turin: Einaudi, 1998.

Žižek, Slavoj. "The Spectre of Ideology: Introduction." In *Mapping Ideology*, ed. Slavoj Žižek, 1–33. London: Verso, 1995.

Index

www.ingramcontent.com/pod-product-compliance
Lightning Source LLC
LaVergne TN
LVHW090157080826
844660LV00013B/841/J

* 9 7 8 1 4 4 2 6 4 9 2 2 4 *